The Law in Nazi Germany

Related Titles of Interest

Jewish Life in Nazi Germany: Dilemmas and Responses
Edited by Francis R. Nicosia and David Scrase

The Arts in Nazi Germany: Continuity, Conformity, Change
Edited by Jonathan Huener and Francis R. Nicosia

Business and Industry in Nazi Germany
Edited by Francis R. Nicosia and Jonathan Huener

Medicine and Medical Ethics in Nazi Germany: Origins, Practices, Legacies
Edited by Francis R. Nicosia and Jonathan Huener

The Law in Nazi Germany

Ideology, Opportunism, and the Perversion of Justice

Edited by
Alan E. Steinweis
and
Robert D. Rachlin

berghahn
NEW YORK • OXFORD
www.berghahnbooks.com

First published in 2013 by
Berghahn Books
www.berghahnbooks.com

©2013, 2015 The Miller Center for Holocaust Studies
at the University of Vermont
First paperback edition published in 2015.

All rights reserved. Except for the quotation of short passages
for the purposes of criticism and review, no part of this book
may be reproduced in any form or by any means, electronic or
mechanical, including photocopying, recording, or any information
storage and retrieval system now known or to be invented,
without written permission of the publisher.

Library of Congress Cataloging-in-Publication Data

The law in Nazi Germany : ideology, opportunism, and the perversion of
justice / edited by Alan E. Steinweis and Robert D. Rachlin.
   p. cm.
   Includes bibliographical references and index.
   ISBN 978-0-85745-780-6 (hardback : alk. paper) — ISBN 978-1-78238-921-7 (paperback : alk. paper) — ISBN 978-0-85745-781-3 (ebook)
   1. Justice, Administration of—Germany—History. 2. Law—Germany—History. 3. National socialism—Moral and ethical aspects. 4. Holocaust, Jewish (1939–1945) 5. Germany—Politics and government—1933–1945. 6. Jewish lawyers—Germany—History—1933–1945. 7. Jews—Persecutions—Germany—History. I. Steinweis, Alan E. II. Rachlin, Robert D.
   KK3655.L39 2012
   349.4309'043—dc23

2012027604

British Library Cataloguing in Publication Data

A catalogue record for this book is available from the British Library

Printed on acid-free paper.

ISBN: 978-0-85745-780-6 hardback
ISBN: 978-1-78238-921-7 paperback
ISBN: 978-0-85745-781-3 ebook

Contents

Preface	vii
List of Abbreviations	ix
Introduction: The Law in Nazi Germany and the Holocaust *Alan E. Steinweis and Robert D. Rachlin*	1
1. The Conundrum of Complicity: German Professionals and the Final Solution *Konrad H. Jarausch*	15
2. Civil Service Lawyers and the Holocaust: The Case of Wilhelm Stuckart *Hans-Christian Jasch*	37
3. Roland Freisler and the Volksgerichtshof: The Court as an Instrument of Terror *Robert D. Rachlin*	63
4. Guilt, Shame, Anger, Indignation: Nazi Law and Nazi Morals *Raphael Gross*	89
5. Discrimination, Degradation, Defiance: Jewish Lawyers under Nazism *Douglas G. Morris*	105
6. Evading Responsibility for Crimes against Humanity: Murderous Lawyers at Nuremberg *Harry Reicher*	137

7. Judging German Judges in the Third Reich: Excusing and Confronting the Past — 161
Kenneth F. Ledford

Appendixes

    A. Article 48 of the Weimar Constitution, 11 August 1919 — 191

    B. Decree of the Reich President for the Protection of the People and State (Reichstag Fire Decree), 28 February 1933 — 192

    C. Law to Remove the Distress of the People and the State (The Enabling Act), 23 March 1933 — 194

    D. Hitler's Call for a Nazi Lawyers' League, 12 September 1928 — 196

    E. Circular No. 8/1938 from Dr. Karl Leitmeyer, League of National Socialist Guardians of the Law, 4 March 1938 — 197

    F. Law Amending Criminal Law and Criminal Procedure (Excerpts), 24 April 1934 — 199

    G. White Rose - Leaflet 5, February 1943 — 202

    H. The Sentencing of Hans and Sophie Scholl and Christoph Probst, 22 February 1943 — 204

    I. The Fate of Markus Luftglass: Excerpt from the Record of the Nuremberg Justice Case, October 1941 — 208

    J. Opinion and Sentence of the Nuremberg Special Court in the Case of Leo Katzenberger, 13 March 1942 — 211

    K. Testimony of Curt Rothenberger at the Nuremberg Justice Case (Excerpts), 1947 — 224

    L. Gustav Radbruch, "Statutory Lawlessness and Supra-Statutory Law" (excerpt), 1946 — 230

Contributors — 233

Selected Bibliography — 236

Index — 241

Preface

Five of the essays in this book are based on lectures delivered at a symposium on "The Law in Nazi Germany," which took place at the University of Vermont in April 2009. Organized by the Carolyn and Leonard Miller Center for Holocaust Studies at the University of Vermont, this was the fifth symposium bearing the name of Carolyn and Leonard Miller, generous supporters of the Center's work, and great friends of the university.

Established to honor the legacy of Professor Raul Hilberg, who served on the faculty of the University of Vermont for more than three decades, the Miller Center for Holocaust Studies is committed to furthering research and education about the Holocaust, and to serving as a forum for the presentation and discussion of new perspectives on the subject. Hilberg's pioneering scholarship remains a model and a standard for scholars, and is an inspiration for the Center's programming and for publications such as this book. The Miller Symposia have contributed significantly to the Center's efforts to explore insufficiently charted areas in the history of the Third Reich and the Holocaust. Our goal in organizing them has been to address topical, or even controversial, themes in that history, relying on the expertise of some of the most accomplished scholars and other authorities in the field.

The first Miller Symposium, held in April 2000, convened some of the world's leading scholars in the history of eugenics and the German medical establishment during the Third Reich. It resulted in the anthology *Medicine and Medical Ethics in Nazi Germany: Origins, Practices, Legacies,* published by Berghahn Books in 2002. The second Miller Symposium, with its focus on German business and industry under Nazism, took place in April 2002. It brought together scholars who are among the most respected and innovative analysts of German business, industry, and finance in the years of the Third Reich. The resulting volume, *Business and Industry in Nazi Germany,* was published by

Berghahn Books in 2004. The third Miller Symposium in 2004 featured some of the most important scholars in the history of the arts in Nazi Germany. Their contributions to the volume *The Arts in Nazi Germany: Continuity, Conformity, Change,* published by Berghahn in 2006, address, among other subjects, the activities of artists, writers, musicians, filmmakers, and Jewish cultural institutions during the Nazi era. The fourth Miller Symposium brought some of the world's leading scholars of the history of German Jewry to the University of Vermont in 2006. Their papers addressed research and controversies in the tragic history of German Jews from Hitler's appointment as chancellor in January 1933 to the initiation of the "Final Solution" in 1941. The volume was published by Berghahn Books in 2010 under the title *Jewish Life in Nazi Germany: Dilemmas and Responses.*

The present volume is the product of collaboration between historians and practitioners of the law. Four of its seven contributors are active in the legal profession, either in private practice, in government, or in the non-profit sector. The editors—one an academic historian, the other an attorney with extensive law school teaching experience—hope that the book will prove useful to scholars and students in a variety of educational and institutional settings, and more generally to readers with an interest in Nazi Germany, the Holocaust, and the history of law and legal professionals in extreme circumstances.

Abbreviations

BAB	Bundesarchiv-Berlin (German Federal Archive, Berlin)
BDC	Berlin Document Center
BGB	*Bürgerliches Gesetzbuch* (The German Civil Code)
BGH	Bundesgerichtshof (Supreme Court of the FRG)
GDR	German Democratic Republic
FRG	Federal Republic of Germany
IMT	International Military Tribunal
NS	National Socialist
NSDAP	National Socialist German Workers Party (The Nazi Party)
POW	Prisoner of War
RGBl	*Reichsgesetzblatt*
RMI	Reich Ministry of the Interior
RSHA	Reichssicherheitshauptamt (Reich Security Main Office)
RVL	*Reich, Volksordnung und Lebensraum*
SA	Sturmabteilung (The Nazi Brownshirts or Stormtroopers)
SPD	Social Democratic Party of Germany
SS	Schutzstaffel (The Nazi Blackshirts)
VfZ	*Vierteljahrshefte für Zeitgeschichte*
VGH	Volksgerichtshof (The Nazi-era People's Court)

Introduction

THE LAW IN NAZI GERMANY AND THE HOLOCAUST

Alan E. Steinweis and Robert D. Rachlin

THE LEGAL HISTORY OF NAZI Germany has not attracted a great deal of attention from scholars, especially when compared to the huge body of publications available about other aspects of that regime.[1] Moreover, much of the important scholarship that does exist in this area has not been translated from German into English.[2] This is unfortunate, as both the law and the conduct of legal professionals did much to influence the tragic course of German history in the twentieth century. There are several factors that may explain this lacuna. Legal history has been out of fashion among academic historians on both sides of the Atlantic for several decades, having been displaced by approaches to the past that have eschewed a focus on the state and its powers. Additionally, the challenges involved in mastering the technical and theoretical aspects of legal history may have deterred some scholars from tackling the subject. Finally, scholarship may have suffered from the erroneous perception that the law did not matter in Germany during the Nazi period.

Indeed, a book about the law in Nazi Germany might strike some readers as an exercise in contradiction. They understand the Nazi regime as a tyranny, characterized by arbitrary rule, enforced through intimidation and terror. The hallmark of Nazi society, as they understand it, was not law, but lawlessness. In many respects, they are correct. Under Nazi rule, Germany largely ceased being a *Rechtsstaat*—a nation of laws—as millions of people, both German and non-German, were deprived of their property, their freedom, and their lives as the result of measures implemented entirely outside of the framework of traditional, codified

German law. At the same time, however, much of the German legal system continued to function in a manner that would have been recognizable to observers before 1933. To be sure, the formal administration of justice grew increasingly dependent on the dictates of a Nazi leadership that was motivated by racist ideology, as well as on the prosecutors, judges, and civil servants who, for one reason or another, accommodated themselves to such political interference. Moreover, important elements of Nazi ideology, most notably its biological racism, were gradually insinuated into the legal code. Many—probably most—Germans who lived through the Nazi years acknowledged the constitutional and legal legitimacy of dictatorial rule and of the racist and repressive laws that extended from it.

The simultaneous existence of a traditional legal system (Nazified as it was) with that of an extra-legal system of terror was the focus of an early work of scholarship on the Third Reich, *The Dual State,* published in 1941 by Ernst Fraenkel, a Jewish refugee lawyer and legal scholar.[3] This structural analysis of the Third Reich remains highly influential in our understanding of Nazi legal practice today. Fraenkel distinguished two parallel spheres of official authority as they existed in Nazi Germany: the "normative state" and the "prerogative state." The "normative state" consisted of the traditional legal order, including the codes of German law, the Ministry of Justice, and the courts, transformed after 1933 by an infusion of Nazi laws, practices, and personnel. The "prerogative state" was the realm in which the Nazi regime wielded arbitrary power over the freedom and lives of its subjects. When this distinction is applied, most of the mass atrocities for which the Nazi regime is most notorious—the mass murder of Jews, Gypsies, and others during World War II—were carried out mainly by organs of the "prerogative state," most notably the SS. The imprisonment of the regime's critics and political opponents in concentration camps, which also operated outside the traditional legal and penal system, was also a consequence of the "prerogative state" at work. It should be emphasized, however, that the notion of a "dual state" was invented by a legal scholar for analytical purposes, and the Nazi regime itself made no such official distinction. Moreover, the border between the two parts of the "dual state" was often poorly defined in practice. The crimes of the "prerogative state" should not obscure the central role played by a Nazified "normative state" in the creation and implementation of racist policies. The notorious Nuremberg race laws, for example, were products of the "normative state," as were the myriad regulations that were implemented to apply and enforce them. With these caveats in mind, Fraenkel's distinction provides a useful heuristic device that proves useful in several of the essays in this volume.

While the essays in this book have much to say about the laws and the legal system of the Nazi era, their main focus is on the legal professionals of the time—the civil servants, lawyers, and judges. It is important for us to recognize the complex motives of many German legal professionals during the Nazi era. Some were genuine Nazis who were committed to racial purity, authoritarian rule by a single party, and other ideological goals of the Nazi regime. Others were driven more by personal and professional ambition than by ideology. Many believed sincerely in the rule of law, even if the law supported a social order that was racist and a political order that was dictatorial. Carl Schmitt, an influential legal theorist, whose pre-1933 contributions to jurisprudence are still viewed seriously today, joined the Nazi Party in May 1933. His writings from 1933 to late 1936, when he was denounced by the SS, were a shabby defense of anti-Semitism and a time-serving exaltation of Hitler. Scholars continue to debate whether Schmitt embraced the Nazi Party as a matter of conviction or as a calculated, cynical instrument of personal advancement.[4]

As university-trained professionals, lawyers were members of the elite in a society in which higher education and participation in the learned professions were not yet a mass phenomenon. Well educated and (for the most part) economically secure, they often had greater latitude for personal choice than did most Germans when confronted with the ethical dilemmas posed by Nazi rule. But they were also embedded in a political environment in which the exercise of their responsibilities drew them unavoidably into collaboration with odious aspects of official policy. Their intelligence and academic achievement did not immunize them against ideological self-delusion. In fact, their intellects may have enabled them to rationalize their participation in morally questionable activities more easily than most people.

In a country where the legislative function of the parliament had been rendered meaningless by the imposition of dictatorship in 1933, law was decreed directly by Hitler and members of his cabinet. The main responsibility for the drafting of new laws and the revision of existing ones often fell to legally-trained civil servants whose task was to translate the political will of the Nazi leadership into the language of the legal code. Based in a host of ministries and agencies of the German state, these officials were active in formulating decrees that clarified the intent, and influenced the practical implementation, of the legislation.

Legal professionals who served the German state as prosecutors played a vital role in the enforcement of the law. Contrary to the widely held perception, violations of laws regarding race or political dissent did not automatically lead to a concentration camp. Instead, Germans charged with such transgressions were indicted by state prosecutors and tried in established courts. Over time, as the "prerogative state" expanded, it became easier for the Gestapo to bypass the judicial system and imprison people in concentration camps through the use of administrative measures such as "preventive detention." There were members of the German legal community, including committed Nazis, who were disturbed by this deviation from the rule of law. The argument was not over whether Germany should function as a racist dictatorship, but rather over whether the authoritarian, racist order would be maintained by law or by the arbitrary exercise of power. As will be seen below, there was no shortage of German prosecutors willing to apply the law in the most draconian fashion.

This severe disposition was shared by many German judges. Even before the Nazi seizure of power, the German judiciary had comprised a large number of conservative nationalists. After 1933, the Nazi regime found ways to purge liberal judges from the bench, and new judicial appointments were made on the basis of ideological dependability. But sympathy, in whole or in part, with Nazi goals can explain the actions of only some judges. Others, less committed or even opposed to Nazism, may have felt bound to enforce the laws on the positivist premise that only those laws enacted by humans have force and that they, as judges, were obliged to apply and enforce them. For them, performance of "duty" may have overcome their personal opposition or even revulsion in the face of such laws and inhibited them from invoking principles of natural law or universal rights to escape what they saw as their duty. As the law had become infused by the principles of Nazism after 1933, such an objective application of the law, made without ideological bias, inevitably transformed judges into accomplices of the regime. Definitions of race, penalties for violating race laws, the criminalization of dissent and political opposition—all of these provisions had been formally integrated into the German legal code, and judges understood it as their job to enforce them.

One point that requires emphasis is that not all legal professionals collaborated with the Nazi regime's policies of racial and political persecution. Many continued to practice law on a day-to-day basis as they had before 1933. This should be recognized, even if the continuation of such normalcy is less historically interesting than the stories of lawyers and jurists who were complicit in the worst aspects of that period. It should also not be forgotten that many legal professionals were victims of the Nazi regime. During the Weimar Republic many German Jews had undertaken the practice of law, and therefore the systematic purge of Jews from the German professions took an especially high toll on the legal professions. In addition to Jews, who were excluded from the professions for reasons of "race," the victims of Nazi purges also included lawyers, judges, and civil servants whose politics were liberal or left-wing.

The volume's opening essay by Konrad Jarausch, "The Conundrum of Complicity: German Professionals and the Final Solution," places the study of legal professionals in a broader historical and sociological context. Explaining the complicity of legal professionals in Nazism, specifically in the most heinous of Nazism's crimes, requires understanding them not only as individuals, but also as members of an organized profession. Jarausch reviews the extensive recent scholarship on the history of university-trained professionals in Germany before, during, and after the Nazi period. The main "interpretive challenge," as he sees it, is to develop a "complex understanding of professional complicity that accounts for both collaboration and reluctance." Jarausch identifies the various attractions that Nazism held, especially for young professionals of the "war youth generation." Scholarship on Nazi Germany and the Holocaust has pointed to the importance of this generation as the source of many officials who played key roles in Nazi anti-Jewish policy.[5] These were German men born between 1900 and 1910, who experienced World War I as youths but did not themselves fight, and who then lived through the defeat and revolution of 1918 and the tumult of the early years of the Weimar Republic. Their nagging fear of a decline in wealth and status, induced by the economic instability and the rise of the organized influence of the working class, was reinforced by the Great Depression. Many harbored resentment toward Jewish professional colleagues, who were perceived as having benefited from an ostensibly illegitimate Jewish "over-representation" in professions, such as law and medicine. This sentiment was compounded by the perception that Jewish professional students were social climbers whose success would threaten the status of their non-Jewish colleagues, who tended to be of privileged or aristocratic background. Aside from these circumstances that were peculiar to their economic predicament, young professionals also proved susceptible to the ultra-nationalism, militarism, and xenophobia on offer from the Nazis and other right-wing *völkisch* organizations.

In explaining the readiness of German professionals to participate in the "Final Solution," Jarausch argues that genocide provided them with an opportunity to demonstrate their indispensability to the German state in a matter of the highest priority. Jarausch parcels lawyers and other professionals into three concentric circles of involvement in genocide: passive facilitators, active supporters, and killing professionals. Legal professionals were present in all three of these categories, with the highest numbers in the first two. Resistance and dissent did take place, but was infrequent.

Jarausch extends his analysis into the post-1945 period. With the exception of the most heinous perpetrators of atrocities, legal and other professionals had a relatively easy time reintegrating themselves into German society, especially in West Germany. Their skills were needed in the reconstruction process that took place in the context of the Cold War. Their own silence was made possible by the rest of society looking the other way. Only gradually, as a result of the passing of generations and the social and historically critical atmospheres of the 1960s, did a critical remembrance of the past emerge.

In his contribution, Hans-Christian Jasch focuses on a single example of the kind of young professional identified by Jarausch. In "Civil Service Lawyers and the Holocaust: The Case of Wilhelm Stuckart," Jasch describes the life and career of one of the most prominent civil servants involved in Nazi anti-Jewish policy. Wilhelm Stuckart was a young, ambitious, and very capable lawyer. A member of the "war youth generation," Stuckart was born in 1902, joined the Nazi Party well before 1933, and joined the SS in 1936. Well-educated, diligent, intelligent, and well-versed in Nazi ideology, Stuckart served as State Secretary in the Reich Ministry of the Interior, which exercised important powers over the formulation and implementation of racial laws in the 1930s. Jasch characterizes him as the "personification of the new civil servant of the Nazi state."

Jewish policy, Jasch observes, was a prestigious area of policymaking that offered career opportunities for young lawyers. Lawyers in the civil service, like Stuckart, cooperated with each other in proposing anti-Jewish measures and pushing them to the next level of severity, contributing to what one influential scholar has called the "collective radicalization" of National Socialist Jewish policy.[6] Stuckart's Nazi-era career began in 1933, when he was involved in purging Jews from universities in the German state of Prussia. He then began a steady climb through the ranks of the Reich Ministry of the Interior. His expert knowledge of administrative law led to involvement with questions of racial categorization and citizenship policy. He was instrumental in drafting the Nuremberg Laws and other racial legislation and participated in the notorious Wannsee Conference on January 20, 1942, at which German government and Nazi Party officials discussed the logistics of the "Final Solution."

Some have argued that Stuckart was a moderate whose intention in drafting the Nuremberg Laws had actually been to soften the impact of Nazi racial ideology on Jews. Jasch challenges this idea, pointing out that Stuckart and colleagues at the Ministry of the Interior had been at work on anti-Semitic legislation well before the Nuremberg Laws. Jasch also takes issue with the widely held belief that Stuckart objected to the "Final Solution," a notion that has been reinforced by a dramatic depiction of Stuckart in a cinematic reenactment of the Wannsee Conference.[7] Jasch demonstrates that Stuckart was also involved in the mass killing of disabled Germans in the so-called euthanasia program.

Robert Rachlin's contribution also features a case study of a prominent individual. In "Roland Freisler and the Volksgerichtshof: The Court as an Instrument of Terror," Rachlin focuses on perhaps the single most notorious figure of the Nazi legal system. Roland Freisler is best known for his attempt to humiliate the defendants accused of participation in the July 20, 1944 plot to assassinate Hitler. Freisler's frenzied ranting and hectoring of the defendants was captured for posterity on film. Rachlin shows, however, that there was much more to Freisler's Nazi-era legal and judicial career than that one episode.

Freisler was an early zealot of the Nazi movement who, in Rachlin's words, combined a "high intellect" with an "unshakable dedication to Hitler." Freisler's rise as a talented lawyer was closely interwoven with the political rise of the Nazi Party before 1933. His readiness to pervert the German system of justice for ideological and political ends was "extreme even by the standards of the Third Reich." For most of the Third Reich he served as State Secretary in the Reich Ministry of Justice. Like Stuckart, Freisler participated in the Wannsee Conference in January 1942. His career culminated in 1942 with his appointment to the Presidency of the People's Court. Although the autonomy of the German judiciary had been steadily deteriorating since 1933, Freisler's appointment to head the court eliminated any remaining pretense of independence in the administration of justice, particularly as it pertained to politically-tinged acts.

As a result of the widening war, the Nazi regime intensified the severity with which it reacted to cases of dissent and resistance. Under

Freisler, the People's Court handed down thousands of death penalty judgments. These were applied to both Germans and non-Germans accused of dissent and the undermining of morale. As Rachlin describes it, Freisler dispensed with any "outward insignia of impartiality and procedural regularity," and the People's Court became a "naked instrument of Hitler's single-minded aim of mobilizing all institutions of German life, including the judiciary, for the promotion of war aims."

A key argument in Rachlin's essay is that the judicial philosophy applied by Freisler on the People's Court was one that had developed over many years. At the core of this philosophy were two principles: first, the legal system was subordinate to the will of the Führer, and second, the traditional dictum *nullum crimen sine lege* (no crime without a law) should not apply in Germany. This second point meant that defendants could be tried for actions that had not been determined in advance to have been illegal. Taken together, these two principles amounted to a repudiation of the positivist legal tradition in Germany whereby legal norms were defined by specific, clear enactments. Freisler denounced the notion that judges should be bound by written criminal law as un-German. The law, he argued, is what the Führer said it was. Rachlin, therefore, warns against reducing the history of the People's Court to Freisler's widely acknowledged personal odiousness. What was at work was actually an approach to the law that rejected the norms and traditions of the German *Rechtsstaat* and placed the prerogatives of the national leadership above the law.

In his contribution, "Guilt, Shame, Anger, Indignation: Nazi Law and Nazi Morals," Raphael Gross shifts our attention from legal professionals to the law itself. The aim of the essay is to "analyze law in Nazi Germany from the perspective of its moral foundation." As Gross argues, Nazi law was based on a system of moral and ethical values that might be reprehensible to us, but were regarded by the Nazis themselves as virtuous and altruistic. The virtues celebrated by Nazism included honor, loyalty, comradeship, and decency. But these were seen as exclusively "Aryan" virtues, which meant that Jews were, by definition, excluded from this moral universe. In fact, according to Gross, Jews were believed to embody a "counter-morality" to the Aryan morality. From the Nazi perspective, Jewish and Aryan values were polar opposites.

Gross argues that the laws implemented during the Third Reich to exclude Jews from German life were consistent with this Nazi view of the Aryan moral system. The Nuremberg race laws are one example of this phenomenon at work. At the core of Aryan morality was an aversion to all things Jewish, including the Jewish body. It followed that intimacy with Jews was deemed an immoral act and was therefore criminalized.

As Gross shows, the pervasiveness of this moral revulsion toward Jews was such that it often manifested itself in judgments handed down by German courts. Gross illustrates this point through a close textual analysis of the judgment against Werner Holländer by the Special Court in Kassel in 1943. The court convicted Holländer of "race defilement" on the basis of his having had a sexual relationship with an "Aryan" woman despite the fact that Holländer, who had been raised as a Protestant, had not been aware that he was Jewish according to Nazi racial laws. The crime of "race defilement" did not carry the death penalty according to the Nuremberg Laws, but the judges found a way to justify his execution, invoking the language of moral indignation. The court twisted the law to impose a punishment that it regarded as commensurate with the moral gravity of the crime.

One further consequence of Nazi anti-Semitism was the exclusion of Jews from the German legal professions; this is the subject of the essay by Douglas Morris, "Discrimination, Degradation, Defiance: Jewish Lawyers under Nazism." Morris emphasizes that this purge was not only an outcome of anti-Semitic race policy, but it was also closely connected with Nazi attacks on liberal elements in the German legal world. Jews had been closely identified with liberalism in Germany since the nineteenth century, and the emancipation of Jews had been one of the signal accomplishments of liberalism. Jews had come to play an important role in the German legal profession, and for the most part they had promoted liberal notions of the law, which included the rule of law (the *Rechtsstaat*), equality under the law, individual rights, and democratic participation in the legislative process. Eliminating Jews from the legal profession was seen, from the Nazi point of view, as an essential part of the dismantling of liberalism. The Nazi regime replaced legal equality with notions of racial hierarchy, subordinated individual rights to the perceived requirements of the Aryan "*Volk* community," and put an end to democratic participation, creating an authoritarian "Führer State" in its place.

Morris chronicles the measures taken by the regime to remove Jewish lawyers from the legal system. These measures began as physical intimidation and were then gradually institutionalized by laws and decrees. Morris also describes how Jewish lawyers responded to the persecution. Some emigrated quickly. Others attempted to defend their rights, which still seemed possible in the early phase of the regime. For example, President Paul von Hindenburg protected Jewish war veterans from dismissal.

Over time, however, the situation deteriorated as the Nazi movement consolidated its hold on power. Jewish lawyers grew ever more marginalized, were abandoned by their non-Jewish professional colleagues, and were subjected to increasing humiliation by Nazified professional organizations and judicial institutions. The final push to purge Jews from the legal professions occurred in 1938.

In the face of persecution, some Jewish lawyers engaged in intellectual forms of resistance. Morris describes two such cases: Hugo Sinzheimer, who authored a defense of German liberalism and the role of Jews in its development; and Ernst Fraenkel, whose book, *The Dual State,* established itself as a classic analysis of the Nazi legal system. Fraenkel also penned anti-Nazi articles intended to rally readers to defend liberal principles and to inspire them to anti-Nazi resistance.

The final two contributions to the collection deal with attempts after 1945 to judge the behavior of German legal professionals who had been active in the Third Reich. In "Evading Responsibility for Crimes against Humanity: Murderous Lawyers at Nuremberg," Harry Reicher examines the Justice Case, in which sixteen German judges, prosecutors, and civil servants were accused of "having perverted Germany's legal system, and of converting it into an instrument of terror." Reicher's essay describes in detail how several of the defendants attempted to justify their pre-1945 actions before the tribunal in Nuremberg. Their defense relied on the *Führerprinzip*—the Nazi leadership principle—which, they asserted, had functioned as an essential component of the Nazi legal system. It was accepted legal practice in the Third Reich, they argued, that the written law could be overridden by the will of Hitler himself. Ultimately, they argued, they had been accountable not to positive law, but to the will of the Führer, and had had no free choice of their own to interpret the law.

Reicher concentrates on two figures: Franz Schlegelberger and Oswald Rothaug. Schlegelberger had been among the highest-ranking officials in the Ministry of Justice; Rothaug had been Chief Justice of a Special Court in Nuremberg in the late 1930s. At the postwar tribunal, both were indicted for their roles in Nazi-era court cases that had resulted in the execution of Jewish defendants. Schlegelberger was instrumental in the prosecution of Markus Luftglass, who was convicted of stealing eggs, while Rothaug had rendered judgment against Leo Katzenberger, who had been accused of having had an affair with an Aryan woman in violation of Nazi racial laws. These two cases might seem like a drop in the ocean when the magnitude of the Holocaust is taken into account.

But the purpose of trying the responsible German officials after the war was to demonstrate how the German legal and judicial system—the "normative state," in Fraenkel's formulation—had been perverted by Nazism. The Nuremberg court ultimately rejected the defense based on adherence to the *Führerprinzip*. Reicher's concluding point echoes the implicit lesson of Freisler's career as examined by Robert Rachlin; these cases highlight the dangers of placing the prerogatives of the political leadership above the law.

The final piece in the volume is Kenneth Ledford's essay, "Judging German Judges in the Third Reich: Excusing and Confronting the Past." Ledford addresses the long-term aftereffects of the Nazified German judiciary. With a focus on West Germany, he examines the debate over what, if anything, had gone wrong with German judges before 1945. Understanding this debate requires considering the history of the German judiciary since the 1870s. The conservative judiciary of the German Empire survived fairly intact after the collapse of 1918 and the creation of the Weimar Republic. Weimar-era judges often laid down judgments that reflected their sympathy for right-wing political causes, the most notorious example being the lenient sentence meted out to Hitler after the failed Putsch attempt of November 1923. To be sure, liberal judges were also appointed during the Weimar period. Notable among them was Fritz Bauer, a judge of Jewish background in Stuttgart who would later spearhead prosecutions of Nazi criminals in West Germany. However, Bauer and others like him were purged by the Nazi regime, and what remained of the German judiciary after 1933 leaned sharply to the right.

After 1945, the Allies removed many German judges from the bench because of their Nazi-era decisions or political affiliations. But once authority over German courts was returned to the Germans, many of these judges were readmitted to the bench. This was in part a pragmatic (some have argued cynical) decision based on the premise that, without ex-Nazi judges, there would have been nobody to run the court system in postwar West Germany. But, as Ledford shows, the restoration was also justified on the basis of a specific legal tradition: positivism. Judges and their defenders argued that the judges had been compelled by the strong German tradition of positivism to implement laws that may have been objectionable from moral or ethical perspectives. Ironically, one of the chief proponents of this apologia for the German judges was Gustav Radbruch, a Social Democratic legal philosopher. Radbruch's assertions prompted heated debate in international legal circles in the late 1940s.

As essays in this book demonstrate, however, adherence to positivism can go only so far as an explanation of judicial complicity in the crimes of the Nazi regime.

Outside of specialized legal circles, as Ledford shows, little attention was given in West Germany to the Nazi-era past of many judges who remained active on the bench. It was not recognized as a problem. This began to change in the 1960s when the student movement posed disturbing questions about continuities from the Nazi era into post-1945 German society. A body of critical legal scholarship emerged through the 1970s and 1980s. Ledford examines several examples of this genre, most notably Ingo Müller's 1987 book, *Hitler's Justice*.[8] Ledford brings the story up to date, noting that since the 1990 re-unification, there has been an increase in serious critical examinations of the German judiciary in the Nazi period. This body of work attacks the apologetics and exculpatory myths that had proved so persistent in the decades following the war. In contemporary Germany, Ledford concludes, there is little patience with excuses for the complicity of judges in the Nazi regime.

Although these essays deal with the law and the legal professions in a singular historical context, they have important implications for our own time. The essays show how the rule of law can be eroded by allegiance to ideology, by blind obedience to political leaders, and by the pressures of war. They show how a vulnerable minority can be exploited as a scapegoat by well-educated professionals worried about their careers and searching for simple formulas for the restoration of national greatness. And they show how civil servants, lawyers, and judges who had undermined the rule of law can escape accountability for their actions in a society that prefers to move forward rather than to dwell on the unfortunate episodes of the recent past. It is tempting to argue that the case of Nazi Germany is so extreme that it could not possibly serve as a mirror to our own society. It is important, however, to remember that Germans, too, once took great pride in their *Rechtsstaat,* and that no society is immune from the perversion of the law under a fateful combination of circumstances.

Notes

1. Probably the most widely read work, but not the most intellectually rigorous, is Ingo Müller, *Hitler's Justice: The Courts of the Third Reich,* translated by Deborah

Lucas Schneider (Cambridge, 1991). Another popular study is H.W. Koch, *In the Name of the Volk: Political Justice in the Third Reich* (New York, 1989). A collection of essays by a highly regarded German legal scholar is Michael Stolleis, *The Law under the Swastika: Studies on Legal History in Nazi Germany*, trans. Thomas Dunlap (Chicago, 1998). The German legal profession in the Nazi era is examined in Konrad H. Jarausch, *The Unfree Professions: German Lawyers, Teachers and Engineers, 1900–1950* (New York, 1990). A compelling study of how Nazi courts served the political goals of the regime is Nikolaus Wachsmann, *Hitler's Prisons: Legal Terror in Nazi Germany* (New Haven, 2004). Important works on the Weimar Republic that provide important background for understanding the Nazi period are Kenneth F. Ledford, *From General Estate to Special Interest: German Lawyers 1878–1933* (Cambridge, 1996); Douglas G. Morris, *Justice Imperiled: The Anti-Nazi Lawyer Max Hirschberg in Weimar Germany* (Ann Arbor, 2005); and Benjamin Carter Hett, *Crossing Hitler: The Man Who Put the Nazis on the Witness Stand* (New York, 2008).
2. Important German-language studies include the following: Ralph Angermund, *Deutsche Richterschaft 1919–1945: Krisenerfahrung, Illusion, politische Rechtsprechung* (Frankfurt, 1990); Bernhard Diestelkamp, ed. *Justizalltag im Dritten Reich* (Frankfurt, 1988); Rudolf Echterhölter, *Das öffentliche Recht im nationalsozialistischen Staat* (Stuttgart, 1970); Michael Förster, *Jurist im Dienst des Unrechts: Leben und Werk des ehemaligen Staatssekretärs im Reichsjustizministerium, Franz Schlegelberger (1876–1970)* (Baden-Baden, 1995); Lothar Gruchmann, *Justiz im Dritten Reich: 1933—1940: Anpassung und Unterwerfung in der Ära Gürtner* (Munich, 2001); Angelika Königseder, *Recht und nationalsozialistische Herrschaft. Berliner Anwälte 1933–1945: ein Forschungsprojekt des Berliner Anwaltsvereins e.V.* (Bonn, 2001); Helmut Ortner, *Der Hinrichter: Roland Freisler, Mörder im Dienste Hitlers* (Vienna, 1993); Walter Wagner, *Der Volksgerichtshof im nationalsozialistischen Staat* (Stuttgart, 1974); Hermann Weinkauff, *Die deutsche Justiz und der Nationalsozialismus: ein Überblick* (Stuttgart, 1968).
3. Ernst Fraenkel, *The Dual State: A Contribution to the Theory of Dictatorship*, trans. E. A. Shils in collaboration with Edith Lowenstein and Klaus Knorr (New York, 1941).
4. Notable among the many works on Schmitt are Joseph Bendersky, *Carl Schmitt: Theorist for the Reich* (Princeton, 1983); and Raphael Gross, *Carl Schmitt and the Jews: The "Jewish Question," the Holocaust, and German Legal Theory*, trans. Joel Golb (Madison, 2007).
5. See the influential study by Michael Wildt, *Generation des Unbedingten: das Führungskorps des Reichssicherheitshauptamtes*, 2nd ed. (Hamburg, 2003).
6. Hans Mommsen, "The Realization of the Unthinkable: The 'Final Solution of the Jewish Question' in the Third Reich," in Hans Mommsen, ed., *From Weimar to Auschwitz: Essays in German History* (Princeton, 1991).
7. "Die Wannsee-Konferenz," directed by Heinz Schirk, 1987. For a discussion of how Stuckart is depicted in this film as well as a later dramatization of the conference, see Alan E. Steinweis, review of "Conspiracy," a film by Frank Pierson (2001), *American Historical Review* 107 (April 2002): 674.
8. The title of the original German edition of the book was the considerably more sensationalistic *Furchtbare Juristen* (Munich, 1987).

Publicity poster for the 1936 "Day of German Law," the annual meeting of the League of National Socialist German Jurists
Source: Bundesarchiv, Berlin

Chapter 1

THE CONUNDRUM OF COMPLICITY
German Professionals and the Final Solution

Konrad H. Jarausch

FROM THE NUREMBERG TRIALS TO recent media revelations, evidence has steadily accumulated that German professionals were involved in the crimes of the Holocaust to a shocking degree. While the brutality of lower-class concentration camp guards may not be surprising, the betrayal of the Hippocratic oath by murderous doctors like Mengele affronts moral sensibilities.[1] Though the tirades of the anti-Semitic Brownshirts of the Sturmabteilung (SA) were to be expected, the justification of racial discrimination by legal theorists like Carl Schmitt continues to baffle observers. Even if the book-burning by Nazi students might be attributed to misguided enthusiasm, the drawing up of ethnic cleansing plans by *völkisch* professors like Albert Brackmann disgusts intellectual sensibilities. Perhaps this outrage is a result of disappointed expectations based on the implicit assumption that academics ought to be held to a higher ethical standard, possess greater competence, and behave in a more humane manner.[2] Behind this revulsion lies the central question: How could apparently decent, competent professionals become Hitler's accomplices?

The emergence of the Holocaust perspective has transformed educated involvement in the Third Reich into a cautionary tale, which now suspects virtually all professionals of being accomplices in genocide. In a remarkable reversal of fronts from earlier apologias, a younger generation of German intellectuals is no longer content to treat their predecessors as occasional accomplices, but accuses them of being the actual "masterminds of mass destruction."[3] Though appealing, such a blanket condemnation oversimplifies the complexity of collaboration in turn.

Interestingly enough, survivors' accounts rarely mention professionals—only sometimes referring to prison doctors—but they rarely address the engineers who designed the camps or the lawyers who organized the genocide.[4] For all his "shame over Germany" because it was suddenly turning back into a violent fourteenth century Romania, Victor Klemperer noted in his diary a range of academic behaviors extending from base opportunism to courageous resistance.[5] A closer look reveals not only an appalling amount of nationalist collusion but also instances of opposition against war and repression.

Older explanations, initially put forward by contemporaries, tended to emphasize the dictatorial character of the Third Reich that left professionals no choice but to cooperate with the regime. Distressed by the betrayal of their colleagues and frightened by the rise of communism, émigrés like Hannah Arendt or Carl Friedrich developed the notion of totalitarianism that emphasized the terrorist character of the racial dictatorship. Historians like Karl-Dietrich Bracher investigated the reasons for the collapse of the Weimar Republic, sought like Michael Kater to account for the rise of the Nazi movement, or tried like Henry Ashby Turner to analyze the alliance of German conservatives with the Nazi upstarts that put them in power.[6] Other scholars have, like Ian Kershaw, focused on Hitler's "charismatic authority" and interpreted his appeal to the masses through the notion of "working towards the *Führer*," while Hans-Ulrich Wehler endeavored to provide a socio-structural explanation for the workings of Hitler's charisma.[7] Though these larger interpretations sketch the context of the Third Reich, they say little about the specific role of professionals in the Nazi regime.

More recent research that differentiates the monolithic picture of a "consensus dictatorship" makes more room for an analysis of academic collusion by examining the changing pattern of voluntary cooperation from below. Transcending the black and white categories of de-Nazification, Robert Gellately's or Eric Johnson's studies of everyday interactions stress the ambiguity of individual roles and uncover a complex mixture of complicity and reluctance, pointing out that reactions ranged from enthusiastic nationalism to Catholic or Socialist reservations.[8] More suggestive is Ulrich Herbert's exploration of the strange mixture of ideological commitment and professional competence in the biography of SS leader Werner Best, while Michael Wildt has painted a collective portrait of an entire cohort of university graduates who formulated the murderous policies of the RSHA.[9] Finally, a number of scholars have also started to examine the actions of individual professions like doctors, lawyers, and teachers more closely in order to get at the complicated mixture of support, collaboration, or resistance among academics as a group.[10]

The interpretative challenge, therefore, consists of developing a complex understanding of professional complicity that accounts for both collaboration and reluctance. Perhaps the perspective of "critical historicization" that addresses the contradiction between Communist terror and everyday lives in the second German dictatorship might provide such a nuanced approach.[11] In order to assess the precise extent to which individual academics or entire professions were involved, it might help to break down the overall question into some of its component parts: Why did a growing number of professionals respond to Nazi appeals during the Great Depression? What was the role of anti-Semitism in the subsequent displacement of their Jewish colleagues? How did the Second World War speed the abandonment of moral standards and facilitate mass murder? Which memories did the collusion of academics with the Third Reich leave after its collapse? The following reflections will draw both on recent scholarship and on some documentation from my own family history in order to examine how similar to or different professionals were from ordinary Germans.[12]

The Attraction of National Socialism

Due to the social distance between the educated middle class and lower class rowdies, most professionals initially looked askance at the "crude anti-intellectualism" of the Nazi movement. In Weimar Germany, the academic professions consisted largely of male university or technical school graduates who were steeped in a neo-humanist tradition of the classics, oriented towards scholarly research, and initiated into the practical requirements of their later pursuits. Though they had much freedom to study, they were generally subjected to a rigorous set of state examinations that tested their theoretical knowledge as well as their practical competence. While many chose the independence of the free professions (*freie Berufe*) by becoming lawyers and doctors, even more gravitated towards state employment in the legally-oriented bureaucracy, neo-humanist Gymnasia, or proliferating research institutes. Graduates of the natural sciences, technical subjects, or commercial fields also flocked into the laboratories and board-rooms of the knowledge-based industries. Though rarely wealthy, the some 350,000 university graduates were respected for their competence and envied for their security.[13]

One educated group which was particularly vulnerable to right-wing appeals was the "war youth generation." Like my father, these young men were born between 1900 and 1910 and experienced the First World War in school, where they were subjected to a stream of incessant patriotic propaganda and longed to prove their mettle in action. Since they lacked the personal experience of combat that disillusioned many of their older brothers, many were keenly disappointed in the military defeat and never really arrived in the leftist Weimar Republic. Traumatized by "the terrible collapse of our childhood world," they flocked to *völkisch* causes that provided a populist form of nationalism, which seemed more modern and egalitarian than the hierarchical Empire. The radical fringe volunteered, like Ernst von Salomon, for the Free Corps, fighting foreign and domestic enemies, while moderate youths joined rightist student groups that banned Jews and hounded liberal professors. Some of them might have outgrown the male-bonding fantasies of the Youth Movement, had they not completed their training just when the bottom dropped out of the economy.[14]

By exposing the shallowness of the postwar recovery, the Great Depression plunged aspiring and established professionals into a crisis that often threatened their very survival. Due to the lack of alternatives, the number of students soared, overcrowding the universities and also renewing the oversupply of graduates desperately looking for jobs. Since the government had little revenue left to hire, most law probationers had no choice but to swell the number of attorneys desperately competing for clients. Several thousand teacher trainees, like my parents, had to wait for up to a decade before they could find a position. Massive layoffs in industry created an annually doubling pool of tens of thousands of unemployed who had to get by on their shrinking savings, losing much of their self-respect. Even bureaucrats were hard hit, since successive pay cuts, imposed by the Brüning government, reduced their previous income by about one-third. Though most established professionals resented their longer work hours, shrinking remuneration, and declining social status, the Depression hit the younger generation especially hard, since it denied them entry into their chosen field.[15]

No wonder the result of such dislocation was a widespread "crisis of professional consciousness." Overcrowding, unemployment, and impoverishment seemed to practitioners to be a betrayal of expectations and values for which the failure of the system, i.e., the Weimar Republic, and not their individual mistakes, must be responsible. It hardly helped that the democratic parties were unable to offer any workable remedies, since the Social Democrats suggested spreading the pain by sharing poverty. Struggling lawyers were disappointed that Liberals could only counsel a redoubling of efforts to win the competition for the few remaining commissions. In this confusion, the previously dismissed radical suggestions of various *völkisch* nationalists gradually began to seem more credible: Could the acute crisis not be overcome by eliminating unwanted competitors such as the newly admitted women, the studious Jews, or the subversive foreigners? Some embittered teacher-trainees without a job even contemplated suicide.[16] In effect, the suffering of the depression discredited liberal conceptions of professionalism and made harried academics search for more drastic alternatives.

The chief beneficiaries of the crisis were zealous Nazi practitioners who founded their own competing associations. Fed up with traditional corporations, *völkisch* students created an anti-Semitic NS German Student League; they campaigned against Leftist professors, brawled with their competitors, and won enough campus elections so they could take over the national student association in the summer of 1931![17] In order to provide legal defense for their violent SA thugs, Nazi lawyers established a League of NS German Jurists, a vocal pressure group that had attracted about 1500 members, i.e., 5 percent of all lawyers, by early 1933. Similarly, radical pedagogues created a Nazi Teachers League that preached the Nazification of education and mushroomed to about 11,000 adherents by seizure of power. More complicated was the creation of an engineering organization, but eventually a "Fighting League for German Architects and Engineers" coalesced, which drew several thousand technicians.[18] By publishing their own journals, holding congresses, and spreading racism, these Nazi affiliates proselytized their professional colleagues for the Nazi cause.

Initially reluctant, professionals began to respond to Nazi appeals due to the electoral breakthrough of 1930, and began to flock in increasing numbers into the party after the seizure of power when thousands of opportunists joined. Among the different age groups, it was especially the war-youth cohort that followed Hitler's message, since for them the material crisis was most acute. Similar to the population at large, Protestants were also overrepresented, while Catholics remained reluctant and Jews were excluded. Interestingly enough, before 1933 veterinarians, foresters, and technicians were more likely to enter the party than members of established pursuits, perhaps also due to legal prohibitions. Among frustrated jurists, modestly marginal practitioners, including some with a doctorate, joined the League. However, among teachers, primary pedagogues and trainees were the most likely Nazis. In spite of the prevalence of nationalist resentment, only a small but growing minority of German professionals, like the brother of my aunt, Hermann Kauba, responded to Hitler before 1933, prompted by the rhetoric of *völkisch* nationalism and the fear of becoming an "academic proletarian."[19]

Nationalism and Anti-Semitism

The "fateful alliance" between traditional conservatives, *völkisch* nationalists, and Nazis created much support for the so-called "national awakening," even among professionals. In the universities, Nazi-inspired purges shifted the already truncated political spectrum even further to the Right by eliminating the few remaining democrats and socialists. In the professional organizations, self-coordination toppled the pro-Republican leadership, dropped all Jewish board members, and transferred their membership into the appropriate Nazi professional organization. The remaining nationalists agreed with the Nazi leadership on the need for domestic economic recovery and international resurgence by repudiating the restrictions of the Treaty of Versailles.[20] Conservative historians had few qualms about polemicizing against the "war guilt lie" or in buttressing calls for frontier revision, so as to return the lost provinces to the fatherland.[21] Legal theorists like Carl Schmitt began to elaborate justifications of German hegemony, while pastors among the German Christians preached a renewed *völkisch* version of a national mission.[22] In short, most professionals joined the rightist consensus on national rebirth.

Within the wider enthusiasm for the Third Reich, specific anti-Jewish policies had a narrower base because the new racial anti-Semitism, spreading since the late 1870s, had not yet infected all professionals. Though Heinrich von Treitschke's claim that "the Jews are our misfortune" was rejected by liberal defenders of tolerance like Theodor Mommsen, the rantings of *völkisch* outsiders like Langbehn and Largarde transformed older religious resentment into a quasi-scientific, racial prejudice. Nationalist students played an important role as multipliers by founding the Association of German Students in order to propagate Christian, patriotic, and imperialist ideas. Due to the patronage of Prince Otto von Bismarck, as well as its ingenious agitation tactics, the Association managed to compel prestigious student corporations like the *Burschenschaft* to accept anti-Semitism into their programs, forcing Jewish students to create their own associations in defense. Though defenders of the Weimar Republic continued to support assimilation, after 1918 social anti-Semitism became part of the nationalist resentment against Versailles and began to dominate campus atmosphere and student self-government.[23]

A key argument among the proponents of anti-Semitism was the charge of Jewish overrepresentation in German intellectual life and the professions. Racist propaganda fastened upon the discrepancy between the Jewish share of less than 1 percent in the population and the 9.4 percent proportion in the Prussian student body in 1894–95, ignoring its subsequent decline to 4.7 percent in 1931–32. Critics liked to point out that Jewish students concentrated in urban institutions like Berlin (11.5 percent in 1926), Frankfurt, or Breslau, preferred some disciplines like medicine (22.2 percent in 1911–12) or law (11.1 percent) over others, and that in some institutions like Berlin departments like medicine (37 percent in 1911–12) or law (20.2 percent) were heavily Jewish. Ironically, this uneven distribution was itself a product of the contradiction between legal emancipation and social prejudice that opened the free professions to Jewish practitioners, but restricted government careers like the military, the diplomatic service, or the bureaucracy. As a result, about one-third of German doctors and lawyers came from Jewish backgrounds, though Jews continued to find it quite difficult to become professors.[24]

In the crisis atmosphere of the Great Depression, racial nationalists began to turn their social and cultural prejudices into a demand for legal exclusion of Jewish students, professors, and professionals. The difference in social habits between some newly emancipated Jewish youths, eager to learn in order to advance, and Christian students, intent on enjoying student life, tended to create tension. The cultural resentments of guardians of traditional cultivation against modernist experiments and the advancement of mass entertainment, often associated with Jews, produced pessimistic warnings against decadence and decline. But it took the multiple threats of the World Economic Crisis to turn these fears into demands for actual de-assimilation, barring the further entry of Jewish trainees or excluding already established practitioners. In Berlin, Nazi students loudly promoted a purge: "We demand the selection of students and professors on the basis of proof that they think in a German spirit." At the same time, Nazi professional associations like the Lawyers' League called for the expulsion of Jewish colleagues in order to make room for new Christian graduates.[25]

Though still fearful of foreign opinion, the Nazi government was happy to oblige with an escalating series of legal discriminations that can only be briefly summarized. The first blow was a law, euphemistically for "the restoration of professional civil service," which purged political enemies on the Left and excluded non-Aryans from the bureaucracy, as well as the professions, via a dubious construction of designating even lawyers a public office. The second strike was another law "against the overcrowding of German universities" that restricted Jewish matriculations to 1.5 percent overall and the Jewish share to 5 percent at any given institution, thus forcing the expulsion of hundreds of students.[26] The Nuremberg racial laws of 1935 rescinded the initial exceptions that covered those appointed before 1914 or who had served at the front in World War I, while a myriad of petty edicts sought to squeeze Jews out of the universities through administrative practice.[27] The final assault came with the disbarment of the remaining Jewish professionals in 1938 that left only a few legal consultants or doctors to practice in the Jewish community alone.[28] In the brief span of five years, Nazi activists legally reversed over a century of civic emancipation, ending Jewish contributions to German intellectual life and precipitating their former colleagues into untold personal tragedies.[29]

The ease with which racist zealots succeeded in overturning humanist traditions of tolerance continues to puzzle. While a few courageous scholars like the physicist Max Planck protested against the illegality of the exclusions, the majority reacted with deafening silence to the dismissals. Suddenly, Victor Klemperer felt quite alone: "An animal is not more outlawed or hunted down."[30] Perhaps the noisy agitation of radical students kept some timid academics from speaking out; perhaps the illusion of national rebirth misled some respected figures like Eduard Spranger to pardon Nazi measures as youthful excesses; perhaps some desperate practitioners saw the exclusion of competitors as the only way out of their personal crisis. But the lack of protest also points to the force of prior prejudice in the social isolation of the victims and the cultural stigmatizing of their difference. Moreover, even baser motives of envy of Jewish success among the frustrated Aryan rivals, of greed that sought to profit from taking over an abandoned practice, or of cunning that hoped to open career chances by creating vacancies were rarely put on paper though nonetheless quite real.[31] Even if some academics like my father sought to protect their Jewish pupils, the complicity of the majority was a result of their pact with Hitler's regime that gave anti-Semitism free reign.[32]

Professional Involvement in the Final Solution

Several factors moved professionals to abandon their remaining scruples and move from anti-Semitic discrimination to actual genocide. This escalation was prepared by the emphatic advocacy of anti-Jewish policies by the fanatics of the Nazi professional auxiliaries, such as the younger members of the NS-Dozentenbund (League of University Instructors) or the leadership of the Lawyers' League.[33] Nazi planners also used the funding of the German Research Council to initiate research in racial science, ethnography, arms technology, and other ideological priorities.[34] In the social sciences, Nazified academics like the archivist Albert Brackmann created a whole series of new working groups, such as the networks of Eastern and Western Research, which radical nationalists could join with outright Nazis in waging ethnic warfare and preparing schemes for racial cleansing or resettlement.[35] The core of "Jewish research," which sought to generate statistical information as well as propaganda support for the final solution, nonetheless, remained outside of academe in new party institutes that were staffed by previously marginal academics.[36]

Decisive for abandoning all moral reservations was the unleashing of World War II and the attack on the Soviet Union, since this "war of annihilation" served as a convenient cover. The surprising extent of the initial victories transformed a limited nationalist revisionism into a much wider project of an ethnic reordering of Europe along racial lines. Moreover, the occupation of an increasing number of countries demanded help from area specialists in setting up a military, civilian, or actual Nazi administration. Hitler's growing domain allowed previously fantastic plans of a reconsolidation of ethnic Germans into areas contiguous to the Reich to become a reality, an effort that was organized by legal specialists within the upper echelons of the SS. At the same time, the bloodshed of mechanized warfare created an extralegal realm that permitted the infamous *Einsatzgruppen* (mobile killing squads) to begin the process of killing Polish elites and Jews, thinly camouflaging it as anti-partisan retaliation.[37] The support of most professionals for the war effort allowed a minority of radical anti-Semites to move from civic discrimination to ethnic cleansing and actual genocide.

In a somewhat stylized typology, three different levels of involvement in the Final Solution may be distinguished within the professions, clustered around similar responses. Scholars have largely ignored the many passive facilitators who competently did their duty or enthusiastically supported the war effort. Into this category fall the efficient managers like the Krefeld industrialist Paul Kleinewefers who did his best to produce rare steel alloys needed to build weapons.[38] Legally trained officials also kept the state functioning by implementing the myriad of Nazi decrees, although the dynamism of the racial dictatorship resisted codification because it would hamper spontaneity. Similarly, teachers who inculcated militaristic values, stressed past German greatness, and propagated racial distinctions helped prepare their youthful charges for service on the battlefield or behind the lines. Finally, Protestant pastors who preached a curious mixture of *völkisch* superiority and Christian tradition also played an important role in promoting nationalist values and maintaining a fighting spirit.[39] Even professionals, such as my father, who refused to join the party, created with their commitment to the war effort the precondition for more radical Nazi policies.

More involved, but fewer in number, were the active supporters of German hegemony over Europe who provided intellectual expertise for ethnic resettlement and racial cleansing. Research has shown an appalling degree of academic justification for Hitler's New Order that built upon older Pan-German dreams to found Aryan domination upon a vast scheme of colonizing living space in the East. Whole new branches of historical research studied ethnic patterns, in order to prepare schemes of population transfer or border corrections. Geographers, ethnologists, and historians also cooperated in order to determine the extent of German influence in the East and to suggest policies of consolidating the *Volk*. Typified by Theodor Schieder's 1939 memorandum, these expert papers isolated the Jews as a disintegrative factor that would need to be eliminated in one way or another.[40] While scholarly works like the research of my uncle Franz Petri on the Franco-German language frontier only rarely influenced decisions, they created a climate of opinion in support of ethnic resettlement. While legal experts transformed some of these suggestions into administrative measures, lawyers like Hans Frank supervised their ruthless implementation in the General Government.[41]

Most heavily implicated was the minority of killing professionals who, as trained experts, directly participated in annihilationist warfare or genocidal extermination. Recent studies of the *Einsatzgruppen* have revealed the importance of mobile police forces for the initiation of mass murder, while the controversy swirling around the Wehrmacht exhibition has shown the large degree of complicity of the regular armed forces.[42] Equally disturbing has been the fresh evidence on the cool planning of genocide by an elite corps of young lawyers in the SS and Gestapo under the direction of the talented Werner Best that transformed somewhat haphazard violence into a bureaucratic process.⁴³ Similarly, the admissions by managers like my father-in-law Friedrich Flessa of having exploited slave labor in arms production show a startling combination of rationality and ideology among engineers that served the dual goals of producing weapons and killing racial inferiors.⁴⁴ Finally, the revelations on the role reversal of doctors from healers to killers in preferring the eugenic goal of preserving the health of the body politic through sterilization, euthanasia, selection, and medical experiments document unspeakable crimes.⁴⁵

These increasing degrees of commitment to the Third Reich functioned as an interlocking system in which each level supported the next. Perhaps the image of concentric circles, starting with a broad ring of apolitical expertise, but narrowing through a second circle of nationalist supporters towards an annihilationist core might illustrate this fateful interrelationship. Most widespread was the support for the war effort that stabilized Nazi rule at home and made military conquest abroad possible. Such an outlook at least tolerated anti-Semitic discrimination by failing to protest in public against it. Less prevalent, but still quite popular among professionals, was a radical nationalist justification for ethnic resettlement and racial cleansing as a biopolitical base for ensuring German hegemony in Europe. This *völkisch* mind-set singled out Jews and Slavs as racial inferiors to be expelled from the professions and displaced from Germany into some undefined Eastern ghettos. Least widespread, but most fatal was the direct participation of military, legal, technical, and medical professionals in the Final Solution. Whether acting from opportunist motives or ideological conviction, these experts narrowed their ethical outlook to service to their own *Volk,* oblivious of the untold human suffering which their actions created in those excluded from its community.⁴⁶

Though well trained and widely respected, professionals raised surprisingly few objections to participating in a genocidal regime. In my own family, the brother of the wife of my father's brother had a golden party badge, indicating that he was an enthusiastic Nazi who had joined the party well before 1933. While my mother's brother Franz Petri clashed with the SS on specific issues like the treatment of Flemish separatists, as a party member since 1937 and part of the Belgian military government, he failed to oppose the murderous policies of the Third Reich in general.⁴⁷ Only my father was so shocked by the systematic starvation of Russian POWs that he tried to distribute the scarce food more evenly and expressed human solidarity with the regime's victims—an action that cost him his life in January 1942.[48] Tied to service to the national or *Volk* rather than to universal principles of human rights, their conception of professionalism as expertise provided no ethical grounds for objecting to participation in systematic killing. Based on lingering Christian precepts, some professionals might have developed qualms about racist genocide, but, exceptions like Jochen Klepper notwithstanding, these failed to coalesce into effective public resistance.[49]

Living with Nightmare Memories

Once the killing stopped, the victims, perpetrators, and bystanders developed quite different recollections of what had actually transpired. To cope with their prior suffering, the few surviving Jewish professionals dedicated themselves to keeping memory alive so as to prevent the recurrence of such atrocities; some, like Victor Klemperer, even joined the Communist Party as the most resolute anti-fascist group.[50] Those fortunate academics who had managed to flee in time and struggled to continue their calling in a new country were understandably bitter about their expulsion, and demanded some restitution for their many material losses as well as psychological traumata.[51] In international opinion, relief about the impending end of the war overshadowed the shock over the racist genocide due to the discovery of the horrors of concentration camps such as Buchenwald or Dachau by the American army. It took the organization of depositories like the Leo Baeck Institute to preserve the scattered records of the persecuted and to overcome the reluctance to talk about the Holocaust within the Jewish community.[52]

The overwhelming physical, photographic and written evidence of mass murder forced the reluctant Germans into an acknowledgement of the existence of such crimes. The documentation of the Nuremberg prosecutors like the émigré lawyer Robert Kempner, the gripping testimony of survivors, and the accounts of anti-fascists like Egon Kogon made it impossible to deny that many officers, lawyers, doctors, or managers had been involved in atrocities. Since the democratic politicians of the West and the Communists in the East had themselves been persecuted, the successor states adopted competing versions of anti-Fascism, with the GDR emphasizing the Third Reich's structural roots in the landed and business elites, and the FRG instead stressing the criminal disposition of the Nazi leadership. Ironically, both interpretations opened the door to exculpation, since the former ignored the question of individual guilt while the latter held only a small minority responsible, thereby absolving the majority of accomplices.[53] As long as professionals conformed to these explanations, they could rewrite their CVs and continue to practice, minimizing their personal role.

The amnesia of the 1950s that allowed experts to suppress their own responsibility was largely a result of their indispensability for the occupation authorities and the successor states. In a thoroughly devastated country the pragmatic needs of survival, such as providing electric power, tending to the sick, or restoring public order, required the reinstatement of previously dismissed specialists without dwelling too much on their tarnished record.[54] The bureaucratic nature of the de-Nazification process engendered so much resentment that the vetting boards eventually turned to reducing major crimes into minor misdemeanors, thereby becoming an infamous *Mitläuferfabrik* (fellow-traveler factory).[55] Caught up in the general plight of flight and expulsion, and the hunger and homelessness of being a POW, most professionals focused on their own suffering and helped to elaborate a sense of victimhood that fostered oblivion. While the public insistently debated the general question of responsibility, prominent academics were rarely willing to admit personal guilt, retreating behind a discussion of impersonal forces. Finally, the ideological polarization of the Cold War spread a mantle of silence over the issue.[56]

All the more surprising was the eventual return of a critical memory that transformed the recollections of the victims into the official public memory of the Federal Republic. Against the resistance of compromised judges, the litigation of committed prosecutors like Fritz Bauer forced West Germany to create a central clearinghouse in Ludwigsburg, while a series of well publicized cases like the Eichmann trial in Jerusalem and the Auschwitz trial in Frankfurt produced damning testimony of wider involvement. The media broadcast of radio-plays and television documentaries on the Third Reich and the rewriting of teaching guidelines also improved public awareness of the magnitude of collaboration. Part of the generational conflict in the late 1960s revolved around the suppression of individual guilt among the parents, even if radicals used the accusation of fascism rather indiscriminately.[57] For the professions, it was crucial that a few committed individuals within their own ranks leveled accusations, created scandals, and mounted exhibitions like "Terrible Jurists" that tore away the cover of silence. Precipitating a difficult process of soul-searching, such critical interventions broke through the barrier of denial and forced experts to confront their own complicity.[58]

What does this brief sketch suggest about the painful evolution of memories? Since Maurice Halbwachs already pointed out that remembering is a social process, it should not be surprising that the recollections of the same atrocities differed fundamentally according to the respective roles in the Holocaust.[59] Chancellor Konrad Adenauer's controversial joining of material restitution to Israel with the reinstatement of all but the most discredited specialists into their former positions according to paragraph 131 of the Basic Law illustrates that recollection is a highly political process with enormous financial implications, not just a value-free scholarly enterprise.[60] The discrepancy between an officially critical stance towards the Nazi dictatorship and the survival of a private set of more positive recollections among many Germans of the older generation also shows the limits of imposing a minority memory onto an unwilling majority.[61] Since most judges and legally trained administrators had themselves collaborated in the Third Reich, they were willing to censure the most egregious cases, preferring instead to cover their own actions with the merciful mantle of silence.

Critical remembrance must ultimately be the result of honest self-examination from within, which reflects on the consequences of complicity. It took a younger generation of scholars and journalists who were neither involved in the crimes nor personally beholden to compromised mentors to break the cartel of silence and establish groups like "critical jurists." Also, consistent pressure by international public opinion, sometimes increased by sensationalist reporting, made it impossible to sweep embarrassing revelations under the rug. Some scandalous cases, like the discovery of the transformation of the SS Germanist Schneider into the democrat and European Schwerte, have focused attention on the postwar transformation of perpetrators. Similarly, the apology of the Max Planck Society to the victims of the Auschwitz twin experiments and the invitation of the Humboldt University to its expelled students are small but important steps towards admitting guilt and reconciling memories. But much remains to be done in individual families, academic institutions, and professional associations in order to unearth the full extent of the Nazi roots of postwar society.[62]

Explaining the Inexplicable

Analyzing the failure of the professions to live up to their presumed ethical standards is a daunting challenge, because the historian finds himself implicated both in scholarly and personal ways. It is painful to recognize that well-trained legal practitioners like Justice Minister Otto Thierack became "political soldiers,"[63] masterminding the Nazi perversion of law, while others actively promoted fantasies of German superiority, and the rest at least supported the war effort. It is similarly difficult to deal with the involvement of one's own family members whom one has known as decent human beings in so repulsive a process. For many younger Germans this predicament has produced feelings of intense ambivalence, alternating between shame and sympathy, and not knowing how to relate to their own ancestors.[64] In wrestling with the dilemmas of her own youth in the Third Reich, the East German writer Christa Wolf has skeptically remarked that "we shall not succeed in explaining why it happened thus and not differently." But she nonetheless concludes correctly: "We ought not to shy away from at least doing preparatory work for future explanations."[65]

What then were some of the reasons for the surprising degree of professional complicity in the Nazi seizure of power, expulsion of Jewish colleagues, and racial genocide? Among the various interpretations, the powerful pull of social factors can hardly be overstated: For professionals steeped in a culture of "academic illiberalism," the loss of the First World War and the partly punitive peace of Versailles came as unexpected shocks. The subsequent hyperinflation and the Great Depression created a pervasive crisis of overcrowding, pay cuts, and unemployment that threatened their future careers as well as their respected social position. Its effect was especially pronounced on the generation that had grown up during the nationalist hysteria of the First World War. The failure of the liberal leaders to provide adequate solutions to these problems made ordinary practitioners receptive to the radical proposals of Nazi fanatics who promised a return of stability by purging the professions of undesirables, such as Jewish competitors. Neo-humanist cultivation provided inadequate reservations against such inhumane policies, since competent practice rather than ethical commitment defined the core of German professionalism.[66]

Overlapping ideological commitments, narrowing from patriotism to racial fanaticism, also facilitated professional collusion. Most practitioners merely did their duty and supported the war effort without directly persecuting their Jewish neighbors. More problematic were radical nationalists who worked actively for German hegemony by military armament, ethnic research, or racial propaganda, and who took anti-Semitic measures in stride. Their aims were closer to the Nazi project of restoring a national community and returning the country to predominance, although they retained some respect for professional standards and were reluctant to resort to ruthless means. Most dangerous were those professionals, like People's Court Judge Roland Freisler, who completely blended their expertise with racist ideology, growing unquestioningly ready to kill whenever the Führer demanded it. These fanatical followers completely instrumentalized their competence to maintain power and eliminate all presumed enemies. Since potential liberal or Marxist critics were purged, few professionals were left who might, like Sebastian Haffner, challenge the compliance of patriots and the collaboration of radical nationalists with the fanatical racists in the implementation of genocide.[67]

It is also important to recognize that involvement in the Third Reich was an incremental process, which deepened over time. In the beginning, members of the conservative elite could support the national revival, since Nazi propaganda emphasized "peace and freedom" to a skeptical international community. Even a few eventual victims, like the lawyer Max Hachenburg, found some initial measures of discrimination appropriate, since he, himself, warned against an excessive "Jewish forwardness."[68] With each step the Nazi project grew clearer, but Hitler cleverly bided his time, occasionally even reining in local zealots who precipitated violence, such as in the initial anti-Semitic boycott. Moderates could, therefore, delude themselves about the final aims and hope that some form of legality might be restored.[69] Only the outbreak of the World War and the brutal partisan warfare stripped away the last Nazi reservations—but by this time there was no more turning back for accomplices, since they had gotten ever more deeply compromised. Instead of viewing the process as a product of a deep-seated "eliminationist anti-Semitism," it might be more realistic to see it as a vortex into which professionals were drawn step by step.[70]

My father's war correspondence reveals that recognizing consequences of complicity was a difficult process that came too late to prevent the atrocities. Since he initially supported the war as a chance to conquer "living-space for future decades," the plight of refugees, hanging of partisans, and exploitation of Jews seemed regrettable, but necessary. Only when he was put in charge of feeding a camp with thousands of Russian POWs in the fall of 1941, he began to realize that the systematic starvation of enemy prisoners violated not only the Hague convention, but his own Christian ethics. Moved by their "horrible misery," he began to meet with educated prisoners, learn Russian, and to discuss how he might help. The shock of the "dull dying" around him, which he was unable to stop, finally caused him to "question the purpose of the entire" war: "Here true humanity is needed between the peoples and races, if a better world is to arise out of this excess of blood and destruction." Just when he started to denounce the futility of the carnage, he contracted typhoid fever and died.[71] All too few German professionals understood the full consequences of their complicity in time to prevent the untold suffering caused by the perversion of their ideals.

Notes

1. Robert Jay Lifton, *The Nazi Doctors: Medical Killing and the Psychology of Genocide* (New York, 1986), 337 ff.
2. Konrad H. Jarausch, *The Unfree Professions: German Lawyers, Teachers and Engineers, 1900–1950* (New York, 1990), 226 ff.
3. Götz Aly and Susanne Heim, *Vordenker der Vernichtung. Auschwitz und die deutschen Pläne für eine neue europäische Ordnung* (Hamburg, 1991). See also Rüdiger Hohls and Konrad H. Jarausch, *Versäumte Fragen. Deutsche Historiker im Schatten des Nationalsozialismus* (Stuttgart, 2000).
4. Elie Wiesel, *Night, Dawn, Day* (New York, 1986); Tadeusz Borowski, *This Way to the Gas, Ladies and Gentlemen and Other Stories* (New York, 1967); and Primo Levi, *Survival in Auschwitz: The Nazi Assault on Humanity* (New York, 1961).
5. Victor Klemperer, *Ich will Zeugnis ablegen bis zum letzten. Tagebücher 1933–1941* (Berlin, 1995), 1: 15 ff.
6. Karl Dietrich Bracher, *Die deutsche Diktatur. Entstehung, Struktur und Folgen des Nationalsozialismus* (Frankfurt, 1971); Michael H. Kater, *The Nazi Party: A Social Profile of Members and Leaders, 1919–1945* (Cambridge, MA, 1983); Henry Ashby Turner, *Hitler's Thirty Days to Power: January 1933* (Reading, MA, 1996).
7. Ian Kershaw, *Hitler: A Biography* (New York, 2008), one volume edition, and Hans-Ulrich Wehler, *Deutsche Gesellschaftsgeschichte,* vol. 4: *Vom Beginn des Ersten Weltkriegs bis zur Gründung der beiden deutschen Staaten, 1914–1949* (Munich, 2003).
8. Robert F. Gellately, *Backing Hitler: Consent and Coercion in Nazi Germany* (New York, 2001); and Eric Johnson, *Nazi Terror: The Gestapo, Jews and Ordinary Germans* (London, 1999).
9. Ulrich Herbert, *Best. Biographische Studien über Radikalismus, Weltanschauung und Vernunft, 1903–1989* (Bonn, 1996); Michael T. Allen, *The Business of Genocide: SS Business Administration, Slavery and the Concentration Camps* (Chapel Hill, 2002).
10. Michael H. Kater, *Doctors under Hitler* (Chapel Hill, 1989); Jarausch, *Unfree Professions,* passim. and Charles Lansing, *From Nazism to Communism: German Schoolteachers under Two Dictatorships* (Cambridge, 2010).
11. Konrad H. Jarausch, Matthias Middell, and Martin Sabrow, "Störfall DDR-Geschichtswissenschaft. Problemfelder einer kritischen Historisierung," in idem

and Georg G. Iggers, eds., *Die DDR-Geschichtswissenschaft als Forschungsproblem,* Beiheft 27 of the *Historische Zeitschrift* (Munich, 1998), 1 ff.
12. Christopher R. Browning, *The Path to Genocide: Essays on the Launching of the Final Solution* (Cambridge, 1992), and *Nazi Policy, Jewish Workers, German Killers* (Cambridge, 2000).
13. Charles E. McClelland, *The German Experience of Professionalization: Modern Learned Professions and their Organizations from the Early Nineteenth Century to the Hitler Era* (Cambridge, 1991); Werner Conze and Jürgen Kocka, eds., *Bildungsbürgertum im 19. Jahrhundert* (Stuttgart, 1985); and Geoffrey Cocks and Konrad H. Jarausch, eds., *German Professions, 1800-1950* (New York, 1990).
14. Konrad H. Jarausch, "Vatersuche" in idem and Klaus Arnold, eds., *"Das Stille Sterben…" Feldpostbriefe von Konrad Jarausch aus Polen und Russland, 1939–1942* (Paderborn, 2008), 20 ff. Cf. Michael Wildt, *Generation des Unbedingten. Das Führungscorps des Reichssicherheitshauptamtes* (Hamburg, 2002), 41 ff.
15. Konrad H. Jarausch, *Deutsche Studenten* (Frankfurt 1983), 141 ff.
16. Jarausch, *Unfree Professions,* 80 ff. Cf. also idem, "Die Not der geistigen Arbeiter. Akademiker in der Berufskrise, 1918–1933," in Werner Abelshauser, ed., *Die Weimarer Republik als Wohlfahrtsstaat* (Wiesbaden, 1987), 280 ff.
17. Michael Kater, *Studentenschaft und Rechtsradikalismus in Deutschland 1918–1933* (Hamburg, 1975); and Anselm Faust, *Der Nationalsozialistische Studentenbund. Studenten und Nationalsozialismus in der Weimarer Republik* (Düsseldorf, 1973), 2 vols.
18. Literature in Jarausch, *Unfree Professions,* 92 ff. Cf. Stefan König, *Vom Dienst am Recht. Rechtsanwälte als Strafverteidiger im Nationalsozialismus* (Berlin, 1987); Willi Feiten, *Der Nationalsozialistische Lehrerbund. Entwicklung und Organisation* (Frankfurt, 1981), and Karl Ludwig,
19. Kater, *The Nazi Party,* 51 ff; and Jarausch, *Unfree Professions,* 100 ff. Hermann Kauba was killed during the last fighting in the Rhineland in the spring of 1945.
20. Michael Grüttner, "Die 'Machtergreifung' als Generationskonflikt. Zur Lage der deutschen Hochschulen 1933–1936" (MS. Berkeley, 2001). Cf. also Peter Chroust, *Gießener Universität und Faschismus. Studenten und Hochschullehrer 1918–1945* (Münster, 1994), 2 vols. Term from Hermann Beck, *The Fateful Alliance: German Conservatives and Nazis in 1933* (New York, 2008).
21. Ulrich Heinemann, *Die verdrängte Niederlage. Politische Öffentlichkeit und Kriegsschuldfrage in der Weimarer Republik* (Göttingen, 1983); and Wolfgang Jäger, *Historische Forschung und politische Kultur in Deutschland. Die Debatte 1914–1980 über den Ausbruch des Ersten Weltkrieges* (Göttingen, 1984).
22. See the discussion about Raphael Gross, *Carl Schmitt und die Juden, Eine deutsche Rechtslehre* (Frankfurt, 2000) in H-Sozu-Kult, April 2001. Cf. Doris Bergen, *Twisted Cross: The German Christian Movement in the Third Reich* (Chapel Hill, 1996).
23. Konrad H. Jarausch, *Students, Society and Politics in Imperial Germany: The Rise of Academic Illiberalism* (Princeton, 1983) and Norbert Kampe, *Studenten und "Judenfrage" im Deutschen Kaiserreich* (Göttingen, 1988).
24. Konrad H. Jarausch, "The Expulsion of Jewish Professors and Students from the University of Berlin during the Third Reich," in Larry E. Jones, ed., *Crossing Boundaries: The Exclusion and Inclusion of Minorities in Germany and America* (New York, 2001), 9 ff. Cf. also Fritz Ringer, "The German Academic Community, 1964-1938," *Central European History* 25 (1983), 251–280.

25. Theses against the un-German spirit, first published in Leon Poliakov and Josef Wulf., eds., *Das Dritte Reich und seine Denker* (Berlin, 1959), 117 ff., Geoffrey Giles, *Students and National Socialism in Germany* (Princeton, 1985).
26. Goetz von Olenhusen, "Die 'nichtarischen' Studenten an den deutschen Hochschulen. Zur nationalsozialistischen Rassenpolitik," *Vierteljahrshefte für Zeitgeschichte* 14 (1966), 175–206. While the Jewish share of the over-all population was already sinking to .75 percent, this reduction was nonetheless a severe hardship.
27. Andreas Fijal, "Die Rechtsgrundlagen der Entpflichtung jüdischer und politisch mißliebiger Hochschullehrer nach 1933 sowie der Umbau der Universitäten im nationalsozualistischen Sinne," in: Wolfram Fischer et al., eds., *Exodus von Wissenschaften aus Berlin* (Berlin, 1994), 116 ff. Cf. Jane Caplan, *Government without Administration: State and Civil Service in Weimar and Nazi Germany* (Oxford, 1988); and Jarausch, *Unfree Professions*, 130 ff.
28. Jarausch, *Unfree Professions*, 145 ff. and idem "Jewish Lawyers in Germany, 1848-1938: The Disintegration of a Profession," *Leo Baeck Yearbook* 26 (1991), 171–190.
29. Mark M. Anderson, ed., *Hitler's Exiles: Personal Stories of the Flight from Nazi Germany to America* (New York, 1998); and Saul Friedländer, *Nazi Germany and the Jews* (New York, 1997), 1: 41 discusses the churches and the university.
30. Klemperer, *Ich will Zeugnis ablegen*, 1: 19 ff. Cf. Jarausch, "The Expulsion," 16.
31. Günter Grau and Peter Schneck, eds., *Akademische Karrieren im "Dritten Reich." Beiträge zur Personal- und Berufungspolitik der medizinischen Fakultäten* (Berlin, 1993). Cf. Jarausch, *Unfree Professions*, 156 ff. Cf. Götz Aly, *Hitler's Beneficiaries: Plunder, Racial War and the Nazi Welfare State* (New York, 2007) overstates his case.
32. Unsolicited testimony of one of his former students, 2000.
33. Michael Grüttner, *Studenten im Dritten Reich* (Paderborn, 1995).
34. Notker Hammerstein, *Die deutsche Forschungsgemeinschaft in der Weimarer Republik und im Dritten Reich. Wissenschaftspolitik in Republik und Diktatur* (Munich, 1999).
35. Michael Fahlbusch, *Wissenschaft im Dienst der nationalsozialistischen Politik? Die Volksdeutschen Forschungsgemeinschaften von 1931 bis 1945* (Baden-Baden, 1999). Cf. Ingo Haar, *Geschichtswissenschaft im Nationalsozialismus. Die deutschen Historiker und der "Volkstumskampf" im Osten* (Diss., Halle, 1998).
36. Alan E. Steinweis, *Studying the Jew: Scholarly Antisemitism in Nazi Germany* (Cambridge, 2006).
37. Omer Bartov, *Murder in our Midst: The Holocaust, Industrial Killing, and Representation* (New York, 1996); Christian Gerlach, *Kalkulierte Morde. Deutsche Wirtschafts- und Vernichtungspolitik in Weissrußland, 1941 bis 1944* (Hamburg, 1999). Cf. Michael Geyer's chapter on "War, Genocide, Extermination: The War Against the Jews in an Era of World Wars," in Konrad H. Jarausch and idem, *Shattered Past: Reconfiguring German Histories* (Princeton, 2003), 111 ff.
38. Paul Kleinewefers, *Jahrgang 1905. Ein Bericht* (Stuttgart, 1977).
39. Manfred Heinemann, ed., *Erziehung und Schulung im Dritten Reich* (Stuttgart, 1980), 2 vols; and Bergen, *Twisted Cross*, passim.
40. Michael Burleigh, *Germany Turns Eastward: A Study of Ostforschung in the Third Reich, 1933-1945* (Cambridge, 1988); and Willy Oberkrome, *Volksgeschichte. Me-*

thodische Innovation und völkische Ideologisierung in der deutschen Geschichtswissenschaft 1918–1945 (Göttingen, 1993).
41. Karl Ditt, "Die Kulturraumforschung zwischen Wissenschaft und Politik. Das Beispiel Franz Petri (1903–1993), " *Westfälische Forschungen* 46 (1996): 73–176.
42. Hannes Heer, *Vernichtungskrieg. Verbrechen der Wehrmacht 1941–1944* (Hamburg, 1995).
43. Herbert Ziegler, *Germany's New Aristocracy: The SS-Leadership, 1925–1939* (Princeton, 1939); Herbert, *Best,* 191 ff.
44. Allen, *The Business of Genocide,* chapter III ff. Except for spectacular cases like Werner von Braun, the engineers have largely escaped public criticism.
45. Michael Kater, "Medizin und Mediziner im Dritten Reich. Eine Bestandsaufnahme," *Historische Zeitschrift* 244 (1987): 299–352. Cf. also Michael Greve, *Die organisierte Vernichtung des "lebensunwerten Lebens," im Rahmen der "Aktion T4,"* (Pfaffenweiler, 1998).
46. Jarausch, *Unfree Professions,* 196 ff.
47. Peter Schöttler, ed., *Geschichtsschreibung als Legitimationswissenschaft 1918–1945* (Frankfurt, 1997); and Winfried Schulze and Otto Gerhard Oexle, eds., *Deutsche Historiker im Nationalsozialismus* (Frankfurt, 1999). After losing his chair at Cologne and two years of internment, Petri was able to resume his career, culminating as director of the Institut für geschichtliche Landskunde in Bonn.
48. Jarausch and Arnold, eds., *Das Stille Sterben,* 284 ff. My father-in-law Friedrich Flessa might have treated his POW laborers decently, but he continued to produce ammunition for the war effort without apparent qualms.
49. Theodore S. Hamerow, *On the Road to the Wolf's Lair: German Resistance to Hitler* (Cambridge, MA, 1997). Cf. also Jochen Klepper, *Überwindung. Tagebücher und Aufzeichnungen aus dem Kriege* (Stuttgart, 1958).
50. Victor Klemperer, *So sitze ich denn zwischen allen Stühlen. Tagebücher 1945-1949* (Berlin, 1999), 1: 7 ff.
51. Fritz Stern, *Five Germanys I Have Known* (New York, 2008).
52. Frank Stern, *Im Anfang war Auschwitz. Antisemitismus und Philosemitismus im deutschen Nachkrieg* (Göttingen, 1991), and oral testimony of Irmgard Mueller, an Auschwitz survivor.
53. Jeffrey Herf, *Divided Memory: The Nazi Past in the Two Germanys* (Cambridge, 1997) and Annette Weinke, *Die Verfolgung von NS-Tätern im geteilten Deutschland: Vergangenheitsbewältigung 1949–1969* (Paderborn, 2002).
54. Christoph Klessmann, *Die doppelte Staatsgründung. Deutsche Geschichte 1945–1955* (Göttingen, 1982); and Peter Graf Kielmannsegg, *Nach der Katastrophe. Eine Geschichte des geteilten Deutschland* (Berlin, 2000).
55. Lutz Niethammer, *Die Mitläuferfabrik. Die Entnazifizierung am Beispiel Bayerns* (Berlin, 1989).
56. Norbert Frei, *Vergangenheitspolitik. Die Anfänge der Bundesrepublik und die NS-Vergangenheit* (Munich, 1996), is more persuasive than Manfred Kittel, *Die Legende von der "Zweiten Schuld." Vergangenheitsbewältigung in der Ära Adenauer* (Berlin 1993).
57. Konrad H. Jarausch, "Critical Memory and Civil Society: The Impact of the Sixties on German Debates about the Past," in Philipp Gassert and Alan E. Steinweis, eds., *Coping with the Nazi Past: West German Debates on Nazism and Generational*

Conflict, 1955–1975 (New York, 2006); Peter Reichel, *Vergangenheitsbewältigung in Deutschland. Die Auseinandersetzung mit der NS-Diktatur von 1945 bis heute* (Munich, 2001).

58. Alexander Mitscherlich, *Doctors of Infamy: The Story of Nazi Medical Crimes* (New York, 1949); Bundesminister der Justiz, ed., *Im Namen des deutschen Volkes. Justiz und Nationalsozialismus. Katalog zur Ausstellung des Bundesministers der Justiz* (Cologne, 1989); and Karl-Heinz Ludwig, *Technik und Ingenieure im Dritten Reich* (Düsseldorf, 1974).
59. Manfred Hettling, "Die Historisierung der Erinnerung—Westdeutsche Rezeptionen der nationalsozialistischen Vergangenheit," *Tel Aviver Jahrbuch für deutsche Geschichte* 29 (2000): 357–378; and Aleida Assmann und Ute Frevert, *Geschichtsvergessenheit—Geschichtsversessenheit. Vom Umgang mit deutschen Vergangenheiten nach 1945* (Stuttgart, 1999), 21–52.
60. Frei, *Vergangenheitspolitik,* passim.
61. Konrad H. Jarausch, "Zeitgeschichte und Erinnerung. Einleitende Bemerkungen," in idem and Martin Sabrow, eds., *Verletztes Gedächtnis. Erinerungskultur und Zeitgeschichte im Konflikt* (Frankfurt, 2001).
62. Hohls und Jarausch, *Versäumte Fragen,* passim. Cf. Nikolas Berg, *Der Holocaust und die Westdeutschen Historiker. Erforschung und Erinnerung* (Göttingen, 2003).
63. Allen, *The Business of Genocide,* Chapter I. Cf. also Wolfgang Bialas and Manfred Gangl, eds., *Intellektuelle im Nationalsozialismus* (Frankfurt, 2000), and Jonathan Petropoulos, *The Faustian Bargain: The Art World in Nazi Germany* (New York, 2000).
64. Niklas Frank, *Der Vater. Eine Abrechnung* (Munich, 1987) is typical of the children of perpetrators syndrome. For a more measured effort see Wibke Bruhns, *Meines Vaters Land. Geschichte einer deutschen Familie* (Berlin, 2005), 249 ff.
65. Christa Wolf, *Kindheitsmuster. Roman* (Berlin, 1976), 189.
66. Jarausch, *Unfree Professions,* 196 ff.
67. Sebastian Haffner, *Geschichte eines Deutschen. Die Erinnerungen 1918–1933* (Stuttgart, 2000).
68. Max Hachenburg, *Lebenserinnerungen eines Rechtsanwalts und Briefe aus der Emigration* (Stuttgart, 1978), ed. by Jörg Schadt.
69. Marion Kaplan, *Between Dignity and Despair: Jewish Life in Nazi Germany* (New York, 1998).
70. Daniel Goldhagen, *Hitler's Willing Executioners: Ordinary Germans and the Holocaust* (New York, 1995) versus Peter Longerich, *"Davon haben wir nichts gewusst!" Die Deutschen und die Judenverfolgung* (Munich, 2006).
71. "Aus den Briefen von Dr. K. Jarausch" to Dr. Korth, November-December 1941; "2. Folge von Auszügen aus den Briefen von Konrad Jarausch" compiled by O. Ziegner, in the author's possession. Cf. Also Thomas Vogel, ed., *Wilm Hosenfeld. "Ich versuche jeden zur retten." Das Leben eines deutschen Offiziers in Briefen und Tagebüchern* (Munich, 2004).

Wilhelm Stuckart, undated photo (probably mid-1930s)
Source: Bildarchiv preussischer Kulturbesitz, Berlin/Art Resource, New York

Chapter 2

CIVIL SERVICE LAWYERS AND THE HOLOCAUST

The Case of Wilhelm Stuckart

Hans-Christian Jasch

A SERIES OF STUDIES HAS demonstrated that the formulation of the Jewish policy of the Third Reich was not merely the work of ideologically motivated members of the Nazi Party and the SS, but also of officials in the more "traditional" ministerial bureaucracies.[1] The systematic deportations and the industrialized genocide would not have been possible without the complicity of an efficient civil service, which created the legal framework for depriving Jews of their fundamental rights. The genocide depended on a division of labor that was typical for modern and complex administrations. To overstep any moral boundaries required not only a murderous ideology spread by Nazi propaganda to incite "willing executioners," but also a highly developed organizational and legalistic framework—a sort of administrative consensus—to ensure that the communication, the logistics, and the distribution of tasks among all actors involved would function almost seamlessly.

Given its closeness to the very core of Nazi ideology, Jewish policy quickly evolved into an important and prestigious field of policymaking in the Third Reich. Officials competed for political influence and power, triggering a process of "cumulative radicalization," a murderous dynamic that eventually culminated in genocide.[2] This area of policy offered career opportunities to ambitious bureaucrats—most of them trained in the law—in the newly created special agencies of the SS and the Nazi Party, and also in the more traditional branches of government, such as the national ministries[3] and local administrations. As a strategy for career advancement, they would compete to outdo each other with ever more radical proposals targeted at Jews.[4]

Biographical research on civil servants suggests that the differences between such officials and those of the Nazi Party and SS might have been much less significant than some civil servants depicted them to be in their apologetic postwar memoirs.[5] Some of these memoirs have shaped postwar historiography.[6] As trained lawyers, many of the officials in the upper echelons of the "traditional" civil service were better educated and experienced than their counterparts in the newly established party and SS agencies. They knew and valued existing structures and legal techniques and often had a better sense of political judgement about what was practically achievable without alienating the majority of the population. This "pragmatism" made them appear to lack ideological zeal and to be less radical. The example of Wilhelm Stuckart, however, shows that there were civil servants in key positions who sought to implement Nazi ideology with the same ideological conviction as their peers in the party and the SS. Their defense of traditional legal methods and institutions did not necessarily imply that they were less radical than their comrades who worked in the party institutions. To the contrary, men like Stuckart were well aware of the advantages and efficiencies that could be achieved using a legalistic approach to implement measures of structural violence. Furthermore, there were high numbers of SS and party members in the upper echelons of the traditional ministerial administration because of a routine exchange of staff among these organizations. This suggests that differences between party and state bureaucracies were less driven by ideological disagreement than by competition for influence and power.[7]

Despite the frequent attacks by Hitler and Himmler on "intransigent lawyers and bureaucrats in the state-apparatus"—in one of his Reichstag speeches on 26 April 1942, Hitler declared: "I will not rest until every German understands that it is a disgrace to be a lawyer"—as well as Hitler's aversion to a "legal corset" limiting his exercise of power, the Nazi leadership relied on an effective and well-organized civil service to implement its policies. Young, high-flying lawyers in the public administration like Stuckart were needed to translate anti-Jewish intentions into law. The regime could count on their loyalty, diligence, legal expertise, administrative experience, and imagination.

Despite the efforts of the US military prosecution at Nuremberg to draw attention to the role of high-ranking civil servants and their complicity in the genocide, in particular in the last of the Nuremberg trials, the "Wilhelmstrasse or Ministries case,"[8] many were able to continue their careers in postwar West Germany; they played a major role in rebuilding the administration of the future NATO member and outpost of the West in the Cold War. Eager to protect themselves against prosecution, they formed powerful networks that successfully lobbied against the continuation of de-Nazification and cuts in their salaries or pensions.[9] They benefited from the general political climate, which called for "normalization" and forgetfulness, in order to rebuild an effective and stabilizing administration in divided, Cold War Germany. Even former émigrés, who took offices in the new administration, sometimes closed their eyes to the "re-Nazification" of the civil service, in part because they genuinely believed in the potential for change, in part because they were pressured, and in part because they thought that old expertise was needed to build the new system.[10]

Continuity in the civil service after 1945 was also a consequence of the half-hearted efforts of the German administration and judiciary to investigate the criminal involvement of various professional groups in the Holocaust. Continuity of personnel in the postwar judiciary did not differ much from the situation in the civil service. In many cases, the old generation of judges and prosecutors continued to stay in their posts to serve the emerging West German democracy. It took nearly a generation for changes to set in and for the "old guard" to be replaced by younger lawyers not complicit with Nazism.[11] It is, therefore, hardly surprising that the first West German attempts at criminal prosecution in the 1950s and 1960s were largely limited to rank and file policemen who had shot Jewish families in German-occupied Eastern Europe—as was the case in the *Einsatzgruppen* trial in Ulm in 1958–59—or limited to guards in Nazi extermination camps—as was the case in the Auschwitz trial in Frankfurt in 1963 or the Majdanek trial in Düsseldorf in 1977. The "desk perpetrators" (*Schreibtischtäter*), i.e., perpetrators in the civil service or in the judiciary, largely benefitted from impunity.

Some of them even managed to make themselves indispensable, as is suggested by the example of Stuckart's aide Dr. Hans Globke, who became Chancellor Konrad Adenauer's confidant and a trusted informer of the US intelligence service. Men like Globke nearly managed to escape even historical scrutiny by influencing, and in part silencing, contemporary historical research.[12] The German historian Norbert Frei has pointed to the fact that blind spots in early postwar historical scholarship are telling: they emerged everywhere where closer scrutiny would have adversely affected the powerful group interests of judges, civil servants, or members of the armed forces. These groups successfully managed to create the myth of a "clean" *Wehrmacht* or a "clean civil service." However, it was clear after the Nuremberg trials that these institutions had been deeply entangled in anti-Jewish policies or even in genocide.[13] It took until the 1980s and 1990s for such myths to be exploded in Germany.

The respectable public image of civil service lawyers did not comport with that of mass murderers, as is shown by the negative public reactions to the sentencing of Ernst von Weizsäcker, the former state secretary in the Foreign Office, in the Wilhelmstrasse Trial mentioned above.[14] The crimes that civil servants had committed from their desks in the ministries in Berlin appeared less overt than the murders that had been perpetrated by the *Einsatzgruppen*. The genocide was perceived as an excessive and barbarian act, which was difficult to reconcile with the image of highly-educated and well-mannered civil servants and legal experts in the ministries of the Reich. It was only later that Hannah Arendt coined the term "banality of evil" to describe the "clerks" in the service of genocide.[15] In his haunting book, *Modernity and the Holocaust*, Zygmunt Bauman went a step further, interpreting the genocide as a "product" of modernity. Rather than resort to barbarian behavior or "suspend" civilization by anti-Semitic propaganda, the Nazis used "modern" structures, including an efficient and dehumanizing bureaucracy, to commit genocide.[16]

The popularity of Ernst Fraenkel's theory of the Nazi regime as a "Dual State,"[17] according to which a "prerogative state" and a "normative state" coexisted in parallel, may also have unintentionally contributed to the post-1945 self-exculpatory claims of civil-service lawyers, allowing them to minimize their complicity in the anti-Jewish policies of the Nazi era. Policies against Jews culminating in genocide were generally perceived as part of the exceptional or "prerogative state," which had been severed from the traditions and legal protections of the "normative state." The genocide was seen as an "act of excess" and an exceptional phenomenon, rather than as a product of the civil service operating within a normative framework.

Franz L. Neumann offered an interpretation different from Fraenkel's. Neumann characterized the Nazi state as a Behemoth.[18] This concept suggested an arbitrary and fluid system of government, which went beyond all other forms of governance and thus also distinguishesd itself from the Hobbesian vision of a total state, the Leviathan. In contrast to Fraenkel's "Dual State," no remnants of legality remained in the state of the Behemoth. In the Nazi Behemoth state, justice and law degenerated into mere technical norms without any lasting validity or ethical content. Every rule was at the disposition of the Führer's will, leading to a permanent state of emergency. The Ministry of the Interior and its lawyers—in particular Wilhelm Stuckart—were part of this Behemoth-like structure. They played a key role in defining, ostracizing, and eventually deporting the biggest group of its victims by designing the legal framework for the implementation of anti-Jewish policies.

The Reich Ministry of the Interior and its State Secretary, Dr. Wilhelm Stuckart

After the seizure of power by the Nazi Party in 1933, the Reich Ministry of the Interior (RMI) emerged as an important actor in the process that allowed the new government to consolidate its grip on power. Officials in the RMI drafted the new civil service legislation, providing for the removal of persons who were considered non-Aryan or politically unreliable. This created job opportunities for followers of the Nazi movement.[19] They also prepared the legislation for the "coordination" (*Gleichschaltung*) of the German states (*Länder*), which were politically neutralized and deprived of the autonomous powers they had exercised previously.[20] At the same time, the RMI was in charge of introducing racial and eugenic legislation designed to implement Nazi ideology.[21]

During the Weimar Republic, the RMI had primarily been in charge of formulating legislation and had virtually no direct executive powers—it emerged from the process of "coordination" as a powerful new agency. It merged with the former Prussian Ministry of the Interior, gained direct control over the interior ministries of the other German *Länder,* and came to exercise executive responsibilities reaching down even to the local level.[22] In addition, the RMI was placed in charge of health matters, sports, citizenship, civil service legislation, and the police sector. In 1936, the police were placed under the authority of Heinrich Himmler, the leader of the SS, who held the office of State Secretary in the Interior Ministry with cabinet rank. Himmler, later, detached the police from the ministerial administration by integrating its diverse components into the apparatus of the SS.[23] As the Third Reich expanded its borders both before and during World War II,[24] the RMI was responsible for coordinating administrative matters in the newly acquired territories,[25] for selecting administrative personnel,[26] and for formulating legislation governing the process of "Germanization."[27]

From 1933 to 1943, the RMI was led by a former Bavarian civil servant, Dr. Wilhelm Frick, an early supporter of Hitler. Himmler replaced Frick in the summer of 1943, when the surrender of Italy stirred fear in the Nazi leadership that Frick was too weak to cope with the challenges on the home front. In the polycratic power struggles of the Third Reich, Frick had not been able to defend the initially strong position of his ministry. The transfer of control over the police to the SS was the most notable defeat, but not the only one. Frick also attempted to implement a "Reich Reform" that would have further centralized the administrative structure of the country. This initiative was blocked by Hitler's regional party leaders, the Gauleiter, who feared for their influence and their local "kingdoms."[28] There were, nonetheless, areas where the RMI remained an important actor. These included race and citizenship legislation and health matters. The ministry's continued importance in these areas resulted largely from the effectiveness of its ambitious and politically well-connected State Secretary, Wilhelm Stuckart (1902–1953), who was regarded by many at the time as the de facto minister.[29]

Stuckart was the personification of the "new" civil servant of the Nazi state. An ambitious, young, intelligent, and diligent lawyer, Stuckart had been a member of the Nazi Party since at least 1930, as well as a member of the SS since 1936. He was well-versed in Nazi ideology and did not hesitate to impose it on the civil administration. His professionalism and the backing he enjoyed within the SS and among his staff in the ministry helped him to defend his sphere of competencies against encroachments by other state and party agencies.

Born on 16 November 1902 in Wiesbaden, Stuckart was, like many important officials in the Nazi Party, a member of the "war youth generation" (*Kriegsjugendgeneration*).[30] The members of this generation, born in the decade 1900–1910, had experienced the war only at home, as they were too young to have served in the army. They felt that they had missed the hardening experience of the trenches; their youth and early adult years were influenced by the experience of political and economic instability. Like many of his generational peers, the young Stuckart had oriented himself towards the racist right, the "*völkische Rechte.*" While still in high school, he joined the *DNVP-Jugend,* the youth organization of the conservative-nationalist German National People's Party. Despite his working-class background—his father had been a railroad worker—he was able to study law at the universities of Munich and Frankfurt from 1922 to 1926. He claimed to have joined the Freikorps Epp paramilitary organization and then the Nazi Party in Munich as one of the

"Old Fighters" (*alte Kämpfer*) of Hitler's movement.³¹ According to his own (probably exaggerated) account, he lost his Nazi Party membership card while committing acts of sabotage against French forces in the occupied Rhineland.³² In October 1926, Stuckart completed his legal studies with excellent grades and started his legal training practicum (*Referendariat*). As a *Referendar*, Stuckart had to take an oath to the democratic constitutions of the Weimar Republic and the State of Prussia. Although Prussian civil servants were banned from being members of, or actively promoting the aims of, the anti-democratic Nazi and Communist parties before June 1932, Stuckart nevertheless worked as a legal advisor for the Nazis.³³ At the same time, he worked in the Wiesbaden firm of the Jewish lawyers Max Liebmann and Dr. Fritz Hallgarten.

In 1928, Stuckart finished his doctorate with a treatise on commercial law and became an assistant judge in Wiesbaden and Rüdesheim. He lost his job when the judicial authorities learned about his involvement with the Nazi Party. Stuckart then moved to Stettin, where he worked as a defense counsel for Nazi Stormtroopers undergoing prosecution for acts of violence. In 1932 he married Lotte Gertrud Köhl, the daughter of a merchant from Saarbrücken.

In the spring of 1933, Stuckart participated in the Nazi Party's accession to power, becoming a member of the Pomeranian Provincial Parliament, Acting Governing Mayor of Stettin, and State Commissioner for Pomerania. As a member of the local Nazi leadership, Stuckart approached Kurt Daluege about purging civil service positions in Stettin from elements that did "not deserve the title civil servant" or "were even married to Jews."³⁴ At the time, Daluege was in charge of personnel matters in the Prussian Ministry of the Interior and would later rise to the rank of SS General and head of the German Order Police.

The accession to power by the Nazi Party offered further career opportunities to the young lawyer. At age thirty-one, Stuckart was called to Berlin and appointed a department head in the Prussian Ministry for Culture and Education. Only weeks later, he was appointed State Secretary by the Prussian Minister President, Hermann Göring, who also included Stuckart in his exclusive Prussian State Council (*Staatsrat*). As a State Secretary, first in the Prussian administration and, as of the summer of 1934, in the newly created Reich Ministry of Education, Stuckart played a key role in church matters,³⁵ and in reforming the training curriculum for lawyers.³⁶ He was also involved in purging the Prussian educational service and the universities of non-Aryan and "politically undesirable" staff. By the spring of 1935, 234 university professors who were classified as non-Aryan were removed by Stuckart and his staff at the University of Berlin alone.[37]

Stuckart's role in the purge of Prussian universities cannot be explained simply by obedience to orders or by an apolitical responsibility to implement Nazi law, as he pretended after the war. His handling of the cases shows that he was well aware of the political dimensions of his actions, and that he frequently exercised his discretion in an ideologically motivated manner.[38] Excerpts from a brochure he published in 1934 suggest that Stuckart adhered to the biological anti-Semitism of the Nazi movement. In his text, he highlighted the need to use history lessons as a method "to educate German youth to become genuine members of the 'people's community'" (*Volksgemeinschaft*). This would require that pupils be taught about the "racial characters" and "racial souls" of different peoples. The mixing of races would lead to "racial decay," demonstrable by the decline of empires, as highlighted by the British-German race theorist Houston Stewart Chamberlain. Preventing "racial decay" could therefore be used as a valid "moral justification" (*sittliche Rechtfertigung*) for measures introduced by the Nazi state in the field of "racial hygiene." In this context, Stuckart explicitly referred to the introduction of the "Aryan clause" in the civil service as well as to the eugenically motivated laws for mandatory sterilization and abortion introduced by the RMI.[39] According to Stuckart, it was the "battle between racial forces" that had determined the course of world history. "Jewish influence" had prevented genuine "German thinking and acting" (*deutschgemässes Denken und Handeln*). And while the "best bearers of Germandom" had been sacrificed at the front during World War I, the Jews and their followers had attemped a final blow against Germandom in the November 1918 revolution, seeking to eliminate the German spirit and seize power.

The excerpts cited here were typical in the writings and utterings of Nazi activists. They also shed light on Stuckart's political convictions and hint at the high degree of "ideologization of reality," which Hannah Arendt asserted was a typical feature of totalitarian rule.[40] Stuckart's ideologization of reality was not limited to building an all-encompassing belief structure in order to address political grievances. His conviction that racial struggle determined the course of history became one of the guiding principles of his actions. It is therefore hardly suprising that Stuckart applied for membership in the SS as early as December 1933, although his membership was only approved in 1936 after a personal encounter with Heinrich Himmler.[41]

Stuckart's career in the Nazi administrative apparatus did have its rough moments. In the autumn of 1934, he was removed from his position on account of tension with Education Minister Bernhard Rust.[42] After intervention by Hermann Göring, Rudolf Hess, and the powerful head of Hitler's Chancellery, Hans-Heinrich Lammers, Stuckart was granted a meeting with Hitler in January 1935. Stuckart skillfully exploited the growing conflict among the various factions of the Protestant church in presenting to Hitler a radical proposal for the reorganization of state control over religious institutions.[43] Although his proposal was never implemented, Stuckart made a positive impression on Hitler and was rehabilitated. After a short interval as President of an upper district court in Darmstadt, he was called back to Berlin in March 1935 as head of the constitutional department of the Ministry of the Interior.[44] He kept his grade and his salary as a State Secretary and headed a department of about one hundred civil servants. Stuckart was in charge of several important policy areas: state-party relations; constitutional and organizational reform; administrative law; armed forces and civil defense legislation; citizenship law; and racial law and racial policy.[45]

At the age of 33, Stuckart had also become a central figure in discussions of administrative and constitutional reform of the German Reich[46] and played a central role in creating the legal framework for Germany's later territorial expansion.[47] In 1938, he traveled to Linz at Hitler's request, just after German troops had occupied Austria, and drafted the law for the "Reunification of Austria with the German Reich."[48] His achievements in the course of the *Anschluss* led to his promotion to the rank of a full State Secretary in March 1938.[49] After the adoption of the "Second Law on the Reich's Defense" of 4 September 1938, and Frick's nomination as Plenipotentiary for Reich Administration,[50] Stuckart was appointed to lead Frick's staff.[51] On 16 March 1939, Stuckart accompanied Hitler to Prague, where he drafted the decree for the creation of the "Protectorate of Bohemia and Moravia."[52]

Upon the German attack on Poland on 1 September 1939, Stuckart became a member of the short-lived war cabinet[53] led by Göring.[54] Stuckart contributed to the destruction of the Polish state by drafting the "Decree for the Structure of the Administration of the Eastern Territories" of 8 October 1939[55] and the "Decree for the Administration of the Occupied Polish Territories" of 12 October 1939, which created the Nazi colonial regime for a large part of Poland, the so-called General Government.[56] On 17 October 1939, Stuckart participated in a confidential meeting in which Hitler unveiled radical plans for the treatment of the defeated Poles.[57]

After the defeat of France in the spring of 1940, Stuckart provided Hitler with a proposal for annexing large parts of the French territory.[58] After the occupation of Yugoslavia, he drafted a proposal for the treatment of various ethnic groups and the annexation of parts of Slovenia.[59] He traveled to further occupied countries, including Norway and Denmark, and published comparative collections of administrative law in those areas.[60] In May 1942, he founded an "International Academy for State and Administrative Sciences" on the basis of the archives of the *Institut International des Sciences Administratives*, which had been requisitioned in Brussels on his orders.[61]

Stuckart was also closely involved in the Germanization policy in the occupied territories, which sought ethnic cleansing by separating out and "re-settling" ethnic groups according to racial, political, and other social or economic criteria.[62] He and his staff drafted one of the most important legal instruments in this field: the "Decree for the German Population List" of 4 March 1941, designed to classify Poland's population by five categories, ranging from ethnic Germans, who were to receive German citizenship, to "lesser" ranks to be targeted for re-settlement or exploitation.[63] Stuckart also belonged to the "High Tribunal for Population Questions in the Eastern Territories," presided over by Himmler in his capacity of Reich Commissioner for the Strengthening of Germandom, and which rendered final decisions on the racial classification of individual Poles.[64]

These responsibilities did not prevent Stuckart from becoming one of the leading experts on administrative law in Nazi Germany. After joining the RMI, he was appointed head of the administrative law branch of the Nazi Lawyers League (*NS-Rechtswahrerbund*) and chairman of the committee on administrative law of Hans Frank's official legal think-tank, the Academy for German Law. He was a frequent speaker at events organized by the Academy, especially the German Jurist Assemblies;[65] he published extensively, and became the editor of the journal *Deutsche Verwaltung* (*German Administration*). His explanatory overviews of important fields of racial and administrative law proved popular, and presented Nazi legal thinking in an easily accessible format. In the autumn of 1941, Stuckart co-founded the quarterly journal *Reich, Population Order, and Living Space* (*Reich, Volksordnung und Lebensraum—RVL*), which was published in six volumes until autumn 1943.[66] The official aim of *RVL* was to develop new concepts for the administration of Germany and its new European empire.⁶⁷ *RVL* was thus to become a forum for discussion about the racial "New Order" for Europe, as well as a bridge between Nazi administrative science and imperialist practice.⁶⁸ Stuckart used *RVL* to present his ideas on issues such as citizenship, Germanization,⁶⁹ and the training of German colonial administrators, who, he argued, should fill the roles of "promoters of culture, colonizers and economists."⁷⁰

Stuckart can be seen as a prototype for a generation of young, dynamic, and ideologically committed administrators who became state secretaries in various Reich ministries after the Nazis came to power: Fritz Reinhard in the Ministry of Finance; Roland Freisler and Curt Rothenberger in the Ministry of Justice; Martin Luther in the Foreign Office; Paul Körner in the Agency for the Four Year Plan; Wilhelm Kritzinger in the Reich Chancellery; Albert Ganzenmüller in the Ministry of Transportation; Herbert Backe in the Ministry of Agriculture; Leonardo Conti in the Ministry of the Interior (responsible for health issues); and Werner Naumann in the Ministry of Propaganda. They formed a distinctive part of the Nazi elite and implemented ideologically-driven policies in their ministries. Additionally, they played an important coordinating role after Hitler held the last ordinary cabinet meeting in February 1938 with the Reich ministers.⁷¹ With the exception of Göring's short-lived war cabinet, formal and informal meetings of the State Secretaries—such as the infamous Wannsee Conference—became the main forum for inter-agency coordination on all policy matters.⁷²

Wilhelm Stuckart and the "Legal" Framework of the Holocaust

Stuckart's department in the RMI was responsible for several areas that were at the heart of the anti-Jewish policies of the regime. These included not only racial law and racial policy, but also citizenship law and the laws governing personal names. Activity in these areas of the highly politicized struggle against the "racial enemy" promised visibility and career opportunities to civil servants. Stuckart played a central role in drafting and negotiating the legislation, which formed the framework for defining Jews, excluding them from public life, depriving them of their political and social rights, expropriating their property, and eventually deporting and murdering them.

Shortly after Stuckart had moved to the RMI, the Nuremberg Laws were adopted at the 1935 Nazi Party rally in Nuremberg. The "Reich

Citizenship Law" and the "Law for the Protection of German Blood and German Honor" of 15 September 1935[73] formed the core of the racial legislation of the Third Reich and the legal basis of the systematic segregation of German Jews. The laws introduced a new status of political citizenship—the so-called *Reichsbürgerschaft*—which excluded Jews from citizenship and banned marriages or extra-marital sexual intercourse between non-Jews and Jews. The Grand Senate of the Reich Court (*Reichsgericht*), as well as the legal literature, later celebrated the laws as "foundational norms of the Nazi state" (*Grundgesetze des nationalsozialistischen Staates*).[74]

For many years, understanding of the role of the RMI and its officials in masterminding and implementing the Nuremberg Laws was obscured by the self-absolving memoir of Bernhard Lösener, the head of the unit for racial matters in Stuckart's directorate. His memoir was published in the prestigious *Vierteljahrshefte für Zeitgeschichte* (*Quarterly for Contemporary History*) in 1961.[75] According to the "Lösener Memoir," the Nuremberg Laws were the result of hasty law-making following a sudden and unexpected request from the Führer, who ultimately made his choice from a set of differing proposals presented to him by Stuckart and his staff. The RMI officials, Lösener claimed, gathered in Nuremberg on the eve of the party rally and had to work day and night to draft the proposals, scribbling on restaurant menus due to a lack of paper. Lösener insisted that their only concern had been to keep the laws as moderate as possible, in particular by limiting their scope to so-called "full Jews" (*Volljuden*). After the laws and pertinent implementation orders had entered into force, the RMI continued to defend the Nuremberg Laws as the "mildest instrument" possible to resist demands by the Nazi Party for tougher measures against people of "mixed race" (*Mischlinge*). Eventually, Lösener argued, the moderate civil servants in the RMI were outmaneuvered by the ideological zealots in the SS (specifically the Reich Security Main Office, or RSHA), which achieved complete control over Jewish policy. Nevertheless, by their insistence on the strict application of the definitions adopted under the Nuremberg Laws, Stuckart and his colleagues in the RMI managed to resist demands from the party and the SS to widen the scope of wartime deportations (Lösener insisted), thus sparing the "Half Jews" and "Quarter Jews" from "evacuation to the east" and almost certain death.

Lösener's account was based on the carefully coordinated defense strategy that Stuckart and his colleagues had developed for the Wilhelmstrasse Case in Nuremberg in 1947. By presenting the initiative for the

Nuremberg Laws as an unexpected and sudden order of the Führer, and the laws, themselves, as the mildest possible option in the face of more radical demands from the party, Lösener and his colleagues intended to minimize their own decisive role in the anti-Jewish measures. They managed to turn their complicity in the persecution and oppression of the Jews into an act of mitigation or even resistance, suggesting that the process was unstoppable and beyond the influence of the officials of the RMI, who were merely "reacting" to orders from the almighty Führer and demands of the party.[76]

Lösener's credibility rests, in part, on the fact that, despite having been an early member of the Nazi Party, he requested to be released from his duties when learning about the genocide in 1941, and was later imprisoned by the Gestapo for helping to hide a member of the conspiracy to kill Hitler in July 1944. But his account is belied by the fact that the officials in the RMI had been involved in discussions of racial legislation since 1933.[77] They were not simply driven by events, as Lösener claimed, but rather influenced events on the basis of careful and meticulous preparation. The presentation of the legalistic approach of the RMI as "mitigation" of radical party demands for deportations during the war is also problematic—it ignores the importance of the legal framework for the definition of the victims and the deprivation of their civil and political rights, all of which preceded the deportations. Even after the deportations had started, the RSHA routinely referred to the racial classification contained in the Nuremberg Laws.[78] Legal definition of the victims was indispensable for the efficient cooperation of the manifold actors involved in the genocide. The laws also segregated the German Jews from their non-Jewish neighbors, creating an atmosphere in which all bonds of societal solidarity were destroyed, and in which it became acceptable to expropriate and deport the Jews as "lawless beings." In 1941, Stuckart and his colleagues even prepared a legal framework for the deportations in the form of the "11th Decree for the Reich Citizenship Law." This decree definitively stripped the Jews of their German nationality by turning them into stateless subjects once their deportation trains crossed the Reich's frontier on their way to ghettos and death camps in the East. The 11th Decree also facilitated the expropriation of Jewish-owned property by linking the loss of citizenship to a loss of property in the Reich. According to section 3.2 of the decree, the property of the expropriated Jews was to be used to "promote the solution of the Jewish question."[79] It therefore seems doubtful that Stuckart and his staff really intended to avert a radical solution to the "Jewish Question" through deportation. Instead, it seems that the "normative state" (RMI) and the "prerogative state" (SS and RSHA) worked hand in hand to achieve the "Final Solution of the Jewish Question." The defense strategy reflected in the "Lösener memoir" was nonetheless extremely successful and continues to influence historiography in the present day.[80]

Between 1935 and 1937, Stuckart published a series of articles to explain and interpret the Nuremberg Laws. He also wrote the preface to a 287-page commentary of his colleague Hans Globke, which was published in 1936.[81] This commentary became an important tool for judges and administrators in applying the new laws and finding authoritative answers to questions about citizenship, racial classification, marriage, and sexual relations. Stuckart's writings, and especially his highly ideological preface to the "Stuckart-Globke" commentary, resonated with the same rhetoric of "racial decay" and "bastardization" that had characterized the brochure that he had published in 1934. In defending the Nuremberg Laws from foreign criticism, Stuckart justified the new regulations in an article published in *Deutsches Recht*, the official journal of the Academy for German Law, in December 1935.[82] Invoking language from Hitler's *Mein Kampf*, Stuckart painted the defenders of racial equality as enemies of the newly created *Volksgemeinschaft*. The "protection of the race," Stuckart maintained, was of fundamental importance for the German people. He characterized accusations from abroad that Germany would be falling back into barbarism as an attempt to denigrate the country. The majority of the German people, however, as an "organic and historic community of blood," had always sensed the boundaries established by race, and had intuitively refused everything that was foreign, including Jews. The egalitarian notion of mankind had to be replaced by recognition of the existence of a multitude of racial groups. Only a "people defined by race" (*rassenbestimmtes Volk*) could generate cultures and authentic beliefs. Jewry, in contrast, was marked by "racial alienation" and "rootlessness," and therefore represented an alien and divisive presence among all European peoples, as could be demonstrated by Jewry's years of domination of Germany. In Stuckart's view, this historical background justified depriving Jews of their rights.

Stuckart's involvement in "Jewish Policy" was not limited to interpreting or justifying the Nuremberg Laws that he and his staff had drafted. He was also actively involved in their implementation, and in additional initiatives that were directed at solving the "Jewish Question." Beginning in March 1936, Stuckart served as President of the "Reich Committee for the Protection of German Blood" (*Reichsaus-*

schuss zum Schutze des deutschen Blutes), which considered permissions for marriages between "Mischlinge" and those of "German blood."[83] In a series of interministerial meetings, he impelled new initiatives and measures that would further limit the legal status of Jewish Germans. On 29 September 1936, he hosted such a meeting on the "fundamental direction of Jewish policy."[84] The participants discussed limiting "Jewish influence in the economic life" and the forced emigration of Jews from Germany, which would require a careful balancing of fiscal and foreign policy concerns.

After the deportations and the genocide had begun, following the invasion of the Soviet Union by German forces in June 1941, Stuckart was invited to represent the RMI at the Wannsee Conference on 20 January 1942.[85] According to the minutes of the conference, Stuckart objected to Reinhard Heydrich's plans for including "Mischlinge of the First Degree" (i.e., half Jews) in the deportations. Stuckart believed that such a step would generate an unmanageable administrative burden, and would not be conducive to the overall aim of achieving a "Final Solution of the Jewish question" within the carefully designed legal framework of the Nuremberg Laws. Stuckart proposed instead that "Mischlinge" be sterilized, which would neutralize the "racial danger" that they presented while averting interventions by their non-Jewish relatives. Regarding "mixed marriages" that had been entered into before the Nuremberg Laws went into force on 15 September 1935, Stuckart suggested a law that would allow state prosecutors to request divorce proceedings. He worried about administrative and morale problems that could arise from the deportation of one partner while the other remained in Germany.[86] Stuckart, who was promoted to the rank of *SS-Gruppenführer* (major general) ten days after the Wannsee Conference, was no less ardent an anti-Semite than Heydrich. His insistence that the deportations be carried out in an orderly, legalistic manner was intended to protect the turf of the Interior Ministry and to minimize the risk of breeding political discontent in the majority population.

That he did not have fundamental objections against the Final Solution is evident from a memo by Bernhard Lösener relating to a conversation between Lösener and Stuckart on 19 December 1941, about a month before the Wannsee Conference.[87] Lösener had complained to Stuckart that the RMI's unit for racial matters, which he led, had gradually lost influence to the RSHA. In this context, Lösener told Stuckart that he had been infomed by one of his aides about the horrifying executions in Riga of deported Jews from Berlin.[88] Lösener told Stuckart that under these circumstances he would ask to be released from his responsibilities and given another job outside the RMI, since he could not reconcile such acts with his conscience and did not want to be associated with them.[89] Stuckart replied that the "procedure against the evacuated Jews" had been adopted following a "decision at the highest level" and that Lösener would have to accept it:

> The final solution of the Jewish question has to be regarded from a higher standpoint. In the last weeks alone, 50,000 German soldiers have fallen on the Eastern front; millions more will fall, because, Mr. Lösener, the war will last a very long time. Remember that the Jews are responsible for every German death, for it is the fault of the Jews that we have to fight this war. Jewry has forced it upon us. If we strike back with toughness, one has to see the world historical necessity for this toughness and should not fearfully inquire, if this or that Jew, who is meeting his fate, is personally guilty."[90]

This exchange, shortly before the Wannsee Conference,[91] suggests that Stuckart knew about the mass murders in the East, even if he might not yet have grasped the scale and systematic dimension of the killings. He had no scruples about justifying these abominable acts to his subordinate on the basis of the "historical" argument of an "ongoing racial struggle," which he had advanced in his publications in the early 1930s, and which had been used by Hitler and Goebbels for the same purpose.

Another document which is telling with regard to Stuckart's knowledge about, as well as his attitude toward, the Final Solution has been noted by the legal historian Diemut Majer. She has pointed to the 1942 edition of Stuckart's educational overview of the racial legislation, *Rassen- und Erbpflege in der Gesetzgebung des Reiches* (*Race and Heredity Protection in the Legislation of the Reich*), published together with his colleague Dr. Rolf Schiedermair. The edition from 1942 contains a barely concealed reference to the genocide: Jews are "a race, as has been highlighted by the Führer ... which is inferior through and through. The extermination of the Jews (*Judenvernichtung*) is therefore justified not only by their being different but also by their being of a lesser value."[92] Stuckart does not use the words "annihilation" or "extermination" in the 1943 edition of the same work, in which he wrote:

> "The objective of racial legislation can be regarded as having been achieved and the racial legislation can therefore be seen as essentially

closed. It has [c]ontributed to a preliminary solution of the Jewish question and at the same time prepared the way for a definitive solution. Many regulations will gradually lose their practical importance as Germany approaches its final objective in the Jewish question."[93]

Stuckart's involvement in crimes was not limited to the genocide of the European Jews. He was also complicit in another murderous area of Nazi policy, the so-called Euthanasia Program—the murder of disabled Germans.[94] On 18 August 1939, he signed a confidential decree regarding the "Reporting Obligations for Deformed Newborns."[95] Officially, this decree aimed at "clarifying scientific questions regarding the dysfunctional development of newborns," but in reality it was the starting point of the "Children's Euthanasia," the systematic killing of newborns, babies and toddlers with disabilities. Stuckart's own one-year-old son, Gunther, became a victim of this program on 15 June 1941. According to his younger brother, Rüdiger Stuckart, Gunther, who suffered from Down's Syndrome, was handed over to the "euthanasia" pediatrician Prof. Werner Catel in Leipzig.[96]

In the closing days of the Third Reich, Stuckart was appointed Reich Minister of the Interior and Education in the government of Admiral Karl Dönitz. He was arrested by the Allies in Flensburg on 26 May 1945. In 1947, he was indicted in the Wilhelmstrasse Case together with Ernst von Weizsäcker, Hans-Heinrich Lammers, and other leading civil servants and diplomats of the Nazi era. When he was asked about his knowledge of the systematic killing of Jews by his defense counsel,[97] he responded that Lösener had never told him about the mass killings and that his understanding of the term "Final Solution" had been that Jews would be "concentrated on a reservation in the East." The "extermination of Jews" (*Ausrottung der Juden*) had, he claimed, "never entered my imagination." [98] He testified that he never received the minutes of the Wannsee Conference, which, in any event, would convey a distorted image of the meeting. Heydrich, he said, had never mentioned the "extermination of Jews through labor."[99] He claimed credit for having saved Mischlinge and persons living in mixed marriages from deportation.

The Nuremberg judges were only partially convinced by Stuckart's defense. They found him guilty under the count for crimes against humanity. They were convinced that he knew about the fate of the Jews in the East, and they believed that the laws and regulations that he had drafted were part of a programme for the systematic and complete extermination of the Jews. They held that he was as guilty as the commanders of the death camps, as he had put his expertise and legal knowledge at the disposal of the organizers of the mass murder.[100] The judges looked positively on his role in the Wannsee Conference and his initiatives to prevent Mischlinge from being included in the Final Solution.[101] In view of his bad state of health at the time of the trial, the judges sentenced him to three years, ten months and twenty days of imprisonment—the time he had spent in Allied custody since his arrest in 1945. This meant that Stuckart was released in 1949. He died four years later on the eve of his fifty-third birthday.

Notes

1. Léon Poliakov and Joseph Wulf, *Das Dritte Reich und seine Diener. Dokumente*, 1st ed. (Berlin, 1956); Raul Hilberg, *The Destruction of the European Jews* (London, 1961); Hans-Günther Adler, *Der verwaltete Mensch. Studien zur Deportation der Juden aus Deutschland* (Tübingen, 1974); Uwe D. Adam, *Judenpolitik im Dritten Reich* (Düsseldorf, 1979, new edition 2003); Diemut Majer, *Non-Germans under the Third Reich: The Nazi Judicial and Administrative System in Germany and Occupied Eastern Europe*, trans. Peter Thomas Hill et al (Washington, 2003); Hans Mommsen, "The Civil Service and the Implementation of the Holocaust. From Passive to Active Complicity," in *The Holocaust and History: The Known, the Unknown, the Disputed, and the Reexamined*, eds. Michael Berenbaum and Abraham J. Peck (Bloomington, 1998), 219–27; Cornelia Essner, *Die "Nürnberger Gesetze"oder die Verwaltung des Rassenwahns 1933–1945* (Paderborn, 2002); Michael Mayer, *Staaten als Täter. Ministerialbürokratie und "Judenpolitik" in NS-Deutschland und Vichy-Frankreich* (Munich, 2010). On the SS see Michael Wildt, *Die Judenpolitik des SD 1935–1938. Eine Dokumentation* (Hamburg, 1995), and *Generation des Unbedingten. Das Führungskorps des Reichssicherheitshauptamtes* (Hamburg, 2002); as well as Peter Longerich, *Politik der Vernichtung. Eine Gesamtdarstellung der nationalsozialistischen Judenverfolgung* (Munich, 1998) and *Heinrich Himmler. Biographie* (Munich, 2008).
2. Hans Mommsen, "Die Realisierung des Utopischen. Die 'Endlösung der Judenfrage' im Dritten Reich," *Geschichte und Gesellschaft* 9 (1983): 381–420 (387 et seq.).
3. On the Foreign Office, see Christopher Browning's research on the domestic directorate: "Referat Deutschland," *Yad Vashem Studies* 12 (1977): 37–73; "Unterstaatssekretär Martin Luther and the Ribbentrop Foreign Office," *Journal of Contemporary History* 12 (1977): 313–344; *The Final Solution and the German Foreign Office: A Study of Referat D III of Abteilung Deutschland 1940–1943* (New York, 1978); "The Government Experts," in *The Holocaust: Ideology, Bureaucracy, and Genocide: The San José Papers*, eds. Henry Friedlander and Sybil Milton (Millwood, NY, 1980), 183–97; Hans-Jürgen Döscher, *Das Auswärtige Amt im Dritten Reich. Diplomatie im Schatten der "Endlösung"* (Berlin, 1987); Sebastian Weitkamp, *Braune Diplomaten. Horst Wagner und Eberhard von Thadden als Funktionäre der*

"*Endlösung*" (Bonn, 2008); *Das Amt und die Vergangenheit. Deutsche Diplomaten im Dritten Reich und in der Bundesrepublik,* eds. Eckart Conze, Norbert Frei, Peter Hayes and Moshe Zimmermann (Munich, 2010). See also the extensive bibliographical references in Deutscher Bundestag, Drucksache 17/8134, 17. Wahlperiode, *Antwort der Bundesregierung auf die Große Anfrage der Abgeordneten Jan Korte, Sevim Dağdelen, Ulla Jelpke, weiterer Abgeordneter und der Fraktion Die Linke. Umgang mit der NS-Vergangenheit,* in: http://dipbt.bundestag.de/dip21/btd/17/081/1708134.pdf.

4. Wolf Gruner, *Der geschlossene Arbeitseinsatz deutscher Juden. Zur Zwangsarbeit als Element der Verfolgung 1938 bis 1943* (Berlin, 1997), 311–26; "Die NS-Judenverfolgung und die Kommunen. Zur wechselseitigen Dynamisierung von zentraler und lokaler Politik 1933–1941," *Vierteljahrshefte für Zeitgeschichte (VfZ)* 48 (2000): 75–126.

5. A flagrant example is the testimony of the head of unit for "Racial Matters" in the Reich Ministry of the Interior, Dr. Bernhard Lösener. "Das Reichsministerium des Innern und die Judengesetzgebung. Aufzeichnung von Doktor Bernhard Lösener," *VfZ* 9 (1961): 262–313. It took more than 20 years before Lösener's account was questioned by Otto Dov Kulka, "Die Nürnberger Rassengesetze und die deutsche Bevölkerung im Lichte geheimer NS-Lage- und Stimmungsberichte," *VfZ* 32 (1984): 582–624, and another two decades before it was critically analyzed in its historical context by Cornelia Essner, *Die "Nürnberger Gesetze."*

6. On the "antagonism" between the party and the state, see Edward N. Peterson, *The Limits of Hitler's Power* (Princeton, 1969) and "Die Bürokratie und die NSDAP," in *Der Staat* 6 (1967): 151–73; Peter Diehl-Thiele, *Partei und Staat im Dritten Reich. Untersuchungen zum Verhältnis von NSDAP und allgemeiner innerer Staatsverwaltung 1933–1945* (Munich, 1969); Dieter Rebentisch, *Führerstaat und Verwaltung im Zweiten Weltkrieg. Verfassungsentwicklung und Verwaltungspolitik 1939–1945* (Stuttgart, 1989); Michael Mayer, *Staaten als Täter.*

7. Jane Caplan, "The Politics of Administration. The Reich Interior Ministry and the German Civil Service 1933–1943," *Historical Journal* 20 (1977): 707–36; *Government without Administration: State Civil Service in Weimar and Nazi Germany* (Oxford, 1988); and "Recreating the Civil Service: Issues and Ideas in the Nazi Regime," in *Government, Party and People in Nazi Germany,* ed. Jeremy Noakes (Exeter, 1980).

8. *Trials of War Criminals before the Nuernberg Military Tribunals under Control Council Law No. 10,* Vol. XII-XIV: *The Ministries Case, October 1946–April 1949* (Washington n.d.) (hereafter *TWC*); Robert M.W. Kempner and Carl Haensel, *Das Urteil im Wilhelmstraßenprozess* (Schwäbisch Gmünd, 1950); R.M.W. Kempner, *Ankläger einer Epoche. Lebenserinnerungen* (Frankfurt, 1986), 310, 312. On *Kempner* see Dirk Pöppmann, "Robert Kempner und Ernst von Weizsäcker im Wilhelmstraßenprozess: zur Diskussion über die Beteiligung der deutschen Funktionseliten an den NS-Verbrechen," in *Im Labyrinth der Schuld: Täter, Opfer, Ankläger,* eds. Irmtrud Wojak and Susanne Meinl (Frankfurt, 2003), 163–99.

9. Norbert Frei, *Vergangenheitspolitik. Die Anfänge der Bundesrepublik und die NS-Vergangenheit* (Munich, 1996), and Ulrich Herbert, *Best. Biographische Studien über Radikalismus, Weltanschauung und Vernunft 1903–1989,* 3. ed. (Bonn, 1996); Deutscher Bundestag, *Antwort der Bundesregierung.*

10. Klaus-D. Godau-Schüttke, "Von der Entnazifizierung zur Renazifizierung der Justiz in Westdeutschland," pubished at: http://www.rewi.hu-berlin.de/online/fhi/zitat/0106godau-schuettke.pdf. See also Friedemann Utz, *Preuße, Protestant, Pragmatiker. Der Staatssekretär Walther Strauß und sein Staat* (Tübingen, 2003) on the example of W. Strauß and his (re-) employment policy in the justice sector.

11. Annette Weinke, *Eine Gesellschaft ermittelt gegen sich selbst. Die Geschichte der Zentralen Stelle Ludwigsburg 1958-2008*, 2 ed. (Darmstadt, 2009); Hubert Rottleutner, *Karrieren und Kontinuitäten deutscher Justizjuristen vor und nach 1945* (Berlin, 2010).

12. On the controversial personality of Hans Globke see Klaus Gotto, ed., *Der Staatssekretär Adenauers. Persönlichkeit und politisches Wirken Hans Globkes* (Stuttgart, 1980), and Erik Lommatzsch, *Hans Globke (1898–1973) Beamter im Dritten Reich und Staatssekretär Adenauers* (Frankfurt, 2009), as well as the more critical work of Jürgen Bevers, *Der Mann hinter Adenauer. Hans Globkes Aufstieg vom NS-Juristen zur Grauen Eminenz der Bonner Republik* (Berlin, 2009), who also gives an account of Globke's efforts to silence the student activist Reinhard-M. Strecker, *Dr. Hans Globke. Aktenauszüge, Dokumente* (Hamburg 1961).

13. Norbert Frei, "Abschied von der Zeitgenossenschaft. Der Nationalsozialismus und seine Erforschung auf dem Weg der Geschichte," in *Werkstatt Geschichte* 20 (1998): 69–83.

14. Rainer A. Blasius, "Fall 11: Der Wilhelmstraßenprozess gegen das Auswärtige Amt und andere Ministerien," in *Der Nationalsozialismus vor Gericht. Die alliierten Prozesse gegen Kriegsverbrecher und Soldaten 1943–1952*, ed. Gerd R. Ueberschär (Frankfurt, 1999), 187– 98.

15. Hannah Arendt, *Eichmann in Jerusalem. A Report on the Banality of Evil* (New York, 1963; revised and enlarged edition, 1970).

16. Zygmunt Bauman, *Dialektik der Ordnung. Die Moderne und der Holocaust* (Hamburg, 1992).

17. Ernst Fraenkel, *The Dual State. A Contribution to the Theory of Dictatorship* (New York, 1941). On Fraenkel see Simone Ladwig-Winters, *Ernst Fraenkel- ein politisches Leben* (Frankfurt, 2009).

18. Franz L. Neumann, *Behemoth. Struktur und Praxis des Nationalsozialismus 1933– 1944* (Munich, 1984; originally published Oxford, 1942).

19. *Gesetz zur Wiederherstellung des Berufsbeamtentums* of 7 April 1933, *Reichsgesetzblatt* (RGBl) I, 175. For further details see Jane Caplan, "The Politics of Administration," 714 et seq.; Günther Püttner, "Der öffentliche Dienst," in *Deutsche Verwaltungsgeschichte, Vol. IV: Das Reich als Republik und in der Zeit des Nationalsozialismus*, ed. Kurt G.A. Jeserich (Stuttgart, 1985), 1082 et seq. (1084 f.); Hans Mommsen, *Beamtentum im Dritten Reich* (Stuttgart, 1966). On the use of the civil service law for the purging of the universities in Prussia, see Hans-Christian Jasch, "Das preußische Kultusministerium und die 'Ausschaltung' von 'nichtarischen' und politisch missliebigen Professoren an der Berliner Universität in den Jahren 1933 bis 1934 aufgrund des Gesetzes zur Wiederherstellung des Berufsbeamtentums vom 7. April 1933," published at http://www.forhistiur.de/zitat/0508jasch.htm.

20. Walter Baum, "Die Reichsreform im Dritten Reich", VfZ 5 (1955): 52–53.

21. On this issue, see in particular Essner, *Die "Nürnberger Gesetze,"* 86 et seq.; Henry Friedlander, *Der Weg zum NS-Genozid. Von der Euthanasie zur Endlösung* (Darmstadt, 1997).

22. On the history of the Reich Ministry of the Interior, see Günter Neliba, *Wilhelm Frick, Der Legalist des Unrechtsstaats* (Paderborn, 1992).
23. On the development of the police in the Third Reich, see Herbert, *Best*, 133 et seq.; Wildt, *Judenpolitik der SD;* and Longerich, *Politik der Vernichtung*, 157 et seq.
24. On Germany's occupational policy and administration, see Mark Mazower, *Hitler's Empire. How the Nazis Ruled Europe* (London, 2008).
25. Hans-Christian Jasch, "Die Gründung der Internationalen Akademie für Verwaltungswissenschaften im Jahr 1942 in Berlin –Verwaltungswissenschaften als Herrschaftsinstrument und 'Mittel der geistigen Kriegsführung' im nationalsozialistischen Staat," *Die Öffentliche Verwaltung* 58 (2005): 709–722 (71. note 56).
26. Stephan Lehnstaedt, "'Ostnieten' oder Verwaltungsexperten? Die Auswahl deutscher Staatsdiener für den Einsatz im Generalgouvernement Polen 1939-1944," *Zeitschrift für Geschichtswissenschaft* 55 (2007): 701–21.
27. Wilhelm Stuckart, "Probleme des Staatsangehörigkeitsrecht," *Zeitschrift der Akademie für Deutsches Recht* 5 (*ZSdAfDR*) (1938): 401–03; "Die Staatsangehörigkeit in den eingegliederten Gebieten," *ZSdAfDR* 8 (1941): 233–37, and "Staatsangehörigkeit und Reichsgestaltung," *Reich Volksordnung Lebensraum (RVL)* 5 (1943): 57–91.
28. On the reform plans see Stuckart, "Partei und Staat," *Deutscher Juristentag 1936*, ed. NSRB (Berlin, 1936), 262 et seq., or his article in the *Frankfurter Zeitung* of 2 November 1937, "Die Zentralgewalt des Reiches. Ein Vortrag von Staatssekretär Stuckart in Frankfurt." See also Jane Caplan, "Recreating the Civil Service," 42; Rebentisch, *Führerstaat und Verwaltung*, 190 et seq.; Uwe Bachnick, *Die Verfassungsreformvorstellungen im nationalsozialistischen Deutschen Reich und Ihre Verwirklichung* (Berlin, 1995); Stephan Lehnstaedt, "Der 'totale Krieg' im Reichsministerium des Innern unter Heinrich Himmler," *Die Verwaltung* 39 (2006): 393–420 (396 et seq.); Hans-Christian Jasch, "Das Ringen um die Verwaltungsgerichtsbarkeit-Verwaltungsgerichtsbarkeit als Instrument der Rechtsvereinheitlichung im Dritten Reich," *Die Verwaltung*, 38 (2005): 546–76.
29. On Stuckart see Hans-Christian Jasch, *Staatssekretär Wilhelm Stuckart und die Judenpolitik. Der Mythos von der sauberen Verwaltung* (Munich, 2012), on which much of the present article is based.
30. Regarding this term, see Herbert, *Best;* Wildt, *Generation des Unbedingten*.
31. See Stuckart's *curriculum vitae* in Bundesarchiv Berlin-Lichterfelde (BAB, German Federal Archives) SSO Stuckart, Wilhelm, 16.11.1902 (former Berlin Document Center, BDC).
32. Ibid. His attempts to obtain a lower and therefore more prestigious party membership number failed, since he could not provide any proof for such an early involvement with the Nazi movement.
33. Mommsen, *Beamtentum*, 21, has highlighted the Nazi Party's success in recruiting followers among civil servants.
34. BAB BDC-Orpo / A 446.
35. On Stuckart's church policy see Klaus Scholder, *Die Kirchen und das Dritte Reich. Vol. 1: Vorgeschichte und die Zeit der Illusionen 1918–1934*, (Frankfurt, 1986), 139 f.
36. See Stuckart's programmatic article "Ziel und Weg einer nationalsozialistischen juristischen Studienreform," *Zeitschrift der Akademie für Deutsches Recht* 1(1934): 53–55, as well as Stuckart's brochure "Nationalsozialistische Rechtserziehung" (Frankfurt, 1935).

37. See note 19. Michael Grüttner and Sven Kinas, "Die Vertreibung von Wissenschaftlern aus deutschen Universitäten 1933–1945," *VfZ* (2007): 123 et seq. (151), have pointed out that the "Manhattan Project" to build the atomic bomb, the biggest research project at the time, employed several leading scientists who had to leave Germany or Italy following the introduction of racial laws, among them Albert Einstein, Leo Szilard, Eduard Teller, Eugen Wigner, Enrico Fermi, and Emilio Segrè.
38. See Jasch, "Das preussische Kultusministerium."
39. See in particular the law on the "prevention of genetically pathologic offspring" (*Gesetz zur Verhütung erbkranken Nachwuchses*) of 14 July 1933, RGBl. I, 529.
40. Hannah Arendt, *Elemente und Ursprünge totaler Herrschaft* (Munich, 1986), 721.
41. BAB SSO Stuckart, Wilhelm, 16.11.1902 (former Berlin Document Center, BDC).
42. BAB R 43 II/1154, p. 20 et seq.
43. Stuckart's 19-page proposal "*Staat und Evangelische Kirche*" of 12 January1935, as well as three draft laws on church questions, can be found in BAB 43 II / 163, p. 134 et seq. See also Gerhard Besier, *Die Kirchen und das Dritte Reich. Spaltung und Abwehrkämpfe 1934–1937* (Berlin, 2001), 58 et seq.
44. Frick addressed to the "Führer und Reichskanzler," 18 March 1935, in BAB R 2/11685; Rebentisch, *Führerstaat und Verwaltung*, 106.
45. BAB R 1501/ 6, Bl. 47 et seq.
46. See Bachnick, *Verfassungsreformvorstellungen*.
47. For further details, see Mazower, *Hitler's Empire*.
48. *Gesetz zur Wiedervereinigung Österreichs mit dem Deutschen Reich*, RGBl. I, 1938, 237–38.
49. See *Pfundtner's* letter of 18 March 1938, in BAB R 2/11687; R 43 II/1126b.
50. See note 28.
51. BAB R 43 II/1293 a, 5 et seq.
52. RGBl. I, 485 et seq. See also Stuckart's article, "Das Protektorat Böhmen und Mähren im Großdeutschen Reich," *Tag des Deutschen Rechts 1939*, ed. by the Deutschen Rechtswahrerbund (Berlin, 1939), 143–62.
53. "Führer's decree," RGBl. I, 1539 f.; Rebentisch, *Führerstaat und Verwaltung*, 117 et seq.
54. For further details see Rebentisch, *Führerstaat und Verwaltung*, 125 et seq.; the meeting reports are printed in IMT vol. 23, 226 et seq., 239 et seq.
55. *Erlass' über die Gliederung und Verwaltung der Ostgebiete*, RGBl. I, 1939, 2042 f; 2057; 2135.
56. *Erlass über die Verwaltung der besetzten polnischen Gebiete*, RGBl. I, 1939, 2077; for background, see Rebentisch, *Führerstaat und Verwaltung*, 172 et seq.
57. See Rebentisch, *Führerstaat und Verwaltung*, 172, and Keitel's note on the meeting, Nuremberg Document PS-864, in IMT, vol. 26, 382. On 23 October 1939 Stuckart informed other state secretaries in a confidential meeting about how Hitler intended to treat the Polish population, see memo from Stuckart's aide Hubrich in BAB R 1501/5401.
58. Printed in Peter Schöttler, "Eine Art 'Generalplan West.' Die Stuckart-Denkschrift vom 14. Juni 1940 und die Planungen für eine neue deutsch-französische Grenze im Zweiten Weltkrieg," *Sozialgeschichte :Zeitschrift für historische Analyse des 20. und 21. Jahrhunderts*, Neue Folge, 18 (2003): 83–131.

59. Institut für Zeitgeschichte, Az. 2948/62, Bestand F 6 83.
60. See Stuckart's report to Himmler about his mission to Norway on 8–15 September 1942 in BAB NS 19/ 1982, and Wilhelm Stuckart, Reinhard Höhn, and Herbert Schneider, *Verfassungs-, Verwaltungs-, und Wirtschaftsgesetze Norwegens* (Darmstadt, 1942).
61. See Stefan Fisch, "Origins and History of the International Institute of Administrative Sciences: From its Beginnings to its Reconstruction after World War II (1910–1944/47)," *Administration Service 1930–2005*, eds. Michael Duggett and Fabio Rugge (Amsterdam, 2005), 35-60; and Jasch, "Die Gründung der Internationalen Akademie."
62. Stuckart, "Staatsangehörigkeit und Reichsgestaltung."
63. *Verordnung über die deutsche Volksliste und die deutsche Staatsangehörigkeit in den eingegliederten Ostgebieten*, RGBl. I,118. On citizenship in the occupied area see Wilhelm Stuckart and Rolf Schiedermair, *Neues Staatsrecht*, 18th ed. (1943), 73 et seq., as well as Stuckart "Staatsangehörigkeit und Reichsgestaltung." Also see the overview by Joachim Neander, "Das Staatsangehörigkeitsrecht des "Dritten Reiches" und seine Auswirkungen auf das Verfolgungsschicksal deutscher Staatsangehöriger," at: http://aps.sulb.uni-saarland.de/theologie.geschichte/inhalt/2008/59.html#fuss2.
64. See Institut für Zeitgeschichte F 129/18. After the war Stuckart told the prosecution in Nuremberg that he had only participated once in a meeting of the tribunal in December 1943. Himmler had taken all the decisions by himself. Stuckart only signed the decisions since they dealt with citizenship issues. See "Die deutsche Volksliste," in BA Koblenz, N 1292/76, S. 3g.
65. See Stuckart's contributions in *Deutsches Recht* 1936, 234 et seq. and *Deutsche Verwaltung*, 1938, 62 et seq.
66. On *RVL*, see Herbert, *Best*, 284.
67. In *RVL* 1 (1941).
68. See Stuckart's programmatic contributions, "Die Neuordnung der Kontinente und die Zusammenarbeit auf dem Gebiet der Verwaltung," *RVL* 1 (1941): 3 et seq., and "Aufgaben und Ziele einer neuen Verwaltungswissenschaft," *RVL* 2 (1942): 53–74.
69. Stuckart, "Staatsangehörigkeit und Reichsgestaltung."
70. Stuckart, "Gedanken zur künftigen Ausbildung des Verwaltungsnachwuchses," *RVL* 4(1943): 105 et seq. For further reference see Stephan Lehnstaedt, "Das Reichsministerium des Innern unter Heinrich Himmler 1943–1945," *VfZ* 54 (2006): 639–672, 654 et seq.
71. While in 1933 the cabinet met every second day, it only met 19 times in 1934, 12 times in 1935, four times in 1936, six times in 1937, and once in 1938. See Hans-Ulrich Wehler, *Der Nationalsozialismus. Bewegung, Führerschaft, Verbrechen 1919–1945* (München, 2009), 65.
72. Hans Heinrich Lammers, the former head of the Chancellery of the Reich told prosecutor Robert Kempner in 1948 in Nuremberg that meetings of the state secretaries became the only forum to deal with daily business, since Hitler had practically prohibited cabinet-level meetings. TWC, vol. 13, 426
73. See the *Reichsbürgergesetz* of 15 September 1935, RGBl. I, 1146, and the *Erste Verordnung zum Reichsbürgergesetz* of 14 November 1935, RGBl. I, 1333, the *Ge-*

setz zum Schutz des deutschen Blutes und der deutschen Ehre of 15 September 1935, RGBl. I, 1146, as well as the *Erste Verordnung zum Gesetz zum Schutz des deutschen Blutes und der deutschen Ehre* of 14 November 1935, RGBl. I, 1146, all modified by Verordnung of 16 February 1940, RGBl. I, 394, and decree of 29 May 1941, RGBl. I, 295. All of these laws were repealed by the *Control Council Law Number 1* of 20 September 1945, *Amtsblatt des Alliierten Kontrolrates*, 3.

74. *Reichsgericht, Großer Senat in Strafsachen,* Decision of 23 February 1938, RG GS St 72, 91, 96.
75. See notes 5 and 12.
76. Ibid.
77. On the various proposals discussed within the Nazi administration prior to the Nuremberg Laws, see Kulka, "Die Nürnberger Rassengesetze;" Neliba, *Wilhelm Frick;* and Essner, *Die "Nürnberger Gesetze,"* 76 et seq.
78. See examples in *Wolf Gruner, Widerstand in der Rosenstrasse. Die Fabrik-Aktion und die Verfolgung der "Mischehen" 1943* (Frankfurt, 2005), 50.
79. *Elfte Verordnung zum Reichsbürgergesetz* of 25 November 1941, RGBl. I, 722. On the negotiations preceding the regulation, see Essner, *Die "Nürnberger Gesetze,"* 292 et seq.
80. See for example, Lommatzsch, Hans Globke, 61 et seq.; Reinhard Mehring, *Carl Schmitt. Aufstieg und Fall. Eine Biographie* (Munich, 2009), 372; Mayer, *Staaten als Täter,* 122 et seq.
81. Wilhelm Stuckart and Hans Globke, *Reichsbürgergesetz vom 15. Sept. 1935; nebst allen Ausführungsvorschriften und den einschlägigen Gesetzen und Verordnungen, Reichs- und Preußisches Ministerium des Innern* (Munich, 1936).
82. Wilhelm Stuckart, "Die völkische Grundordnung des deutschen Volkes," *Deutsches Recht* 5 (1935): 557–564.
83. "Runderlass," MBliV 1936, 11; BAB R 1501/5514, Bl. 153. Minutes of the committee meetings in BAB R 1501/ 125483. See also Essner, *Die "Nürnberger Gesetze,"* 174 et seq.
84. "Besprechungsprotokoll," BAB R 1501/5514, Bl. 199–211.
85. On the Wannsee Conference see Mark Roseman, *The Villa, The Lake, The Meeting. Wannsee and the Final Solution* (London, 2002); Peter Weber, "Die Mitwirkung der Juristen an der Wannseekonferenz," *Schleswig-Holsteinische Anzeigen* (2005): 207–212; Christian Gerlach, "Die Wannsee-Konferenz, das Schicksal der deutschen Juden und Hitlers politische Grundentscheidung, alle Juden Europas zu ermorden," *Werkstatt Geschichte* 18 (1997): 7–44; Eberhard Jäckel, "On the Purpose of the Wannsee Conference," in *Perspectives on the Holocaust. Essays in Honour of Raul Hilberg*, eds. J. A. Pacy and A. P. Wertheimer (San Francisco, 1995), 39–50; Wolf Kaiser, "Die Wannseekonferenz. SS-Führer und Ministerialbeamte im Einvernehmen über die Ermordung der europäischen Juden," in *Täter-Opfer-Folgen*, eds. Heiner Lichtenstein and Otto R. Romberg, 2. ed. (Bonn, 1995), 24–37; Peter Klein, *Die Wannseekonferenz vom 20. Januar 1942. Analyse und Dokumentation* (Berlin, 1995); Peter Longerich, *Die Wannseekonferenz vom 20. Januar 1942: Planung und Beginn des Genozids an den europäischen Juden* (Berlin, 1998); Kurt Pätzold and Erika Schwarz, *Tagesordnung: Judenmord. Die Wannseekonferenz am 20. Januar 1942; Eine Dokumentation zur Organisation der "Endlösung,"* 3rd ed. (Berlin, 1992).

86. Weber, "Die Mitwirkung der Juristen."
87. BAB R 1501/3746a, printed in: Wilhelm Lenz, "Die Handakten von Bernhard Lösener, 'Rassereferent' im Reichsministerium des Innern," *Archiv und Geschichte* 57 (2000): 684–99 (695 et seq.). See also the note about the interrogation of Lösener on 13 October 1947 by R. Kempner in Staatsarchiv Nürnberg, Interrogations, 3 et seq.
88. The account probably refers to the executions of the first transport of Jews from Berlin to Riga by Special Commando II in the forest of Rumbuli. The train had left Berlin on 27 November 1941 and arrived in Riga three days later. See Longerich, *Politik der Vernichtung*, 508.
89. BAB R 1501/3746a.
90. Ibid.
91. Lösener prepared a memo for Stuckart in preparation for the Wannsee Conference, which had initially been planned for 9 December 1941. He described the position of the RSHA and provided Stuckart with arguments for defending the legal *status quo* and preventing the inclusion of Mischlinge in the Final Solution. BAB R 1501/5519, 238–47 (477–95).
92. Wilhelm Stuckart and Rolf Schiedermair, *Rassen- und Erbpflege,* 3rd ed. (Leipzig, 1942), 12, quoted according in Diemut Majer, *Grundlagen des nationalsozialistischen Rechtssystems. Führerprinzip, Sonderrecht, Einheitspartei* (Stuttgart, 1987), 142 et seq.
93. Ibid. 4. edition, p. 14. The author of the present article had direct access only to the 1943 edition, and bases his conclusion on a comparison to Stuckart's text as quoted in Majer, *Grundlagen,* as in the previous note. In the book *Neues Staatsrecht III,* (Leipzig, 1943), p. 24 et seq., co-authored with Harry v. Rosen-v. Hoewel and Rolf Schiedermair, Stuckart refers to the "total removal" (*restlosen Entfernung*) of the Jews in the context of the "racial new order of the European continent" (*Neuordnung des europäischen Kontinents*).
94. On the close connections between Euthanasia and Holocaust, see Friedlander, *Der Weg zum NS-Genozid.*
95. RMI, 18 August 1939, Az. IV b 3088/39-1079 Mi, in BAB R 1501/5586. Stuckart signed the decree on behalf of his minister ("*In Vertretung*").
96. Oral account by Rüdiger Stuckart, Berlin, May 1999. On Werner Catel see Friedlander, *Der Weg zum NS-Genozid,* 84 et seq.
97. BAB Nürnberger Prozesse, Fall XI, Nr. 207, 73–74, quoted in Pätzold and Schwarz, *Tagesordnung,* 156 et seq.
98. Ibid.
99. Ibid. See also Essner, *Die "Nürnberger Gesetze,"* 414 et seq.
100. Kempner and Hänsel, *Das Urteil,* 169.
101. Ibid., 167.

Roland Freisler in 1942
Source: Bundesarchiv, Berlin

Chapter 3

ROLAND FREISLER AND THE VOLKSGERICHTSHOF

The Court as an Instrument of Terror

Robert D. Rachlin

Roland Freisler was in no way a demon rising from hell; rather, he emerged from the midst of the German people. He was a merciless representative of a merciless justice, a consistent accomplice of a murderous system, a showcase murderer in a robe—and the Germans made his deeds, his impact, his career possible.

—Helmut Ortner, *Der Hinrichter:
Roland Freisler—Mörder im Dienste Hitlers*

ONE OF THE ALLIED BOMBS that hit Berlin in early February 1945 smashed into the building in the Tiergarten district housing the *Volksgerichtshof* (VGH)—the People's Court—a murderous tribunal in a murderous regime, ferociously presided over since August 1942 by Roland Freisler. Amidst the wreckage, Freisler lay dead, crushed under a fallen ceiling beam. Freisler, an early zealot of the Nazi movement, deployed his keen intellect and unshakable dedication to Hitler in a perversion of the forms of justice that were extreme even by the standards of the Third Reich. He wreaked retribution on perceived enemies of the state, most notably in the trials of the 20 July 1944 conspirators who plotted the assassination of the Führer. In his proceedings, Freisler abandoned all pretense of judicial impartiality, cast off any veneer of judicial dignity, and remorselessly hectored his hapless defendants with a savagery that actually embarrassed some of the Nazi leadership.

Two and a half years after Freisler's violent end, the Allied Command ordered officials of the city of Berlin and the German prosecutor's office to collect the records of the Volksgerichtshof "on the surface as well as under the debris" of the former court premises.[1] The records were to be transferred to Plötzensee Prison, tracing the route of the 20 July plotters, who were immediately taken from their show trials before Freisler to that prison for swift executions carried out with an exquisite brutality ordered by Hitler himself. Although many VGH records were lost, those that survive reveal a parallel judicial universe functioning alongside the regular, established courts administering the quotidian business of ordinary civil and criminal cases. The functioning of the VGH reflected a theoretical position articulated at length by Freisler in his books and law journal articles. Freisler rejected the notion, fundamental to all civilized legal orders, that laws were to have exclusively prospective effect. It is axiomatic in all legal systems based on the common- or Roman-law traditions that no one should be punished for an act absent advance warning that the act is criminal. The clause in Article I, section 9 of the United States Constitution prohibiting the passage of ex post facto laws was no innovation, but merely a reaffirmation of the firmly-embedded principle *nulla poena sine lege* (no punishment without a law).

The VGH not only inflicted severe penalties, including death, for acts about which the enacted laws were silent; this *a posteriori* criminalization was applied to acts that would be regarded as trifling in any non-despotic society. Such arbitrary ruthlessness was inconsistent with the law-abiding image the Reich wished to convey of itself. The official annual statistical abstract, with its detailed facts and figures covering broad areas of German life, comprised a comprehensive section reporting on judicial administration. That section furnished meticulous statistics of the activities of the regular courts, such as the *Amtsgerichte* (district courts), *Landgerichte* (regional courts), and *Oberlandesgerichte* (higher regional courts). Particulars were set out about specific crimes and misdemeanors adjudged by each court, the occupations of defendants, and the sentences pronounced. The religious affiliations of defendants were tallied. Discrete sections of the penal code were cited. Yet the most potent court in the Reich, with preemptive jurisdiction over cases touching on fluidly-defined treason, and dealing the death penalty to over five thousand men and women in its eleven-year life,[2] was ignored.[3]

The exact number of death penalties is not certain, although a plausible total is 5,266.[4] The VGH spread terror throughout the German population by inflicting extreme penalties for acts that would pass unremarked in a non-totalitarian society. An innocent joke could lead to the guillotine. The court's procedures were calculated to afford the accused no realistic opportunity of defense. Its decisions were little more than vigilante justice executed under the cover of a red robe. Yet after the war, not a single VGH judge was punished. At least twenty-nine of the former VGH judges and at least sixty-nine of the former VGH prosecutors embarked on respectable careers in the postwar German courts, a few even undertook ordinary law practices.[5] The widow of Roland Freisler was granted an enhanced pension on the basis that her husband, had he lived, would possibly have had a career as a lawyer or high official.[6]

Freisler and the Demise of Law

The first hint that a revolution in legal institutions was foreseen emerged thirteen years before Hitler's rise to power. The nineteenth point of the Nazi Party's twenty-five point program, issued in 1920, promised that Roman law, serving a "materialistic world-view," was to be replaced by German common law (*deutsches Gemeinrecht*). A court with the character of the VGH was presaged in *Mein Kampf*,[7] although what Hitler had in mind were trials of the so-called "November traitors" who allegedly brought about Germany's defeat in World War I. No such trials ever took place. Less than two months after Hitler came to power, he gave a further warning that the normative supremacy of the law was to be weakened, if not abrogated. In his 23 March 1933 speech to the Reichstag, Hitler declared that, "Our judiciary must, first and foremost, serve the preservation of the *Volk* community." Aside from the racially-charged term *Volk,* that statement by itself was unexceptional. But he continued with an ominous warning directed at the independence of judges, "The flexibility of judgments calculated to serve the preservation of society must be appropriate in light of the fixed tenure of the judges (*Unabseztbarkeit der Richter*)." Hitler next affirmed the new, subordinate status of individual rights, "Not the individual, but the *Volk* must be the focus of legal concern." If the point was missed by anyone, Hitler added, "In the future, state and national treason will be annihilated (*ausgebrannt werden*) with barbaric ruthlessness."[8] The German people had to be whipped into greater efforts and support, and the Nazi rulers had to take stern measures against anyone whose activities, however trivial, were seen to stand in the way of ultimate victory. Every institution of German life had to be oriented toward the *Endsieg*, the final victory. This included the judiciary, as Hitler made abundantly clear in his 26 April 1942 speech to the Reichstag, in which he presented himself as the supreme judge. The imperatives of survival would no longer be hampered by legal prescriptions or by officials' vested rights. He would no longer tolerate sentences that failed to meet his vision of appropriate severity, relating the case of a man who had abused his wife, driving her to madness and eventually to death. Hitler was outraged that the man had been sentenced to only five years in prison. He promised that in the future he would intervene in cases and remove judges who did not recognize the demands of the hour. Joseph Goebbels, pronouncing the speech as one of Hitler's best, reported that the Führer's demand for absolute authority to do what is necessary to prosecute the war, without regard to the vested rights of others, was greeted by thunderous applause.[9] On the same day, the Reichstag responded with a resolution:

> There can be no doubt that the Führer, in the present time of the war, in which the German *Volk* is in a battle for its very existence, must possess the right he has claimed to do everything that serves or contributes to the struggle for victory. Therefore, the Führer—without being bound by existing provisions of law—in his capacity of Führer of the nation, Supreme Commander of the Armed Forces, Head of Government, and holder of the executive power, must be in a position, as highest judge and leader of the party, to hold every German to the fulfillment of his duty by all means that seem appropriate, whether he is a simple soldier or officer, junior or senior official or judge, leading or subservient functionary of the party, laborer or salaried employee, and when, after diligent inquiry, it is found that such duties have been violated, to remove him from his office, rank, and position without regard to so-called vested rights, without the pertinent compensation, and without the prescribed preliminary procedures.[10]

Inclusion of judges in this inventory of office-holders subject to Hitler's will was not casual, as he made clear in conversations shortly afterwards. Taking aim at the Jehovah's Witnesses, Hitler complained on 7 June 1942 that the VGH was overly cautious about labeling as treason those offenses that were based on idealistic or religious convictions.[11] On 24 June, Hitler expressed himself in favor of the attachment of Nazi emblems to the robes of judges and prosecutors.[12] Hitler's Reichstag speech and the resolution that followed were a clear warning to judges that an independent judiciary was a thing of the past and that their positions—and hence, their income and prestige—depended on conformity to such judicial and legal guidelines as Hitler revealed from time to time as his will. However specific or otherwise these guidelines might be, one thing was plain: it was safer for a judge to err on the side of severity than leniency.[13]

Goebbels's enthusiasm for Hitler's 26 April speech carried over into a speech Goebbels delivered to the VGH on 22 July 1942. He took pains to stress at the outset that his remarks had official sanction: Hitler had personally reviewed and approved his manuscript, thus clothing his observations with *ex cathedra* vigor. Goebbels built on Hitler's threat to remove nonconformist judges, scolding those who persisted in "old ways of thinking" (*alte Denkgewohnheiten*) and criticizing specific VGH decisions. Just as generals can be replaced, warned Goebbels, so can judges. Goebbels then reverted to the familiar devaluation of individual rights and reliance on established legal norms. Judges were to proceed not from statutes, but from the fundamental idea that criminals must be excluded from society. Implicit in this notion is the abstraction of criminality from any antecedent statutory definition. Presumably, a judge would "know it when he sees it." Goebbels then turned to the exigencies of the wartime situation. In wartime, it was less important that a judgment be just or unjust; what mattered was its expediency in the war effort. More explicitly, Goebbels declared that the object of a judgment was not obtaining recompense for a wrong or the rehabilitation of the criminal, but for the preservation of the state. Goebbels referred specifically to the judges' political mandate with respect to the treatment of Jews, in which emotional considerations were to play no part.[14] Otto Thierack, serving his last few weeks as president of the court, expressed his special thanks to Goebbels for his exposition of basic principles and urged him to repeat his energizing lecture in the future.[15]

A decree of the Führer, published in *Deutsche Justiz* on 28 August 1942, following the elevation of Thierack from president of the VGH to Minister of Justice, empowered the new minister to take all measures necessary to bring the administration of justice into line with Hitler's guidelines and directives. Thierack was explicitly authorized to deviate from existing law in pursuit of this mandate (*"Er kann hierbei von bestehendem Recht abweichen"*). Hitler's contempt for the law was matched, as one would expect, by his disdain for lawyers, whom he deemed "defective by nature," and questioned why they should be entitled to the title of "Doctor."[16] But the Führer found an eager and implacable lawyer-collaborator in his drive to subordinate the judiciary to his will. The new order for the judiciary and the concept of law were tailor-made for Roland Freisler, whose posture toward the role of law in the Nazi state had anticipated Hitler's Reichstag speech and 28 August 1942 decree by at least seven years. Hitler's vision of the subservient role of judges was mirrored in the writings and actions of Freisler.

Roland Freisler was born on 30 October 1893 in the city of Celle in Lower Saxony, and was baptized in the reformed Protestant faith. At the age of ten, he entered the Kaiser Wilhelm grammar school in Aachen, where he was an outstanding student and an eager debater. In Kassel in 1912, Freisler completed his *Abitur*, an examination qualifying him for university, finishing first in his class. He entered the University of Kiel to study law, but interrupted his studies at the outbreak of war to enter an infantry regiment as a lieutenant. He was wounded in Flanders and after a few months' convalescence at home, he returned to his regiment, which was sent to the Russian front. There, he was captured while leading a patrol, and spent the rest of the war in a Russian prison camp. The camp authorities, recognizing Freisler's administrative talents, appointed him a commissar in charge of food supplies. While in the camp, Freisler became fluent in Russian. Although there is no evidence that Freisler's appointment had any political overtones, Hitler would later refer to him jokingly as "the old Bolshevik."

He returned from Russia in 1920 and entered the University of Jena as a law student, where he needed only one year to earn his doctorate. In 1923, he took the final bar examination and was admitted to the bar. Between his graduation and the exam, he served as a *Referendar* (judicial intern) and later as an *Assessor* (lay judge) in the *Amtsgericht*, or local court, in his native Celle. In the interval between his return from Russia and Hitler's refounding of the Nazi Party after the failed Beer Hall Putsch in 1923, Freisler joined the extreme right-wing *Völkisch-Sozialer Bund*. In 1924, he opened his own law office with his brother Oswald; Oswald handled civil cases, while Roland specialized in criminal.

Roland Freisler joined the Nazi Party shortly after Hitler reconstituted it. As an advocate, he vigorously and eloquently defended many Nazi Party members charged with criminal offenses. Freisler served as a legislator in the Prussian Diet, and later in the Reichstag. His ascendancy among the ranks of lawyers defending Nazis may have been assisted by the 1928 case in which a propagandist was charged with distributing anti-Semitic literature bearing the colors of the Weimar Republic. Walter Luetgebrune, an able—if opportunistic—lawyer, had undertaken the defense of many members of right-wing and clandestine nationalist organizations and was then engaged to defend the accused propagandist. When the local Nazi organization proved unable to pay a fee, Luetgebrune's ideological fervor was trumped by desire for the fee, and he withdrew from the representation. Roland Freisler immediately stepped into the breach.[17]

Following the Nazi seizure of power on 30 January 1933, Freisler was appointed state secretary in the Prussian Ministry of Justice. From there he advanced in 1934 to state secretary in the Reich Justice Ministry, where he served until his appointment as president of the VGH in 1942. As state secretary in the Reich Justice Ministry, Freisler was listed as one of the attendees of the 20 January 1942 Wannsee Conference, at which the Final Solution of the "Jewish Question" was outlined. The official protocol of that conference does not record anything Freisler then said.[18]

Despite his enthusiastic support of the Nazi Party, his fiery defense of Nazis in the criminal courts and his prolific publications extolling the new legal order, Freisler never advanced to the inner party circles. Ortner skeptically moots one theory for this: Freisler was not sufficiently anti-Semitic, rarely mentioning the Jews in his speeches. Ortner suggests instead that Freisler's political activities were geographically far removed from Berlin and Munich, the hearts of Nazi activity.[19] This explanation is arguable: Freisler's appointment to the Prussian, later the Reich, Ministry of Justice placed him in Berlin from the early days of the Nazi regime, where he had ample opportunity to overcome any obscurity occasioned by his earlier domicile in Lower Saxony.

Freisler made every effort to thrust himself forward by his support of Hitler's vision of the place of law and judges in the new society. As early as 1935, Freisler denounced the traditional reliance on written, promulgated laws as a guide for judges, posing the following rhetorical challenges, demanding

> whether (the judge), given the imperfections of human foresight, of human language as the means of communicating ideas, of human imagination and its capacity to anticipate the progress of life, is bound to ally himself with legislators who, coolly and egotistically, have made all of these shortcomings a springboard of conduct harmful to the *Volk;* whether the judge is summoned to be the knowing

ally of the legislator, viewed as mouthpiece of the *Volk* conscience; whether he is (on the other hand) summoned to call a wrong a wrong, even when the imperfection of foresight, of creative legislative imagination, and of language as the means of communicating ideas has left what is clearly wrong open to argument.[20]

This statement encapsulated a distrust of all forward-looking norms of conduct. Rejection of these norms of conduct is a desertion of the normative basis of positive law, regnant in all civilized countries. "Law, so defined," purports to operate as smoothly *after* the fact as before. Freisler emphasized this with a pair of antinomies: "No punishment without an express corresponding legal command!" versus "Punishment of every punishable wrong!" "Protection of the cool, calculating criminal, in order to secure the 'freedom' of the 'citizen'!" versus "Protection of the *Volk* against every evil-doer, so that it can live and work!"[21] Freisler continued by deprecating the formula *nullum crimen sine lege* (no crime without a law), also traditionally formulated to the same effect as *nulla poena sine lege* (no punishment without a law). This theoretical displacement of the principle that no one should be punished for an act unless institutionally warned in advance that it was a crime was at the heart of VGH judicature, and was the most egregious feature of that court. Underpinning this eccentric view of law was the enthronement of the *Volk* over the individual to the point of abandoning legal worth of the individual other than as a constituent of the *Volk*. For Freisler, there was no national purpose in a state founded on individualism. Every individual had his own goals and could therefore change them at will, which in turn degenerated into the principle that "law and morality are two discrete things" ("*Recht und Moral sind zweierlei*.").[22] Morality was to be understood as a suite of norms deriving from the "*Volk* conscience," however that was to be ascertained.

As the remit of the VGH was treason, Freisler advocated considering all penal law a shade of treason, falling into line with the *Willensstrafrecht* idea, whereby treason was to be judged by the subjective "will" of the perpetrator, rather than by specific acts.[23]

Later, Justice Minister Otto Thierack made it abundantly clear in the first of a series of *Richterbriefe* (letters to judges) that the courts were in no sense to exercise oversight of the government. They were to see themselves as a coadjutor of the executive. Nor were they to avail themselves of what he called the "crutches" (*Krücken*) of statutes.[24] Freisler echoed Thierack's view of statutes as "crutches" in 1938 when he decried traditional jurisprudence, under which an indecent act could be punished "only when it is the complete, concrete mirror image of an express abstract image of the deed, drawn and expressly made punishable in a statute."[25] Freisler argued, on the basis of German legal history, that the commitment of judges to the written criminal law was foreign to German jurisprudence before the Enlightenment and emerged only thereafter.[26] This made the virtually unanimous positivism that prevailed in Germany since the Enlightenment all the more astounding (*erstaunlich*) to Freisler.[27]

Freisler's view of a non-objective normative law was endorsed by a jurist of no less distinction than Carl Schmitt. Schmitt wrote in the same year that "the fiction of a normative commitment of the judge to a statute is, for essential fields of practical legal activity (*Rechtsleben*), theoretically and practically untenable,"[28] and "the fiction and illusion of a statute embracing and subsuming in advance all cases and all situations according to their constituent fact situations cannot be revitalized; indeed the idea of an attempt at a gapless codification or standardization can hardly be accomplished today."[29] For Schmitt, the touchstone of the new jurisprudence was racial equivalence (*Artgleichheit*).[30] In Schmitt's copious pre-Third Reich writings, one finds little that hints at so extensive a dilution of statute-based penal administration.

Freisler was not the only proponent of a legal system free of pre-existing written norms. Others, such as Luetgebrune, Thierack, and Hans Frank expressed themselves to the same effect.[31] Freisler's works were, however, by far the most productive of essays, articles, and books beating the drum for law based on the "healthy conscience of the *Volk*," as embodied in the utterances of Hitler and the party.

Freisler's biographer, Gert Buchheit, arguably turns reality on its head by suggesting that the baneful development of the VGH is traceable to the training of lawyers, who think only in terms of clauses, decrees, and directives.[32] It was precisely the disparagement of written law that permitted and encouraged the VGH, especially in the Freisler years, to dispense with statutes and decide cases on the basis of the "healthy sentiment of the people."[33]

Scope and Operation of the Volksgerichtshof

The VGH was inaugurated on 14 July 1934 in a solemn ceremony in Berlin's recently decommissioned Prussian legislative chamber. SS Chief

Heinrich Himmler, Reich Justice Commissar Hans Frank, Justice Minister Franz Gürtner, and representatives of the SS, SA, and Wehrmacht were in attendance, arrayed before two giant swastika banners stretching from the heights to the floor. The "Röhm Putsch" beginning on 30 June 1934, in which at least eighty-five[34] people were slaughtered by the SS, was fresh in the memory of those present. Gürtner, continuing the myth that the murders were in defense of a coup directed against the Reich, solemnly addressed the gathering: "No *Volk*, however wholesome, no state, however firm, can drop its guard for a moment lest it fall victim to an onslaught such as that of 30 June." In words that were to become a mockery of the true mission of the VGH, Gürtner exhorted the new VGH judges: "Exercise your office as independent judges, obliged only to the law, answerable before God and your consciences."[35]

The VGH was established by the Law for the Amendment of Criminal Law and Procedure of 24 April 1934, specifically Article III.[36] Among other things, jurisdiction over high treason (*Hochverrat*) and state treason (*Landesverrat*),[37] formerly vested in the Supreme Court (*Reichsgericht*), was remitted exclusively to the VGH, except where the Higher Regional Courts retained concurrent jurisdiction. High treason was defined as attacks against the state; state treason was an attack against the country involving a foreign government. The Higher Regional Courts (*Oberlandesgerichte*) retained concurrent jurisdiction with the VGH in prosecutions for preparation for high treason (*Vorbereitung zum Hochverrat*) and certain less serious offenses against the state treason law. Jurisdiction over these fields, formerly granted to the *Sondergerichte* (special courts) by the 28 February 1933 Decree for the Protection of *Volk* and State, was transferred exclusively to the VGH.

Jurisdiction of the VGH was exercised over five categories of crime, which by their nature overlapped. They were, in addition to high treason, state treason, and preparation for high treason, undermining national defense (*Wehrkraftzersetzung*), and favoring the enemy (*Feindbegünstigung*). Undermining national defense and favoring the enemy were categories so inherently Protean that they could and did include activities as diverse as harboring or socializing with enemy prisoners, giving an enemy prisoner a piece of bread, spreading anti-regime propaganda among the German population, or even telling a political joke.[38] For example, a priest was sentenced to death for telling a joke about a soldier who had been gravely wounded and asked to see the faces of the people for whom he was about to die. A picture of Hitler was placed on his right, a picture of Göring on his left. The soldier then remarked that he was dying like Christ.[39] Because of its adaptability to a wide spectrum of acts perceived as anti-government, undermining national defense was the most common charge administered by the VGH.[40]

The VGH was not constrained by statutes or precedent. It functioned as the arm of the Reich executive, exemplifying what Ernst Fraenkel described as the co-existence of the normative state and the prerogative state.[41] Law, as conceived by Hitler and his followers and practiced to near-perfection by Freisler and his VGH colleagues, was the unembarrassed ex post facto imposition of measures selected ad hoc with the sole purpose of promoting the national and military aims of the Reich government.

In spite of the Führer's dismissal of established law as a norm of judicial administration, the VGH and the other *Sondergerichte* observed the forms and externalities of law and orderly procedure, however inevitable the outcome for most of the eleven-year history of the VGH. This conveyed a superficial impression of normalcy. Judgments of the VGH ran an average of 11.5 pages and were carefully divided into sections: the accused, the facts, the defenses, an assessment of the facts and law, and the appropriate punishment,[42] conformable to previous practice. But beneath an integument of regularity lurked an abandonment of formal standards and a total relinquishment of independence from the state and the party. The terror propagated by the VGH was not designed to terrify the broad society in the manner of a pogrom.[43] The terror consisted, rather, in the selective imposition of penal sanctions following criteria that were themselves extraordinary in the light of conventional ideas of proportionality. With the ascension of Freisler in 1942 as the war was turning inexorably against Germany, the proceedings can unreservedly be characterized as arbitrary. This is manifest from the film record of the trials of the 20 July plot defendants, who were deliberately presented in shabby, ill-fitting clothes, bombarded by Freisler with insulting epithets, and denied any opportunity to articulate a defense. By this time, the terror inhered in both applying criteria for infliction of the death penalty and in stripping the veneer of procedural regularity. The disposition of VGH judges toward defined standards of criminal conduct as the exclusive gauge of their actions has been paraphrased this way: "If the judge's task is seen merely to justify legal or other standards by a formal, orderly, and rationally comprehensible proceeding, then justice is available to serve any purpose."[44] The purpose that VGH justice did, in fact, serve is amply shown by a glance at its history, especially as the war turned against Germany.

"Blitzkrieg gescheitert—Terror gesteigert" (Failed Blitzkrieg—Intensified Terror)[45]

Freisler's August 1942 inauguration as president of the VGH coincided with a steep decline in Germany's military fortunes. The lightning successes in Poland, the Lowlands, Norway, Denmark, and France had been overshadowed by the catastrophes of Moscow and Stalingrad. When Freisler entered office as president of the VGH, Hitler's "Night and Fog" (*Nacht und Nebel*) initiative was well underway. This program, decreed by Hitler on 7 December 1941, was directed against dissenters and resisters, chiefly in France, the Netherlands, Belgium, and Norway. Such individuals were to be either executed on the spot or secreted away either to Germany for trial or to concentration camps. A key mandate of the program was that the family and relatives of those kidnapped were to have no knowledge of the cause of the disappearance or the victim's destination. In short, the purpose of "Night and Fog" was to sow terror in the populations of occupied countries. But what court should try those prisoners who were destined to receive a trial? Initially, it was thought that the *Reichskriegsgericht* (Reich War Court, the highest military court) would handle these cases. The War Court was squeamish about undertaking what were expected to be summary, drum-head proceedings. The other regular, German courts also recoiled, and trial of these prisoners became a judicial hot potato. No court wanted to assume the blemish of overt illegality.[46] Freisler, on the other hand, had no such qualms and happily accepted jurisdiction of the VGH over these cases. Trials of "Night and Fog" defendants began in the VGH just a few days after Freisler took office. Some 1,200 such cases had been referred to the VGH. Freisler exercised his transfer authority and referred about three-quarters of these cases to other courts. Of the approximately two hundred cases retained by the VGH, Freisler assigned the majority to his own First Senate. There are no reliable figures for the number of "Night and Fog" trials that were conducted by the VGH, although the tally of over 2,800 death sentences in 1942–1943[47] suggests the outcome. The trials themselves were a sham. The total abandonment of judicial regularity was made inevitable by Justice Minister Thierack, who instructed Freisler that the court must function "in accord with the leadership of the state ... You will have every indictment submitted to you and will recognize ... what is essential for the state."[48]

The focus of Freisler's early cases was largely on foreign, rather than German, nationals. Meanwhile, discontent among the domestic population was growing, and anti-regime conspiratorial sentiments among the military officer corps, which had begun in the 1930s but had lain generally dormant during the heyday of the *Blitzkrieg,* began to take on new life. As the pressure of military defeats and the prospect of final disaster loomed larger, Freisler and the VGH became progressively transformed from a tribunal bearing the outward insignia of impartiality and procedural regularity into a naked instrument of Hitler's single-minded aim of mobilizing all institutions of German life, including the judiciary, for prosecution of war aims. Freisler, for whom the overriding interest of *Volk,* as defined by Hitler and the Nazi Party, took unqualified precedence over the strictures of positive law, began to shift his court's attention from foreign to domestic cases. It was in this context that Freisler found his métier. Walter Wagner writes: "In court proceedings, Freisler developed his full talent for stagecraft (*schauspielerisches Talent*), qualifying him as one of the most effective stage presences of his time."[49]

One case before the VGH, although not with Freisler presiding,[50] was the basis of Hans Fallada's last novel *Jeder stirbt für sich allein,* first translated into English in 2009.[51] The protagonists, Otto and Anna Quangel, are arrested, tried, and executed after distributing anti-Hitler messages around Berlin on postcards and paper. The novel is based on the actual case of Otto and Elise Hampel, who suffered the same fate for the same acts of protest. Shortly after the war, Fallada obtained a part of the Gestapo file on the Hampels through a chain of people, including the poet Johannes Becher. After writing an article about the case in a periodical, Fallada transformed the case into a novel.[52]

In many respects, the fictional Quangels corresponded closely to the actual Hampels, although there were differences of detail. The real Hampels were prompted to undertake their clandestine writing campaign against Hitler by the wartime death of Elise Hampel's brother in France. In the novel, the motivation arises from the death of Anna Quangel's son. However, the most important difference is in the character of the Quangels and the Hampels at the end. It is in this respect that truth is not only stranger than fiction, but more instructive. The actual Hampels were arrested after Otto accidentally dropped one of the writings in the factory where he worked. A co-worker discovered it and turned it over to the Gestapo. The Hampels were tried before the Second Senate of the Volksgerichtshof on 22 January 1943, convicted of preparation for high treason and sentenced to death. The fictional Quangels are likewise sentenced to death. In the Fallada novel, the married couple have a final colloquy in which they bravely accept their fate.[53] But the case of the real Hampels was quite different. Before trial and sentencing, each took the entire blame onto himself or herself, making an effort to exonerate the other. Clearly, they had no expectation that they would be dealt the extreme penalty. After their expectation was dashed and death sentences were handed down, their attitudes completely changed.[54] Otto and Elise were represented by separate counsel, and they submitted separate applications for clemency. But now, unlike the fictional Quangels, each blamed the other and stressed his or her loyalty to Hitler and activities on behalf of the National Socialist state. Elise's father submitted a letter to Hitler describing his daughter as a loyal Nazi who had been misled by her husband. The petitions were in vain. The Hampels were executed by guillotine on 8 April 1943.[55]

The Hampel case reveals an especially poignant and disquieting cost of state terror: the moral disintegration of otherwise brave people when faced with the prospect of violent death. Fallada's fiction excites admiration for the courage of the victims; the truth excites compassion for the all-too-human resort of real people to the instinct of self-preservation even at the cost of damning a beloved spouse. And just what was the crime of the Hampels? What did they write on these postcards? Some examples:

> *Freie Presse! Deutsche Männer und Frauen wir müssen an uns selbst glauben! Nicht den Schurken Hitler! Soldaten schiest [sic] die Hitler Himmler Göring Goebbels Bande nieder!* (Free Press! German men and women, we must believe in ourselves, not in the scoundrel Hitler. Soldiers, gun down the Hitler Himmler Göring Goebbels gang.)

> *Hitler hatt (sic) keine Frau, Der Schlächter keine Sau ... Nieder mit der Hitler Bande.* (Hitler has no wife, the butcher has no sow ... Down with the Hitler gang.)

> *Die Hitlerei bedeutet in der Welt Gewalt geht vor Recht."* ("Hitlerism means that might goes before right in the world.)

Mental illness was no defense for such outbursts. A fifty-year-old psychopathic pensioner was sentenced to death for high treason. Like the Hampels, his crime was distributing about one hundred postcards containing abuse of the Nazi leadership. Among other statements on these cards: "The German people need only one corpse—the Führer's." Although Freisler acknowledged that the accused's condition was the result of hereditary mental disease, he nevertheless sentenced him to death a month after the Hampels were executed with the following singular reasoning: "The First Senate deems mitigation of punishment out of place in such cases. One whose moral capacity (*Verantwortungsfähigkeit*) is diminished by his organic constitution must exert double effort to remain decent (*anständig zu bleiben*)."[56]

Over the years of its existence, the cases that came before the VGH began to change in both character and outcome. Marxen and Schlüter[57] have reproduced in full what they represent as a random sampling of judgments rendered during the life of the VGH. Taking them at their assurance, one gets a sense of how the court and its business evolved over the years, from the relatively peaceful time before 1938, to the uneasy peace with Britain and France in 1938, to the outbreak of war in 1939, to the reversal in Germany's military fortunes in late 1941 and beyond. Here is a sampling:

9 August 1934: a factory worker at I.G. Farben was sentenced to death, one of only four in that year, for espionage, for betraying military secrets to the occupying French in return for money and leniency in a French proceeding charging him with unlawful possession of a firearm.

9 January 1936: a German brick worker and a miner were tried for their participation in activities to promote Esperanto as an international language. Esperanto was then being used by international communist organizations as a convenient means of communication across native language borders. The brick worker was acquitted. The miner was sentenced to one-and-a-half years' imprisonment as an accessory to preparations for high treason. It should be noted that convictions of high treason were far less common over the years than convictions for preparations for high treason. This case is unique among those researched: a defendant was convicted, not of high treason or of preparations for high treason, but of being an accessory to preparations for high treason. Thus, he was punished, although two degrees removed from treason.

31 March 1936: in a case suiting a picaresque novel, a German woman was induced into encouraging a sexual relationship with a soldier stationed in Stuttgart in order to transmit to a source in Switzerland such information about the disposition and armament of troops at that installation as she could obtain by the encouragement of her sexual favors. This is a crime which would, without the slightest doubt, have resulted in the death penalty six or seven years later. Now, in a time of

relative peace, the inept *femme fatale* was sentenced to eight years. With the outbreak of war, severe sentences were handed down for much less than the overt acts of the German miner or the amateur Mata Hari.

20 December 1939: a fiercely anti-Nazi postal worker began displaying anti-Hitler placards: for example, one showing the head of Hitler with the superscription "The guilty one." Language below the image read "Who pushed the world into war? Adolf Hitler. Who is guilty of all the misery? Adolf Hitler. Worker! Rise to battle. Strike the fascists where you find them." The postal worker was sentenced to death. It should be added that, both before and after the outbreak of war, he had been stealing packages from the post office. However, it was the anti-Hitler placards that dominated the Court's written judgment.

6 June 1942: a German iron polisher was sentenced to death for anti-regime graffiti scrawled on the walls of toilet stalls. Examples: "workers, help Russia, strike! Up with the KPD (the German Communist Party)." He also had committed the crime of listening to German language radio broadcasts from London. He was convicted of preparation for high treason.

14 May 1943: a German generator-stoker and a German welder were sentenced to death for undermining national defense. They were quoted remarking, "The poor young soldiers are dying just for the fat bellies. The war is just a capitalist business. We're absolutely going to lose it. We will not profit a bit, whether we win or lose it. The war is an act of desperation by Hitler. Better to live under foreign occupation than under this government."

4 December 1943: two German workers suffered the death penalty for undermining national defense, having asserted that the war was unnecessary and the Nazis' fault. They suggested that enemy airmen would be better advised to drop their bombs on headquarters than on the German population. The war would end more quickly that way.

Perhaps the most renowned trial over which Freisler presided, aside from that of the 20 July plotters, was the trial of twenty-one-year-old Sophie Scholl and her twenty-four-year-old brother Hans, who were students at the University of Munich. In February, 1943, they were summarily tried before Freisler, along with fellow-student Christoph Probst, found guilty of distributing anti-war leaflets as part of the resistance group "White Rose," sentenced to death, and executed by guillotine the same day. In addition to a film treatment, many books have been written about this heart-breaking case.[58]

The VGH Death Toll

Reports of the VGH presidents disclose a total of 5,191 death sentences in the years 1937–1944.[59] For the years 1934–1936, there were 23 death sentences, according to a survey reproduced by Walter Wagner.[60] For the pre-Freisler years (1934–1941), the arithmetic mean of death sentences was 32.9. For the Freisler years, the mean was 1,650.3. Wagner assumes for the sake of a computation that about half of the 1,192 death sentences in 1942 were handed down before Freisler assumed the presidency.[61] Wagner does not assert that this apportionment is an accurate reflection of Thierack's and Freisler's respective contributions to the total, although it is probably close: Hannsjoachim Koch ascribes 649 death sentences out of 1,192, or 54 percent, to Thierack in the first seven months of 1942, the remaining to Freisler.[62] Lest Thierack be deprived of his fair share of "credit," it must be noted that the death sentences jumped dramatically during his presidency, from 1940 to 1941, almost doubling, although the total number of accused persons (1940: 1,091; 1941: 1,237)[63] increased by only 13 percent. If the succession of annual death sentences from 1934 through 1941 are used as independent variables in a regression analysis, the predicted number for 1942 would be 85 (rounded). If one uses only the years 1938 through 1941, the predicted number for 1942 would be 120, which suggests that both Thierack and Freisler reacted to the catastrophic turn of military events and Hitler's demand that judges ramp up the severity meted out to defendants. One can also consider the percentage of accused persons who were sentenced to death in those two years versus the percentage in 1942. In 1940, 4.9 percent of defendants received the death sentence, 8.2 percent in 1941. In 1942 the percentage jumped to 46.3. During the remaining two Freisler years, the percentage remained about the same: 49.8 in 1943, and 47.9 in 1944. The constancy of these percentages in 1942, 1943, and 1944 suggests that it was during Freisler's presidency that the VGH was responsible for the great bulk of the 1,192 death sentences handed down in 1942.

Conclusion

The Third Reich never abandoned the outward trappings of a *Rechtsstaat*, a state governed by law. The Weimar Constitution, while in reality a dead letter, was never formally revoked despite occasional initiatives directed to establishing a National Socialist Constitution. The *Bürgerliches Gesetzbuch* ("BGB"), the civil code, and the *Strafgesetzbuch,* the penal Code, remained in force during the Third Reich. Ordinary civil litigation was conducted by the regular courts in a more or less regular manner, although Jews and other *Untermenschen* (subhumans) were denied access to the courts as unworthy of German law. Thus, even as the VGH and the other *Sondergerichte* carried on their business, the forms and externalities of law were observed. The reality was different. Even in the civil law, certain key concepts contained in the BGB, such as "good morals"[64] and "good faith,"[65] afforded Nazi jurists generous opportunities to reform administration of the laws in a *völkisch* image.[66]

The devaluation of historic legal norms and the perversion of traditional judicial procedure were not merely the spontaneous expressions of malevolence evoked for the occasion, but evolved from an explicit rejection of principles underlying both common and Roman (civil) law systems. Abandonment of *ex ante* norms defining criminality put the individual in a state of uncertainty about the lawfulness of his own conduct. Penal sanctions became a Damoclean sword suspended over the citizen—the protecting thread may break at any moment and on any pretext. When the sword represents the extreme penalty, the unpredictability of its descent creates terror. Peter Hoffmann has justly described the VGH as "an instrument of terror designed for suppression of any form of opposition."[67] On 25 January 1985, the West German Bundestag, itself, labeled the VGH as a *Terrorinstrument.* As Raul Hilberg has written: "... (T)here was an atrophy of laws and a corresponding multiplication of measures for which the sources of authority were more and more ethereal. Valves were being opened for a decision flow."[68] Hilberg's choice of "ethereal" applies not only to the "sources of authority," but to the very acts and events that could energize those sources in deadly measures against the individual. Cloaked with the garments of law, both physically (the judges wore the red robes customarily limited to the highest court in the country) and—in theory—normatively (the VGH administered written laws and decrees, however ill-defined their practical application), the VGH presided over about eighteen thousand cases, although exact numbers are undeterminable.

The VGH dispensed thousands of death sentences, especially during the war. That number has never been definitively established, but a figure of between five and six thousand is credible,[69] based on reports submitted by the court itself. Coupled with an arbitrary and unforeseeable interpretation of legal norms, the infliction of the death sentence was increasingly unpredictable. The VGH, especially under the presidency of Roland Freisler, widely known as "raving Roland,"[70] became a purveyor of lethality disproportionate in a conventional view to the "crime," an instrument of terror. Numerous widely-accessible film clips of Freisler as presiding judge, especially in the prosecution of the conspirators of 20 July 1944, encourage a cartoonish view of him. This one-dimensional conception of the VGH and Freisler, in particular, is comforting, inviting a personal abstraction from the environment that led up to it and a resort to facile pieties, such as "it would never happen here." But as a cartoon distorts reality, it also impedes a realistic grasp of the lessons to be taken from this sorry page of legal history.

The odious excesses of Freisler and the VGH, like the racist ideology of the Third Reich, can be viewed in the context of historical antecedents. The judicial anomie that was the hallmark of the VGH had models, both in the courts and on the streets of Weimar Germany. The turbulent Weimar years offered ample precedent for both. Extreme right-wing paramilitary organizations, such as *Organisation Consul,* murdered opponents and suspected internal spies with few serious legal consequences.[71] Support for parliamentary democracy during the Weimar years was spotty at best and hardly a priority for the conservative judiciary, heavily populated by holdovers from the Wilhelmine years.

The unequal Weimar justice meted out in favor of the right-wing, as distinct from left-wing, accused criminals rendered illusory the *Rechtsstaat* ideal of a nation ruled by law. Similarly, offenses against Jews were treated lightly by the Weimar courts,[72] reflecting the anti-Semitic bias of reactionary judges, itself a continuation of an animus prevailing in German social life since the late nineteenth century.

The extrajudicial murders by bands technically illegal, but winked at by the national government, such as *Organisation Consul* and the *Schwarze Reichswehr* (Black Reich Defense), resonated with the mediaeval institution of the *Feme* courts (*Femegerichte,* also rendered *Vehmgerichte*). These courts operated chiefly in the fourteenth and fifteenth centuries in some parts of Germany, mainly in Westphalia, outside of the established legal institutions and visited death on opponents, suspected traitors, and those who failed to maintain the strict secrecy enjoined on all of the tribunal's members. Composed of lay judges who tried criminal cases and carried out summary executions by the hands of the judges themselves, secrecy applied even to the judges' closest family and relatives. The term "Feme murders" was widely applied to the murders of Foreign Minister Walther Rathenau and other victims of right-wing gangs in Weimar Germany. In fact, the murders perpetrated by right-wing groups in Weimar Germany became known as "Feme murders," often with express or tacit approval of that transplanted antique procedure.[73] The *Feme* mind-set, as indulged in the conflicted society of pre-Nazi right-wing factions, was seamlessly transferred to the judicial and police organs of the Third Reich, particularly when it was faced with military catastrophe. Martin Broszat has described and documented the intercession of the Gestapo in the recapture and internment of perceived enemies of the state who had either been acquitted by the VGH or served out their sentences.[74] What Broszat describes as "the wartime radicalization of criminal justice"[75] can be seen as the natural issue of *Feme*-justice, as practiced during the Weimar years. Even before defeat was seriously threatened, Hitler interfered—Broszat estimates twenty-five to thirty times—in judicial decisions of which he disapproved.[76] The dependence of the institutions of justice on the will or whim of Hitler and his executive agents cannot, therefore, be ascribed wholly to a state of extreme wartime emergency.

At the foundation of institutionalized *Feme*-justice is a rejection of law as the supreme normative force in society. Once the principle of *nulla poena sine lege* is abandoned, the independence of legal institutions vanishes with it. There was Weimar precedent for this as well: after the assassination of Rathenau in 1922, the accused were tried under a law passed after the fact.[77]

Much has been written about resistance in Nazi Germany. Resistance was noteworthy precisely because it was the exception, not the rule. The axiom "government derives from the consent of the governed" can be understood both normatively (this is how governments *should* be established) and descriptively (this is, in fact, how governments *are* established). There is little evidence of popular outcry about the excesses of Freisler and the VGH.[78] The sustained power of the VGH to dispense vengeance in the guise of justice could not have persisted without the express or tacit consent of the German people and the government apparatus. Hitler was not unique in his contempt of lawyers and his distrust of legal institutions. Popular obloquy directed at lawyers and courts predated Hitler at least to Biblical times[79] and endures to this day even in the United States in the ubiquitous lawyer jokes and attacks on "activist" judges. The subtext of these utterances is an impatience with the constraints and delays of the law, impeding as they do the popular passions of the moment. When widespread fear is excited by real threats to the common welfare, as in the contemporary case of terrorism, outcries against normative law can evolve into precipitate surrender of personal liberties along with denigration of the law and courts that are those liberties' sanctuary.

Hegel may have overstated the case when he declared that "what history and experience teach us is this: that peoples and governments have never learned anything from history."[80] It is undeniable that times of perceived national emergency tempt peoples and governments to yield to a restlessness directed to the orderly and often ponderous course of law and justice. And there can be little quarrel with Cicero's dictum: let the public welfare be the highest law.[81] In times of national peril, civil liberties may be justly curtailed to the extent necessary to promote national survival. The reluctance of a society to subordinate its apparatus of justice and the rule of law to perceived threats to survival provides a measure of that society's strength of commitment to those institutions.

Hegel's gloomy assessment must itself be assessed in that light.

Notes

1. *Official Bulletin of the Allied Kommandatura Berlin* 14, 26 September, 1947.
2. Walter Wagner, *Der Volksgerichtshof im Nationalsozialistischen Staat, Die Deutsche Justiz unter der Nationalsozialismus,* vol. III (Stuttgart, 1974), 945–47.
3. An example: Statistisches Reichsamt, *Statistisches Jahrbuch für das Deutsche Reich* (Berlin, 1938), 606–17.
4. Ortner, *Der Hinrichter* (Vienna, 1993), 337, puts the number at 5,243, but lists no death sentences for the years 1934–1936. Wagner, *Der Volksgerichtshof,* 944, gives the number 23 for the years 1934–1936, but omits a tally for 1945, included in Ortner's list. Ortner's 1945 number is 52.
5. A list of these former judges and prosecutors and their postwar careers can be found in Ortner, *Der Hinrichter,* 340–48.
6. *Der Spiegel,* 18 February 1985.
7. Adolf Hitler, *Mein Kampf,* 42 ed. (Munich, 1933), 610–11.
8. Reichstag, 2. Sitzung, March 23, 1933, 28.
9. Joseph Goebbels and Ralf-Georg Reuth, *Tagebücher 1924-1945* (Munich, 2000), 1787.
10. *Reichsgesetzblatt* (RGBl) 1942, I, 247.
11. Henry Picker, *Hitlers Tischgespräche im Führerhauptquartier: Entstehung, Struktur, Folgen des Nationalsozialismus* (Berlin, 1997), 514–515.
12. Ibid., 550.
13. An extended harangue by Hitler on the subject of justice was recorded in a document discovered in the secret files of the Reich Justice Ministry, reproduced with a commentary in Lothar Gruchmann, "Hitler über die Justiz," *Vierteljahrshefte für*

Zeitgeschichte (VfZ) 12 (January 1964): 86–101. Hitler's remarks, at which Otto Thierack, who had just been promoted from president of the VGH to Reich Justice Minister, was present, took place on August 20, 1942, the day that Freisler assumed the presidency of the court. Gruchmann, in his commentary, oddly makes no mention of Freisler, referring somewhat misleadingly to Thierack as "the then-president of the Volksgerichtshof," 86.

14. Günther Wieland, *Das war der Volksgerichtshof* (Berlin, 1989), 75–76, citing Martin Brozsat, "Zur Perversion der Strafjustiz im Dritten Reich," *VfZ* 4 (1959): 438; H.W. Koch, *In the Name of the Volk: Political Justice in Hitler's Germany* (New York, 1989), 156–57, citing "Bericht über die Rede des Reichministers Dr Goebbels vor den Mitgliedern des Volksgerichtshof vom 22.7.1942," *Berlin Document Center*, NG-417. 448 rolls of microfilmed documents from the Berlin Document Center pertaining to the VGH are maintained at the U.S. National Archives in collection A3340, Series "VGH." The author has not examined these microfilms to ascertain whether the report of the Goebbels speech is included.
15. Günther Wieland, *Das War der Volksgerichtshof: Ermittlungen, Fakten, Dokumente* (Pfaffenweiler, 1989), 76.
16. Ibid., 224.
17. Rudolf Heydeloff, "Staranwalt der Rechtsextremisten: Walter Luetgebrune in der Weimarer Republik," *VfZ* 32 (1984): 373–421, at 402. This essay, based as the author tells us on his doctoral dissertation, furnishes an interesting sketch of a talented lawyer, driven by the quest for money and prestige, who found himself drawn to the far right nationalism and racism of the Nazi Party. He served ultimately as chief legal advisor to Ernst Röhm's *Sicherheitsabteilung* (SA) and narrowly escaped death during the "Röhm Purge" of June 30, 1934. He was removed from law practice and reduced to penury. In 1939, through the good offices of Reinhard Heydrich, Luetgebrune was paid 20,000 RM and permitted to resume his practice. He died in obscurity in 1949.
18. The German text of the Wannsee Protocol is available at http://germanhistorydocs.ghi-dc.org/sub_document.cfm?document_id=1532&language=german (accessed 16 January 2012). An English translation is available at http://germanhistorydocs.ghi-dc.org/sub_document.cfm?document_id=1532 (accessed 16 January 2012).
19. Ortner, *Der Hinrichter*, 56.
20. Freisler, *Schutz des Volkes oder des Rechtsbrechers? Fesselung des Verbrechers oder des Richters?* (Berlin, 1935), 2.
21. Ibid.
22. Roland Freisler, *Nationalsozialistisches Recht und Rechtsdenken* (Berlin, 1938), 11.
23. Freisler, "Der Volksverrat," *Deutsche Justiz* 96 (1934): 604, cited in William Sweet, "The Volksgerichtshof: 1934-45," *The Journal of Modern History*, 46/2 (1964): 314–329, here 316.
24. Heinz Hillermeier, herausg., *"In Namen Des Deutschen Volkes!"—Todesurteile des Volksgerichtshofs* (Darmstadt, 1983), 14, 22.
25. Freisler, *Schutz des Volkes*, 17–18.
26. Ibid., 6–7.
27. Ibid., 7.
28. Carl Schmitt, *Staat, Bewegung, Volk* (Hamburg, 1935), 43.
29. Ibid., 44.

30. Ibid. 42–46.
31. Heydeloff, "Staranwalt," 412–13. Thierack's support of this vision of Volk justice is mentioned elsewhere in the present chapter.
32. Gert Bucheit, *Richter in Roter Robe* (Munich, 1968), 123–124, cited in William Sweet, "The Volksgerichtshof, 1934–45, " *Journal of Modern History,* 46 (1964): 314–329, here 328.
33. This formula was specifically sanctioned by the Law for the Amendment of the Penal Code (*Gesetz zur Änderung des Strafgesetzbuchs*) RGBl 1935, I, 839. The law began: "He who commits an act which is punishable by law or which deserves punishment according to the fundamental idea of the law or according to the healthy sentiment of the people (*nach gesundem Volksempfinden*) shall be punished."
34. Ian Kershaw, *Hitler, 1933–45: Nemesis* (New York, 2000), 517.
35. Gürtner speech quoted in Helmut Ortner, *Der Hinrichter: Roland Freisler—Mörder im Dienste Hitlers* (Vienna, 1993), 35–36.
36. RGBl 1934, I, 341–48.
37. *Hochverrat* signifies a violent attack on the existence of institutions of the state; *Landesverrat* applies chiefly to espionage damaging to the security of the state. See *Alpmann Brockhaus Fachlexikon Recht* (Leipzig, 2004), s.v. "Hochverrat" and "Landesverrat," 685, 831.
38. H.W. Koch, *In the Name of the Volk: Political Justice in Hitler's Germany* (New York, 1989), 133.
39. Ibid.
40. Ibid.
41. Ernst Fraenkel, *The Dual State: A Contribution to the Theory of Dictatorship* (New York, 1941). In Ernst Fraenkel and Alexander von Brünneck, *Der Doppelstaat* (Hamburg, 2001), a later German edition translated from the original English, "normative state" and "prerogative state" are translated respectively as *Normenstaat* and *Massnahmenstaat.*
42. Klaus Marxen and Holger Schlüter, *Terror und "Normalität": Urteile Des Nationalsozialistischen Volksgerichtshof 1934-1945* (Düsseldorf, 2004), 5.
43. Marxen and Schlüter, *Terror,* 6.
44. Marxen and Schlüter, *Terror,* 7.
45. Wieland, *Das War der Volksgerichtshof,* 73.
46. Koch, *In the Name of the Volk,* 142–43.
47. Wieland, *Das War der Volksgerichtshof,* 83; Koch, *In the Name of the Volk,* 132.
48. Koch, *In the Name of the Volk,* 127.
49. Wagner, *Der Volksgerichtshof,* 835.
50. Günther Löhmann presided.
51. Hans Fallada, *Every Man Dies Alone,* translated by Michael Hofmann (Brooklyn, 2009).
52. Manfred Kuhnke, *Die Hampels und die Quangels: Authentisches und Erfundenes in Hans Falladas Letztem Roman* (Neubrandenburg, 2001), 16–17.
53. Ibid., 52–53.
54. Ibid., 33–37.
55. Ibid., 38.
56. Heinz Hillermeier, ed., *"In Namen des Deutschen Volkes!"—Todesurteile des Volksgerichtshofs* (Darmstadt, 1983).

57. Marxen and Schlüter, *Terror.* The cases can be found by reference to the dates as noted in the text.
58. Film: *Sophie Scholl, the Final Days,* directed by Marc Rothemund, 2006. Books: Annette E. Dumbach and Jud Newborn, *Sophie Scholl and the White Rose* (Oxford, 2006); Inge Scholl, *Die weisse Rose* (Frankfurt, 1952); Toby Axelrod, *Hans and Sophie Scholl: German Resisters of the White Rose* (New York, 2001); among many others.
59. Wagner, *Der Volksgerichtshof,* 945–947.
60. Ibid., 944.
61. Ibid., 832.
62. Koch, *In the Name of Volk,* 132. Death sentences are attributed to Freisler as president of the VGH and the judge presiding over the influential First Senate. He did not personally hand down all of these sentences.
63. Wagner, *Der Volksgerichtshof,* 945.
64. BGB §148
65. BGB §242
66. Reinhard Zimmermann, "Characteristic Aspects of German Legal Culture," in *Introduction to German Law,* eds. Joachim and Mathias Reimann Zekoll, 2nd ed. (The Hague, 2005), 31.
67. Peter Hoffmann, *The History of the German Resistance 1933–1945,* transl. Richard Barry (Montreal, 1996), 524.
68. Raul Hilberg, *The Destruction of the European Jews,* 3rd ed. (New Haven, 2003), 1063.
69. See note 54.
70. The epithet *"der rasender Roland"* (raving Roland) is the German title of Ariosto's epic *Orlando furioso.*
71. See, for a brief history of this group, Howard Stern, "The Organisation Consul," *Journal of Modern History* 35 (1963): 20–33.
72. See Ilse Staff, ed., *Justiz im Dritten Reich, eine Dokumentation* (Frankfurt, 1978), for pre-Third Reich examples of such uneven-handed justice.
73. Walter Luetgebrune, "Femeprozesse und Recht," *Völkischer Beobachter,* 9 October 1928; Walter Luetgebrune, *Wahrheit und Recht für Feme, Schwarze Reichwehr und Oberleutnant. Schulz* (Munich, 1928).
74. Martin Broszat, "Zur Perversion der Strafjustiz im Dritten Reich," *VfZ* 6 (1958): 390–445.
75. Ibid., 397.
76. Ibid., 400.
77. "Rathenau Case up in Political Court," *New York Times,* 22 October 1922, 5. The article begins: "The Rathenau murder trial began at Leipzig today before Germany's 'Political Supreme Court,' newly established under the law for safeguarding the republic passed by the Reichstag as a result of the slaying of the Foreign Minister." The law referred to was *Gesetz zum Schutze der Republik,* RGBl 1922, I, 585–90.
78. There was some isolated protest. See letter from Melitta Wiedemann, editor of *Die Aktion. Kampfblatt für das neue Europa,* to Justice Minister Thierack, quoted in Koch, *In the Name of the Volk,* 172. Wiedemann criticized Freisler as "so hard, unjust and unfriendly towards the accused, that he was obviously endeavouring to obstruct the man in his defense, although he was as good as sentenced to death

already. …" Even Ernst Kaltenbrunner, the pitiless chief of the police and security apparatus, decried Freisler's courtroom behavior as unsuited to the dignity of the proceedings. Memorandum 57536/44, in *Opposition gegen Hitler und der Staatsstreich vom 20. Juli 1944. Geheime Dokumente aus dem ehemaligen Reichssicherheitshauptamt,* vol. 1, ed. Hans-Adolf Jacobsen. (Stuttgart, 1989), 124ff., cited (by memorandum number only) in Sweet, "Volksgerichtshof," 327.
79. "Woe unto you, lawyers!" *Luke* 11:52.
80. Georg Friedrich Hegel and Theodore Litt, *Vorlesungen über die Philosophie der Geschichte* (Stuttgart, 1975), 45.
81. *"Salus populi suprema lex." De legibus,* III. iii. 8.

A Jewish man and his "Aryan" girlfriend are publicly humiliated in Cuxhaven, 27 July 1933. His sign states "as a Jewish guy, I take only German maidens to my room," while hers reads, "I'm the biggest pig in town, and I hook up only with Jews."
Source: Bildarchiv preussischer Kulturbesitz, Berlin/Art Resource, New York

Chapter 4

GUILT, SHAME, ANGER, INDIGNATION
Nazi Law and Nazi Morals

Raphael Gross

THIS CHAPTER EXAMINES THE LAW in Nazi Germany in the context of its moral foundation and its underlying Nazi moral agenda. It may seem an oxymoron to refer to "Nazi law," and it may seem even more problematic to employ terms like "Nazi morality" or "Nazi ethics."[1] But during the Nazi period, German jurists continually developed new laws and implemented them in German courts.[2] Simultaneously, German society persisted in developing and implementing values rooted in shared moral sentiments such as guilt, shame, anger, or indignation. The desire to govern based on a set of shared moral values can be seen as central to the Nazi era. While Marxism was based on economic notions such as added value, class struggle, and capital, Nazi ideology was based on "moral" notions such as honor, loyalty, comradeship, and decency.[3] To understand the deeper framework of Nazi law, we are compelled to explore what I would call the "moral history" of Nazi Germany.

Towards a History of Nazi Morality

To define its core concepts, this sort of historical research cannot proceed without a framework in moral philosophy and interdisciplinary theoretical ethics. Lacking such a framework, it would be difficult to avoid reconstructing the ethical values expressed in the material upon which we draw. Basic sources in this respect include Adam Smith's *Theory of Moral Sentiments* (1759) and various texts by P.F. Strawson and

Ernst Tugendhat that have developed Smith's theory of moral feelings.[4] These are not, to be sure, the only possible sources we might choose. To those historians who feel that moral philosophy is written more for the purposes of the present day than for understanding the past, and who prefer to rely on common sense for their moral assessments of historical processes: that is fine and good; there is a distinguished tradition of thinking founded in such common sense. But what must be avoided at all costs is the sort of regurgitation of the "facts" of Nazism and the Holocaust without any meaningful evaluative framework whatsoever, as practiced by too many professional German historians through the postwar decades—often, unfortunately, for transparently self-serving reasons.

One conceivable objection to analyzing moral sentiments—in the Nazi context or any other—might arise from the widely held view that such sentiments are purely subjective or beyond human reason. But the opposite is more truly the case. Sentiments are "reasonable"; people can only make judgments and act to the extent that they have feelings,[5] without which the world loses all meaning, and life all significance.[6] Crucially in our context, the moral feelings at play here—the shared sentiments about what constitutes vice and virtue—are drastically different in a society such as Nazi Germany than in one adhering to more traditional values commonly tied to the Western, Judeo-Christian tradition. The same point applies to meanings generated by such feelings. Following this approach, the historical-analytic focus shifts from passing judgment on horrendous Nazi crimes to understanding the society from which they emerged—a society approached in terms of a dense network of shared moral or normative-ethical sentiments, themselves expressed in concepts with their own historical semantics. The central question at work here is how did such sentiments function? How did they both emerge from and vitalize an ideology, not merely legitimizing crimes retrospectively, but making them possible in the first place? There is an inherent connection between the moral history of Nazism and the historical semantics of its central concepts. Nazi morality must be analyzed in the context of the history of moral concepts as they developed and were practiced in Germany.[7] The history of morality must examine the norms and values shared by a social group, and establish their influence on the actions of individuals.

Upon what sources can we draw to understand Nazi norms and values? There are many possibilities: children's books, philosophical and theological texts, private notes and diaries, medical, eugenic, psychological, and pedagogic textbooks, political announcements, political tracts, propaganda, and moral codices of the Wehrmacht and SS. Moral judgments can be found everywhere. They extend well beyond Himmler's notorious secret speech in which he applied the concept of decency—*Anständigkeit*—to the mass murder of the Jews in a way that continues to influence German understanding of that concept. We can analyze these sources with regard to the moral feelings that are presumed, promoted, explicated, or evoked in connection with the Nazi *Volksgemeinschaft*, be they anger, indignation, or guilt. The following discussion will focus on one particular realm of Nazi morals: the realm of law.

Perhaps the most central, and most well-known and odious, piece of Nazi legislation was the "Law for the Protection of German Blood and Honor," the first of the so-called Nuremberg Laws, enacted on 15 September 1935. In the preceding years of Nazi rule, many such legal measures and guidelines had already been issued, some publicly, some secretly. In total, there would be over 1,900 examples of such a "special Jewish law."[8] In view of the volume of this anti-Jewish legislation, and the fact that the laws were so specific in nature as to govern even transports to Auschwitz, the notion, favored by cultural theorists and propagated by Giorgo Agamben, that the persecution and extermination of the Jews unfolded in a more or less law-free space is hardly tenable.[9]

In a survey of this anti-Semitic legal corpus, two of its aspects are especially striking in our context. On the one hand, the laws not only postulate a specifically Aryan morality, but also reinforce the old anti-Semitic notion of a Jewish counter-morality, fixing this idea in the law. They thus attest to a specific ideology and its implementation. On the other hand, these seemingly dry legal texts, either above or below the surface, were infused with a sadistic passion. Although authors like Freud and later, Sartre, have pointed to the passion informing this anti-Semitic thinking, this element has been usually neglected in recent historical-sociological research.[10] But a structural and semantic description of anti-Semitic texts—legal and otherwise—is not sufficient. In the worst case, this approach would produce reconstructive repetition. As Sartre explained, anti-Semitism is "simultaneously a passion and a conception of the world."[11] Especially in the Nazi context, its effects cannot be understood outside the framework of its emotional contents.

At the same time, a psychological analysis of this anti-Semitic passion does not do justice to the general societal effects and articulations of Nazi anti-Semitic ideology. Rather, the passion's explosiveness stems from its grounding in a complex mix of mutually-dependent moral feelings of guilt, anger, and indignation. Sartre did not address this dimension of his subject. In our investigation, it ties in closely with a question rarely raised by historians: why did so many Germans follow Hitler with such enthusiastic devotion?

In trying to understand the socio-historical phenomenology of Nazi morals, engaging in a project of reconstruction based on, say, "error" or "confusion" is insufficient. It will never be sufficient to analyze one key term inside the Nazi "moral system." Rather, we need a broad approach examining both different key terms and a broad range of empirical materials. As with etiological research on Nazism in general, all single-cause explanations eventually fall apart when confronted with the empirical evidence. A more productive approach involves a close inductive look at the specific ways in which a range of moral feelings—guilt, anger, and indignation—were connected to what the Nazis declared as their quintessential virtues: comradeship, fidelity, self-sacrifice, and decency. The next step is to understand this system of normative categories in terms of its practical expression. How, for instance, was adherence to, or evasion of, the normative system rewarded through "honor," or punished through "shame" and "disgrace"? We should keep in mind that these categories have different normative meanings in different cultural and historical contexts. One can, for example, show loyalty without being a Nazi.

Nazi Morality as the Root of Anti-Jewish Legislation

Before turning to the Nuremberg Laws, let us first consider how earlier Nazi laws were already infiltrated by both anti-Semitism and Nazi morals. In March 1933, local authorities in Berlin issued a decree directed at Jewish lawyers and notaries, who would no longer be allowed to provide legal representation for the city.[12] Already before Hitler's rise to power, many Germans doubted that Jewish lawyers and jurists really saw themselves as duty-bound to the law and, more generally, to justice. Starting in 1933, various Nazi offices worked steadily at battling what they perceived as an enduring, nefarious Jewish presence in the German legal system—a presence inimical to principles of universal justice—through new laws and decrees. The first such decree targeted Jewish lawyers and notaries. Many others followed. On 13 November 1933, it was declared that "non-Aryans cannot be appointed as either lay judges or jury-members." On 4 April 1935, the Berlin Gestapo ordered that "everything must be done to put an end to the appearance that Aryan students are receiving assistance from Jews in preparing their exams." Some seventeen months later, on 2 September 1936, the Justice Ministry decreed that "candidates for the final juridical exam must expressly declare that in preparing the exam they received no assistance from Jews."[13]

What applied to the law was the case as well in a range of other realms. Already in the first year of the Nazi regime, a decree was passed forbidding the "slaughter of animals according to Jewish custom." This reflected the widespread belief—still prevalent in Europe today—that Jewish ritual slaughter was crueler than other forms of the practice. The Nazis posed as the protectors of the welfare of animals that were threatened by Jews. The fluidity of the line of demarcation between this gesture and a deep-seated hatred of Jews[14] would be reflected in 1940 with the appearance of an especially notorious example of cinematic anti-Jewish incitement, the film *The Eternal Jew* (*Der ewige Jude*), which focused on Jewish ritual slaughter. Correspondingly, the use of the Yiddish language in that branch of commerce equated Jewishness with dishonesty.

Another early decree addressed "applications by Jews to change one's name" (3 April 1933).[15] Such applications needed to be checked, the decree succinctly indicated, in order to prevent "one's origins being masked." The fear that Jews camouflaged and concealed themselves, based on the presumption that they were dishonest and deceptive, led to a flood of further legislative measures concerned solely with Jewish names. On 22 April 1933, the Reich Ministry of Transportation took up the matter, issuing a "ban on the use of Jewish names for spelling in the delivery of telegrams by telephone."[16] This measure prohibited, for example, saying "A as in Abraham" when reciting the content of a telegram.

Alongside "truth" and "justice," another conceptual category informing the Nazi moral-normative universe formed a basis for laws aimed at Jewish athletes. On 4 April 1933, Jewish boxers were "excluded from participating in competition." A few days later, an Aryan clause was introduced for all sports organizations by the Reich Commissioner for Sport. In August, Jews were banned from public swimming places, for example, the beach at the Wannsee, one of Berlin's picturesque lakes (22 August 1933). Sartre refers to these special measures in his *Reflections on the Jewish Question* of 1944: "As a first measure, the Germans forbade Jews entry to the swimming pools. They believed the entire pool would be polluted by immersion in it of a Jewish body."[17]

Sartre's observation is important, but arguably the ban on public Jewish bathing reflected more than a delirious obsession with physical purity. These and similar decrees seem to have been inspired by a less complicated motive: the wish to enjoy Aryan sociability free from Jewish contact. There is an interesting precedent for this venue-bound, anti-Semitic legislation in both the Wilhelmine period and the Weimar Republic. In the nineteenth century, it was reflected in the "Borkum Song," which was heard at the beach of the North Sea island of Borkum:

> An Borkums Strand nur Deutschtum gilt,
> nur deutsch ist das Panier.
> Wir halten rein den Ehrenschild
> Germanias für und für!
> Doch wer dir naht mit platten Füßen,
> mit Nasen krumm und Haaren kraus,
> der soll nicht deinen Strand genießen,
> der muß hinaus! Der muß hinaus! Hinaus![18]
> (On Borkum's beach, only Germandom reigns,
> only German is our banner.
> We keep pure the shield of honor
> Of Germania through and through
> But those coming near you with flat feet
> With crooked nose and frizzy hair,
> Should not enjoy your beach.
> They must stay out! Stay out! Stay out!)

It is difficult to understand contagion-centered anti-Semitism—an antipathy perceiving not only heredity, but direct or indirect physical contact as a dire threat—as anything other than a form of delirious paranoia. Since this appears to have been a paranoia that many Germans shared, and that ultimately became anchored in the law, the question of delirium, at least in a clinical sense, seems unresolved. The above song underscores how delirium could be incorporated into a shared normative framework: the conjured-up "shield of honor" renders contagion-focused anti-Semitism into a moral demand. This virulent form of anti-Semitism was aimed at an avoidance of contact—and above all intimacy—between Jews and Aryans. In the context of public bathing, the imperative of Aryan German honor thus meant preserving one's sense of sexual shame—and chastity—in the presence of Jewish men and women.

Adjudicating Blood and Honor

Passed on 15 September 1935, the Nuremberg Laws, in particular the "Law for the Protection of German Blood and German Honor," clothed this sense of shame with its full legal form.[19] Many Jews in Nazi Germany considered this law to have been especially significant.[20] Issued personally by Hitler at the Nuremberg Party rally, the law consisted of a preamble and five key clauses:

> Convinced that the purity of German blood is essential to the continued existence of the German people, and inspired by the uncompromising determination to safeguard the future of the German nation, the Reichstag has unanimously resolved upon the following law, which is promulgated herewith:
>
> § 1: Marriages between Jews and citizens of German or kindred blood are forbidden. Marriages concluded in defiance of this law are void, even if, for the purpose of evading this law, they were concluded abroad.
>
> § 2: Sexual relations outside marriage between Jews and nationals of German or kindred blood are forbidden.
>
> § 3: Jews are not permitted to employ female citizens of German or kindred blood as domestic servants.
>
> § 4: Jews are forbidden to display the Reich and national flag or the national colors.
>
> § 5: A person who acts contrary to the prohibition of Section 1 will be punished with hard labor; a person who acts contrary to the prohibition of Section 2 will be punished with imprisonment or with hard labor; a person who acts contrary to the provisions of Sections 3 or will be punished with imprisonment up to a year and with a fine, or with one of these penalties.[21]

A large number of guidelines for the implementation of this law were issued in the days following. The emotional and legal urgency that informed this legislation, and the norm-setting process that it confirmed and promoted, were underscored in subsequent cases before German courts.

Let us now turn to one such case, a detailed description of which will shed light on the willing cooperation of German jurists involved in the implementation of this unjust law. On 20 April 1943, the Special Court (*Sondergericht*) in Kassel handed down a death sentence in the "criminal case against *Diplom-Ingenieur* Werner Holländer in Kassel born 2 August 1914 in Cologne." Having been raised as a Protestant, Holländer claimed to have been unaware until shortly before his trial that, since the passage of the Nuremberg Laws, he had possessed the status of a Jew in

Germany. "On account of criminal violation of the 'Law for the Protection of German Blood and German Honor,'" he was duly condemned "to death in four cases on account of racial defilement (*Rassenschande*) as a dangerous habitual criminal." Holländer, the court added for good measure, "bears the costs of the proceedings." The presiding judges were *Landgerichtsdirektor* Hassencamp and *Kammergerichtsrat* Dr. Kessler. The formal basis for their ruling was as follows:

> The 28 year old accused man is a full-Jew of Hungarian citizenship. ... Over the years the accused had intimate relations with a series of women. In this way, already as a student, in 1936, he became acquainted with Katharina Wd., a citizen of the state with German blood. A romantic relationship developed between the two that continued for years and led to regular sexual intercourse. ...

The court's judgment devoted the greatest space to Holländer's relationship with Fräulein Wd.:

> He became acquainted with her in a Kassel tennis club, which he joined despite his awareness of having Jewish origins. The relationship of friendship turned into a relationship of love. The young girl, who is in her early twenties, assumed that the accused had serious intentions and gave herself to him sexually as well on these grounds. She brought the accused, who [said] nothing about his Jewish origins, into her parent's house. ... Fräulein Wd., who last had intercourse with Holländer around Easter, became pregnant from him. Only when she let the accused know this and the question of marriage was discussed did the accused inform her that something was not in order with his origins. ... The pregnancy was interrupted.

"The accused," the court summed up, "made himself guilty of racial defilement in four cases." However, Werner Holländer was not condemned to death on the basis of the "blood and honor" law, as violations against that law were not punishable by death. Instead, Hassencamp and Kessler defined Holländer as a dangerous "habitual criminal," justifying the death penalty as follows:

> The balance is tipped by the fact that the accused committed his crime in the second and third years of the war. Hence at a time when Germany's struggle with World Jewry had reached its apogee, as the accused knew very well. ... According to the German sense of law, it is an imperative of just atonement [*ein Gebot gerechter Sühne*] that the accused, who dared, during a war of Germany's, to trample Ger-

man racial honor [*deutsche Rassenehre*] into the mud together with the members of World Jewry, be annihilated [*vernichtet*]. Compelling here is also both the unparalleled baseness and unscrupulousness and the vile breach of trust with which the accused proceeded in the Wd. case as a typical representative of the Jewish race.[22]

Following this judgment, Holländer was sent to the Preungesheim prison in Frankfurt, where—his appeal for clemency having been denied by Reich Justice Minister Thierack—he was kept chained in a cell for a year before his execution on 30 May 1944.[23]

After 1945, proceedings for perversion of justice were opened against the two involved judges.[24] In the course of the trial, it became clear that Holländer had had a relationship with the married daughter of a presiding district-court judge whose husband was in the Wehrmacht—a fact that had been left unmentioned in the proceedings against Holländer. Hence in this particular case, "outrage over a putative injustice inflicted on the family of a high-placed colleague"[25]—a set of circumstances unmentioned in those proceedings out of concern for the same colleague—played a determining role in the death sentence. In other words, he was condemned to death out of outrage at his having penetrated an intimate sphere that was understood to have been morally off limits.

Perhaps more historically significant than this particular act of Nazi injustice (after all, it constituted a mere drop in an ocean of such grievous injustice), while equally revealing when it comes to the Nazi normative system, is the fate of the postwar effort to bring the two Nazi judges to account. On 26 March 1948, a legal opinion from the minister in charge of de-Nazification for the state of Hesse indicated that since "the chairman [Hassencamp] and the rapporteur [Kessler] did not intend to reach a just verdict, but rather were animated by a desire 'to annihilate' the condemned man," the existence of an "intentional perversion of justice" was established.[26] It was proven, the opinion continued, "that the death sentence passed by the judges Hassencamp and Dr. Kessler, who were anti-Semitic and fanatically National Socialist by inclination, was only passed because Holländer was the descendent of Jews."[27]

In 1950, a district court in Kassel, and in 1951, the chief district court of Frankfurt/Main, came to a diametrically opposite verdict. As the findings in the former of the two cases put it, "application of the blood-protection law" was at the time "without a doubt the correct procedure." According to standard judicial practice, crimes committed continuously over time could be broken up into individual offenses. Based on this reasoning—and here the postwar German court even went further than its 1943 counterpart—there were "far more than four offenses in Holländer's case." For the district court, the absence of perversion of justice was based on one salient factor: "The accused were both party members from 1933 onwards. They were convinced—indeed fanatic—National Socialists. They were blinded, allowed themselves to be led, and unconditionally followed the propaganda being thrown out by the party." As it was certain that the accused men believed "that the laws of National Socialism were to be carried out according to the letter, in the sense of the 'Führer,'" they had both to be pronounced not guilty.[28]

Hence, the same factors that had led to a judgment of guilt in 1948 led to exoneration a few years later. In any event, that Edmund Kessler was indeed a fanatic Nazi was made clear in his 1951 interrogation:

> Presiding judge: You would thus continue to say "I consider the verdict correct?"
>
> Kessler: Jawohl! We even insisted on the standpoint that in the war, with German men battling on the front and we having to do our duty at home, punishment had to be meted out without consideration of previous life and origins. Besides I am of the opinion that condemnation of Holländer as a habitual criminal is a discretionary question that can only be judged if one has attended the main trial from start to finish. The witness Wd. was a broken human being who had been completely shattered in her first blossoming.
>
> Presiding judge: Regarding the question of whether to impose the death penalty, didn't you think it necessary to further consider the personality of the accused?
>
> Kessler: Through what he'd done he proved that he was of inferior character [*charakterlich minderwertig*]. That was the very reason I declared him a dangerous habitual criminal. A single deed such as that in the case of Wd. can so characterize a man that the judge has a rounded picture. ... Besides the accused did not restrain himself but rather experienced downright thievish joy in making fun of National Socialism. For example already in 1941 he said the war was lost. ... As the Law for the Protection of German Honor is laid out, what is not decisive is who the individual was but the extent to which German self-respect is affected. If the accused man Holländer trampled the honor of German women and German honor in the mud in this way, thus grievously injuring the self-respect of the German *Volk,* he at the same time gravely injured German self-respect.

Presiding judge: How did he injure the self-respect of the *Volk*?

Kessler: The blood-protection law was a basic law of the state. ... This law needs to be understood as indicating that the legally protected interest is "the honor of the total German *Volk*" and beyond that the honor of the German woman and also racial honor. Clause 1 of this law says that when the self-respect of the German *Volk* is affected, the imperative is to revenge this deed. I was of the judicial conviction that the deed in the Wd. case weighed so heavy, that, with the accompanying circumstances, it demanded the ultimate expiation on grounds of justice.[29]

Thus, in 1951, looking back on his condemnation of Holländer for continued acts of *Rassenschande,* Kessler approached his victim simultaneously on an individual and a prototypical level. On the one hand, he underscored what he felt to be the specifically premeditated character of Holländer's violation of German "racial honor" while the *Volk* was at war, an act carried out with "thievish joy" by a representative of "world Jewry." At the same time, it was not merely the individual honor of Fräulein Wd. that had been violated, but rather the honor of all Germans belonging to the Aryan community of blood. This encapsulates the concept of *Rassenschande* (racial defilement): a crime by one individual against another that also affected the entire *Volksgemeinschaft,* and enduringly so. The defilement inflicted on German honor clung to every individual German.

The centrality of Nazi honor in the judges' decision is confirmed by their avoidance of any mention of the gravest of Holländer's transgressions. For their higher-placed colleague, learning of his daughter's affair with a Jew would have been the deepest possible disgrace. To this extent, in light of the long-term status of anti-Semitism in Christian Europe as an "ordinary" (if sometimes rather ugly) prejudice, their concern with his welfare might be understood as more or less traditional in its normative premises. But its expression in the Third Reich is manifestly Nazi-specific: in the judges' eyes, Werner Holländer acted, consciously or not, "as a typical representative of the Jewish race." Hence his "crimes" were carried out as part of a broader consensus, a planned and organized behavioral pattern, in short a conspiracy, one that could even dispense with the sort of meetings in Jewish graveyards depicted in the *Protocols of the Elders of Zion* (itself a best-seller in the Weimar years). In fact, in the judges' view, the conspiracy functioned on the basis of inheritance alone, which is to say through a chain of intimate relations. And precisely the possibility of intimate relations between Jews and non-Jews was meant to be suppressed by the "Law for the Protection of German Blood and German Honor." From this perspective, we once again confront the overriding reality of twisted moral passion that so often is elided in analyses of the Nazi biological racist world view. The "legal" murder of Werner Holländer, at the deepest level, was propelled by a core of particular outrage, an outrage at his successful incursion into the realm of German intimacy.

Anti-Semitism and Shame

To better understand the dynamic at play here, it may be helpful to consider an essay by the sociological philosopher Max Scheler that was first published in 1913, "On Shame and Feelings of Shame." Scheler is the best known German philosopher to have addressed the subject of shame in depth. A look into his writings helps us to illuminate the close connections between "Germandom," "Jewry," honor, shame, and intimacy that underlay Nazi laws. Scheler's texts did not bear any direct connection to the authors of these laws or to Nazi judges, but they were a clear expression of the relationship between racist anti-Semitic ideas and the concepts of shame and honor. In Scheler's thinking, feelings of shame are central in that they separate human beings from beasts. Human beings feel shame, an emotion that is generated whenever spiritually determined intentions—by which Scheler meant thinking, wanting, or loving—dissolve into "some sort of purely objective entity" and "suprabiological [*überbiologisch*] contents and goals vanish."[30] For Scheler, proximity to the animal-like catalyzed feelings of shame, with "sexual feelings of shame" repeatedly standing in the center. As the philosopher saw it, ethics and sexuality were intimately linked, and formed the context for his construction of the following differentiation between Jews and Christians, and between the Germanic and the Jewish:

> It is a perhaps not uninteresting historical fact that the church's moral principle that the sexual act should only serve reproductive purposes originates neither in the noble Germanic spirit, whose deep feeling of shame we have already underlined, nor in the original Christian lifecycle. Rather, the principle stems from Jewish sexual morality, and long before Jesus' appearance was nothing less than the fundamental principle of their rigid orientation. Perhaps the dry purposefulness

generally constituting the essence of the Jewish spirit is mirrored in no other principle of Jewish morality as in this one. Even that act, which like no other is meant to be pure expression, is here given purposive form. In line with what we underscored earlier about the specifically Jewish lack of feelings of shame, a lack leading to the banishment of all mystery from that people's contemplation of the world and of God, it is easily understandable that even shame, so closely united with awe, has to be replaced here by the surrogate of mandatorily narrow and rigid moral norms.[31]

Establishing a credible path from Kantian moral philosophy to anti-Semitic feelings centered on honor and sexual shame is perhaps impossible. In contrast, numerous authors writing in the 1920s focused on shame and honor in a way clearly anticipating the Nuremberg Laws. Among them, Max Scheler was certainly the most sophisticated, and remains the most respected. As the above passage makes clear, for Scheler, shame had no less a function than rendering sex into something other than a purely physical act—Jewish shamelessness thus distinguishing the Germanic from the Jewish anthropological essence. Inversely, Germanic shame—and consequently Germanic honor—gained its specific contours in its differentiation from that Jewish essence.

From Scheler's perspective, the Jewish spirit was responsible for the Church's moral deviations. But his critique went much deeper than the vulgarized reading of Nietzsche's "Genealogy of Morals" reflected in that perspective. In defining Jews through shamelessness, and by defining humanity on the basis of shame, he was articulating a radical socio-anthropological negation of Judaism and Jewry, a negation located in the zone of intimacy and the sexual. In doing so, he encapsulated the affective dynamic motivating an entire intellectual movement in the pre-Nazi period, a movement that culminated in the "Law for the Protection of German Blood and Honor." If public bathing by Jews was already considered dangerous enough to be legally forbidden, then intruding into the intimate Aryan sphere represented a threat that was deadly. As indicated, the 1935 law was prepared for by hundreds of earlier regulations pointing in its direction, and it was followed by a great many more. A large part of the notorious Wannsee Conference was devoted to an important problem left open in 1935—that of *Mischlinge,* the "mixed raced" Germans. But in truth, the problems tied to protecting Aryans from physical contact with Jews, and especially from any intimacy with them, were endless—and deeply troubling for every anti-Semitic bureaucrat.[32]

This would appear to represent one prominent source of the anti-Semitic passion at the heart of Nazi morals. If one's own honor is based so strongly on remaining untouched by anything Jewish, while honor itself always encompasses not only the individual, but also the entire *Volksgemeinschaft*, then the latter suffers from each and every contact between Jew and Aryan. Such a problem points to only one, theoretically complete, solution. In respect to secret *Mischlinge*, but also in respect to other sorts of secret Jews, there can never be any absolute protection from contact between the *Volksgemeinschaft* and Jewish blood. The phobia can never be fully extinguished. Judges Kessler and Hassencamp were acutely aware of the threat. Even in 1941, it was still possible for a Jew such as Holländer to sleep with an Aryan woman such as Wd., but the real reason for Holländer's judicial murder was a disgrace so great that it had to remain unmentioned.

Translated by Joel Golb.

Notes

1. See Claudia Koonz, *The Nazi Conscience* (Cambridge, 2003). A discussion about the suitability of the term "law" in respect to Nazi rules can be found in Frank Haldemann, "Gutstav Radbruch vs. Hans Kelsen: A Debate on Nazi Law," *Ratio Juris*, 18 (2005): 162–78. After the end of the Nazi regime, a debate about the connection between law and morality arose between the philosophers Hart and Fuler. See H.L.A. Hart, "Positivism and the Separation of Law and Morals," *Harvard Law Review* 71 (1958): 593–629; and Lon L. Fuller, "Positivism and Fidelity to Law — A Reply to Professor Hart," *Harvard Law Review* 71(1958): 630–72.
2. Michael Stolleis, *The Law Under the Swastika: Studies on Legal History in Nazi Germany* (Chicago, 1998).
3. Raphael Gross, *Anständig geblieben: Nationalsozialistische Moral* (Frankfurt, 2010).
4. Ernst Tugendhat, *Vorlesungen über Ethik* (Frankfurt, 1993); idem, *Dialog in Leticia* (Frankfurt, 1997); Peter Frederick Strawson, *Freedom and Resentment and other Essays* (London, 1974).
5. Heiner Hastedt, *Gefühle. Philosophische Bemerkungen* (Stuttgart, 2005), 140–48.
6. Ibid., 141.
7. Reinhart Koselleck, *Begriffsgeschichten. Studien zur Semantik und Pragmatik der politischen und sozialen Sprache* (Frankfurt, 2006).
8. Joseph Walk (ed.), *Das Sonderrecht für die Juden im NS-Staat. Eine Sammlung der gesetzlichen Maßnahmen und Richtlinien—Inhalt und Bedeutung* (Karlsruhe, 1981).
9. Astrid Deuber-Mankowsky, "'Homo sacer', das bloße Leben und das Lager. Anmerkungen zu einem erneuten Versuche einer Kritik der Gewalt," *Babylon. Beiträge zur jüdischen Gegenwart* 21 (2006): 105–21.

10. For the first collection of essays dealing with anti-Semitism from that perspective, see Ernst Simmel, ed., *Anti-Semitism: A Social Disease* (New York, 1946).
11. Jean-Paul Sartre, *Réflexions sur la question juive* (Paris, 1954), 19.
12. Walk, *Das Sonderrecht.*, 5 (18 March 1933).
13. Ibid., 171 (2 September 1936).
14. The Swiss case is instructive is this regard. See Betrix Mesmer, "The Banning of Jewish Ritual Slaughter in Switzerland," *Leo Baeck Institute Yearbook* 52 (2007): 185–94.
15. Dietz Bering, *The Stigma of Names: Antisemitism in German Daily Life,* 1812–1933, transl. Neville Plaice (Ann Arbor, 1993).
16. *Verbot, bei telephonischer Übermittlung von Telegrammen jüdische Namen zum Buchstabieren zu benutzen,*" in Walk, *Das Sonderrecht,* 9.
17. Sartre, *Réflexions,* 29.
18. Michael Wildt, "Antisemitismus in deutschen Nord- und Ostseebädern 1920–1935," *Mittelweg* 36, (2001): 1–25, here 11. In more detail: Frank Bajohr, *"Unser Hotel ist judenfrei." Bäder-Antisemitismus im 19. und 20. Jahrhundert* (Frankfurt, 2003).
19. Cornelia Essner, *Die "Nürnberger Gesetze" oder die Verwaltung des Rassenwahns 1933–1945* (Munich, 2002), and also in a broader context Alexandra Przyrembel, *"Rassenschande." Reinheitsmythos und Vernichtungslegitimation im Nationalsozialismus* (Göttingen, 2003).
20. See the comments of Alfred Hirschberger in October 1935, cited in Avraham Barkai, *"Wehr dich!" Der Centralverein deutscher Staatsbürger jüdischen Glaubens 1893–1938* (Munich, 2002), 342.
21. Gesetz zum Schutz des deutschen Blutes und der deutschen Ehre, 15 September 1935, Reichsgesetzblatt 1935, I, 1146; also in Walk, *Das Sonderrecht,* 127. English text from Jeremy Noakes and Geoffrey Pridham, *Documents on Nazism 1919–1945* (New York, 1974), 463–67.
22. Ernst Noam and Wolf Arno Kropat, *Juden vor Gericht 1933–1945. Dokumente aus hessischen Justizakten mit einem Vorwort von Johannes Strelitz* (Wiesbaden, 1975), 168–73.
23. Ibid., 173.
24. Devin O. Pendas, "Seeking Justice, Finding Law: Nazi Trials in Postwar Europe," *Journal of Modern History* 81 (2009): 347–68.
25. Noam and Kroprat, *Juden vor Gericht,* 173.
26. *NS-Verbrechen vor Gericht 1945–1955. Dokumente aus hessischen Justizakten mit einem Nachwort von Richard Schmid,* eds. Klaus Moritz and Ernst Noam (Wiesbaden, 1978), 306.
27. Ibid.
28. Ibid., 315
29. Ibid. 319 f.
30. Max Scheler, "Über Scham und Schamgefühl," in *Schriften aus dem Nachlaß*. Bd. 1: *Zur Ethik und Erkenntnislehre, Gesammelte Werke* 10 (Bern, 1957), 68.
31. Ibid., 136.
32. On the role of sex in the Nazi *Volksgemeinschaft* see Dagmar Herzog, *Sex after Fascism: Memory and Morality in Twentieth-Century Germany* (Princeton, 2005) especially chapters 1 and 2.

Michael Siegel, a Jewish lawyer, is paraded through Munich by SA-men on 10 March 1933. Siegel had lodged a protest over the treatment of one of his clients who had been taken into custody. The sign reads, "I will never again complain to the police."
Source: Bundesarchiv, Berlin

Chapter 5

DISCRIMINATION, DEGRADATION, DEFIANCE

Jewish Lawyers under Nazism

Douglas G. Morris

ON 11 SEPTEMBER 1933, IN Samaden, Switzerland, outside St. Moritz, a Jewish German lawyer from Berlin shot himself to death.¹ On 30 January, Hitler had become Germany's chancellor; on 27 February, a blazing fire gutted the main chamber of Germany's Reichstag, its parliament building; and in late March, the lawyer's partner had told him that he intended to dissolve their practice together. The partner denied being an anti-Semite, of course, but times had changed and he needed to worry about his own family and responsibilities. Around the same time, a former client, now a member of the SA, the organization of Nazi paramilitary street fighters, warned the lawyer that he was no longer safe in Berlin and must leave. The lawyer did leave, arriving in Switzerland in mid-April. There he suffered a nervous breakdown. He refused opportunities for work, obsessed about events in Germany, lost weight, and spontaneously broke out into tears. Fewer than a dozen people attended the funeral—much like the burial of Willy Loman in *Death of a Salesman,* it was a small affair that did not match the dead man's dreams.²

As with Willy Loman, the final respects for this Jewish German lawyer evoked a grief chilled by loneliness, exhaustion, disappointment, and a sense of injustice. But there the similarity ends. This funeral was not for a professional failure. This funeral was for Max Alsberg—the most celebrated criminal defense lawyer of the time. Berliners knew of Max Alsberg. He was a public figure. When the historian Werner T. Angress and his mother were walking in Berlin one day in the late Weimar Republic, she stopped, pointed and said: "That is the office of Max Alsberg."³ The man was worth noting and the name worth remembering. He represented the rich and the famous. They could not have hired an attorney more knowledgeable in the law or more skilled in courtroom argument. Jurists turned to his legal scholarship, lay people crowded his public lectures. He taught, he edited, and he wrote plays. He accrued a fabulous art collection—auctioned off in January 1934.⁴

We cannot know for sure what drives a man to suicide. Greek heroes sacrificed their lives in the hope of future fame; Alsberg ended his upon the collapse of his renown. He could not go on without the reassurances from adulating surroundings—from his colleagues, from his adversaries, from his clients, from the public, from his audience. And he could not go on without his immersion in German law. Whatever the psychology behind his suicide, this much we can say with confidence: Alsberg's career epitomized the success that Jews had achieved in the German legal profession, and his death marked the roll-back of Jewish emancipation and the collapse of liberal law.

Emancipation: Jewish Lawyers before Nazi Rule

Alsberg's lifetime spanned the rise and fall of an era of liberal law in Germany. He was born in 1877, in the decade of German unification, at the time when legal reform took a quantum leap forward. New national laws—the Penal Code of 1871, and the Constitution of the Courts, the Lawyers' Statute, and the Codes of Criminal and Civil Procedure, all taking effect in 1879—actualized the liberal principles of legal equality.⁵ These laws rationalized court structures, reformed legal procedures, gave rise to a free legal profession (free insofar as it was freed from state control), and opened its doors to Jews. Jews flowed into the legal profession and soon made up a large proportion of practicing lawyers. In theory, Jews could become judges too, but judges were more closely tied to the state, which had persisting traditions of excluding outsiders; Jews only slowly breached the ranks of the judiciary.

The numbers are dramatic. Those numbers for Prussia, by far the largest province in Germany, are illustrative. In 1872, Prussia had 75 Jewish lawyers, 3 percent of the total; by 1880, the number had doubled to 146 lawyers, 7.3 percent of the total; and by 1893, the number had risen six-fold to 885, more than a quarter of the total. From then until 1933, the proportion of Jewish lawyers hovered between 25 and 30 percent of the total. In some cities the numbers were even more stunning. In Berlin almost half the lawyers were Jewish (or by some counts 54 percent), and in Breslau more than a third. The number of Jewish judges increased too, but far less dramatically. In 1872, Prussia had 9 Jewish judges, a fraction of a percent of the total; by 1880, the number had increased to 99 judges, 3.8 percent of the total; and by 1893, the number had increased to 168, or 4.5 percent of the total. The number and the proportion of Jewish judges continued to increase until 1933, when 401 constituted 7.0 percent of the total.[6]

By the time of the Weimar Republic, and for its duration, Jewish lawyers had gained public prominence and professional influence. The historian Benjamin Hett has written that the "great lawyers of Weimar ... represented an array of collective brilliance that formed a fitting counterpoint to the artistic, literary, and scientific glories of Weimar Berlin."[7]

De-Emancipation: The Nazi Attack on Liberalism

Upon gaining power, the Nazi regime reversed Jewish emancipation. It began a five-year process of hounding Jews out of the legal profession. But that tells only part of the story. The reversal of Jewish emancipation and the elimination of Jewish lawyers were like vines entangled with something else, namely, the demise in Germany of liberal law, the transformation of the German legal system, and the creation of a new anti-liberal Nazi legal order. The laws from the 1870s that had ushered Jews into the legal profession did not simply expand opportunities for a specific group. Those laws embodied new liberal principles of equality under the law, individual rights, and democratic participation. In eliminating Jewish lawyers, the Nazi regime was not just uprooting a specific group, it was reversing liberal principles. The Nazis replaced equality with racial superiority, subordinated the individual to the Aryan community, and discarded democratic participation for the dictatorial Führer state.

Uprooting Jewish lawyers and disentangling them from the German legal system took five years. But within months of gaining power in 1933, the Nazi regime struck its first blows, both violently and methodically. By the time Max Alsberg died in September 1933, the regime had already shown that it meant to rid the German legal profession of Jews and rid German law of liberal principles, and that it had an approach for getting the job done. That approach was present in the attacks on Jewish lawyers in the spring of 1933.

The turning point was the Reichstag fire on 27 February 1933, which served as the pretext the following day for an emergency measure titled, "Decree for the Protection of the People and the State." In *The Dual State,* written during the 1930s (although published in 1941), the Jewish German lawyer Ernst Fraenkel aptly described the decree as the "constitutional charter of the Third Reich." Purporting to protect Germany against communist violence, the decree indefinitely suspended civil liberties guaranteed in the Weimar constitution; it empowered the national government to intervene to restore order, whenever and wherever necessary; and it handed Nazi officials enough purported authority ultimately, over the next several years, to transform Nazi rule into a permanent dictatorship with unlimited powers.[8]

With this abrupt transition from the Weimar Republic to Nazi rule, the new regime created what the title to Fraenkel's book suggests, a dual state. This consisted of the prerogative state on the one hand, and the normative state on the other. The prerogative state was the realm of arbitrary power and official violence, against which citizens enjoyed no legal protection. The normative state was the legal order, which included both traditional law and newly enacted Nazi law. Thus, with the emergency decree in place, the new regime delivered a double-punch against Jewish lawyers, a jab by Nazi law, an uppercut by Nazi lawlessness.

Nazi lawlessness burst on the scene the night of the Reichstag fire, as police rounded up 4,000 of the Nazis' political opponents, including politically active, especially leftist, Jewish lawyers. One was a young lawyer named Hans Litten, the son of a Protestant mother and Jewish law professor. In courtrooms in the late Weimar Republic, he had represented working class defendants involved in political brawls, taunted conservative judges as he pushed the law to its limits, and scorned the Nazis to their faces as he exposed their brutality to the public. Most famously, at the Eden Dance Palace trial in 1931, he had caused a sensation when he cross-examined Hitler. In 1933 his mother begged him to get out of Germany, but he refused, saying, "Millions of workers cannot leave, so I must also stay put."[9]

In December 1935, the later Nazi Foreign Minister Joachim von Ribbentrop wrote (maybe not coincidentally in connection with Litten himself), "Revolutions are not fought out and decided in courts of justice or according to the regular rules of legal procedure."[10] After the Reichstag fire, the Nazis bypassed the courts and rules and simply arrested Litten and others. Under the rubric of protective custody, the Nazis empowered themselves to arrest whomever they saw as a threat to the public order, or a future threat. The notion of protective custody was antithetical to liberal law. The arrestee faced no charges and had no legal recourse. No judicial warrants authorized the arrests, and no court orders could end the detentions. Nazi officials could make their decisions secretly and arbitrarily, without heeding any preexisting public rules and without facing any later impartial judicial review. The Nazi regime was creating the prerogative state, a realm of Nazi action independent of law and beyond the reach of judicial scrutiny.[11]

Litten, like others in protective custody, could still ask a lawyer to seek his release. Unable to rely on legal authority, the lawyer could only make ad hoc petitions to those in power, meet with officials, and exploit connections. Seeking a lawyer for her son, Litten's mother asked Max Alsberg. He declined.[12] Alsberg probably simply exercised good sense. When, on 10 March 1933, one Jewish lawyer, Michael Siegel, who was representing a client in protective custody, lodged a complaint at a police station in Munich, SA men seized him, tore his trousers at the knees, and marched him barefoot through the streets with a sign hanging from his neck stating: "I will never again complain to the police."[13]

On the night of the Reichstag fire, the Nazis targeted their political opponents. They arrested Jewish lawyers as political opponents, not as Jews. But within weeks, the Nazis turned their attention to lawyers as well as judges for no other reason than that they were Jewish. Instead of arresting lawyers in the dead of night, they attacked courthouses in the light of day. SA men—the so-called brown shirts, uniformed thugs— stormed courthouses and occupied them, searched for Jews, and chased them away. Invariably, police arrived on the scene too late.[14]

One of the first courthouse attacks occurred on 11 March in the city with Germany's third largest Jewish population, Breslau. Here is one lawyer's description:

> Suddenly—it was exactly eleven o'clock—we heard in the hallway a roaring, as if of wild animals, that got closer and closer. The doors to the lawyers' chambers flew open. Two dozen SA men rushed in ... and screamed, "Jews out." For a moment everyone, Jews and Christians, froze. Then most Jewish lawyers left the room. ... At first I didn't budge. Then an SA man sprang at me and grabbed me by the arm. I shook him away, at which point he pulled out of his right shirt-sleeve

a metal sheath, which he pressed, releasing a spiral with a lead bullet fastened to its end. With this instrument, he struck me twice on the head, which poured forth blood and began to swell. ... There were judges, prosecutors and lawyers, many in their official robes, who were driven onto the street by small hordes of SA men. Everywhere the intruders flung open courtroom doors and bellowed, "Jews out."[15]

Was the attack on Breslau's courthouses an isolated event? The answer came in the following weeks, when SA men stormed other German courthouses. On 29 March, in Görlitz, SA men dragged two Jewish judges and two Jewish lawyers out of the courthouse and displayed them before a jeering crowd. On 31 March, in Cologne, SA men forced Jewish judges and lawyers out of the appeals court and onto a refuse cart, and hooted while driving them around the city. A Nazi lawyer later proudly reported: "No protection by officials; no intervention of colleagues for colleagues! That was the hour of separation!"[16]

If courthouse attacks were brush fires, Nazi officials fanned the flames to spread smoke across the legal landscape. They intended a clear message with their boycott of Jewish businesses, doctors and lawyers planned for April 1. On 31 March, in anticipation of the boycott, Hanns Kerrl— the Reich Commissioner for the Prussian Administration of Justice and soon-to-be Prussian Justice Minister—issued one of his first decrees. He warned that Jewish judges and lawyers were endangering the authority of the justice system because their presumptuous bearing had enraged the German people. If officials failed to remove the causes of the popular rage, the people were bound to take matters into their own hands. Accordingly, he demanded that Jewish judges immediately apply for, and be granted, leaves of absence. He also demanded that bar associations (*Anwaltskammern* or *örtliche Anwaltsvereinen*) limit the number of Jewish lawyers permitted to appear in court to the proportion of Jews in the population as a whole. Otherwise, judges and prosecutors should bar them from entering courthouses.[17]

If arbitrary arrests of individuals and intimidating attacks on courthouses were lawless, what was the legal nature of the Kerrl Decree? Kerrl himself probably did not much care whether his decree constituted law or not, for he stood out as the first Prussian Justice Minister who lacked legal training. For him, the crux of the matter was wielding power— speaking with the authority of his office and inviting compliance through the threat of mob violence. The Appeals Court in Königsberg captured the point. The court wrote that the Kerrl Decree might "not follow the constitutionally prescribed form for formulating law," but since it originated with the "actual holder of state power," and since the SA's presence in the courts secured its enforcement, it was a "thoroughly binding law."[18] Like much Nazi law, the decree was intimidation through other means. And like much Nazi law, the decree diverted attention from the legitimacy of its origins—it had none[19]—to the effectuation of its ends. The decree marked a mid-point between the prerogative state and the normative state.

The Nazi regime also relied on the normative state, the legal system. The prerogative state accomplished many of the regime's goals, but it had limitations. Its terror tactics helped dislodge the liberal order in the short-run, but they jeopardized the Nazi promise of social order in the long-run. Many Nazi power-brokers realized that using the legal system could secure the new government's legitimacy and advance its goals more systematically, consistently, and thoroughly. Of course, they needed to transform the legal system, replacing liberal law with Nazi law. In this process, the government took a major step with two laws of 7 April 1933, which attacked the two professions animating the liberal state, namely the judges and lawyers. The Law on the Restoration of the Professional Civil Service applied to judges, and the Law on the Admission to the Bar applied to lawyers.

With these two laws, the Nazis aimed to stamp the judicial system with the twin principles of racial superiority and Nazi political control. The Nazis intended to be pragmatic about putting these principles into effect, taking measures that were radical but not absolute. Both laws for the first time distinguished Jews from so-called Aryans and discriminated against Jews as a matter of law (anticipating the Nuremberg Laws of 1935). Under these two 1933 laws, Jewish judges had to retire and Jewish lawyers could be disbarred. But even in regard to race, both laws set limits. The disbarments of lawyers had to take place before the deadline of 30 September 1933. However, Jews could continue as judges and lawyers if they fell under one of three exceptions: (1) Jewish judges who had entered the civil service or Jewish lawyers who had been admitted to the bar before 1 August 1914; (2) Jewish judges or lawyers who had fought on the front in World War I; or (3) Jewish judges or lawyers who had a father or son who had fallen in the war.[20]

The two laws—on the Restoration of the Professional Civil Service and on the Admission to the Bar—nailed down not just racial principles, but also political principles. One political dimension was that the laws showed more concern about the authority exerted by judges than about the legal work performed by lawyers; Jewish judges were regarded as more dangerous than Jewish lawyers. Aside from the three exceptions, the law against Jewish judges was mandatory, while the one against Jewish lawyers permissive, i.e., judges had to retire while lawyers could be, but did not have to be, disbarred. While this legal distinction made no difference in practice, the message was clear that the Nazis gave priority to removing Jews from positions of political authority. The two laws also included standards for eliminating judges and lawyers that were political rather than racial. While harsher for judges than lawyers, both standards moved in the same direction. In the broader law, judges could lose their positions if their prior political activity failed to ensure that they would unreservedly and always support the national state. In the narrower law, lawyers could be disbarred who had been active "in a communist way." The political messages were complementary: lawyers may not be subversive and judges must be loyal.[21]

The Law on the Admission to the Bar tackled a problem that had plagued German lawyers for years and solved it with Nazi perversion. The problem was the overcrowding of the legal profession. The fear of overcrowding—of damage to the profession's elitism, standards and prestige—dated back to the 1870s, but became acute during the Weimar Republic. By then many lawyers were economically strapped—first, from clawing their way out of postwar chaos, then reeling from run-away inflation, and finally being beaten down by the Depression. By 1933, three quarters of lawyers earned approximately the same (or less) as the average blue-collar worker. Yet the numbers of lawyers kept increasing, with the largest expansion ever taking place in the last two years of the Weimar Republic.[22] Some reasoned that the more lawyers there were overall, the less business for any one lawyer in particular. The conclusion seemed inevitable: limit the number of lawyers through a *numerus clausus*. Others, such as Max Friedlaender, a Jewish lawyer and nationally respected expert on legal ethics, warned that the proposal threatened to corrode the foundations of the free legal profession. The profession was free because lawyers were free of state control, but a *numerus clausus* would enable the state to control admission to the bar, restoring power to the state that lawyers had earlier wrested away for themselves. In December 1932, with the Weimar Republic in its death throes, the German Bar Association finally voted to recommend a *numerus clausus*. Ironically, the Nazi regime refused to implement the recommendation. Instead, it shrank the legal profession by cutting back the number of Jewish lawyers with the Law on the Admission to the Bar, i.e., not with a merit-based limitation on law applicants but with racial anti-Semitism. In so doing, the regime struck both Jews and the freedom of the legal profession, which it now placed into the noose of the Nazi state.[23]

The Law on the Admission to the Bar jolted the legal profession. Within months, the number of Jewish lawyers in Germany dropped by just over 30 percent, from 4,585 to 3,167; in Prussia by almost 40 percent, from 3,370 to 2,066; and in Berlin, by just over 36 percent, from 1,835 to 1,168, reducing the percentage of Jewish lawyers there, by one count, from 54 percent to 40 percent.[24] From one vantage point, most Jewish lawyers evaded disbarment, either as senior attorneys admitted before World War I or as veterans who had fought on the front. The Nazis were astounded—they never imagined so many "cowardly" Jews had been on the battlefield.[25] Still, many Jewish lawyers abruptly lost their livelihoods. And since Jews could no longer enter the profession, the number of Jewish lawyers remaining represented a ceiling, a number that would decrease, even by attrition alone.

The plunge in the number of Jewish lawyers also had implications for the legal profession overall. The total number of lawyers, i.e., of both Jewish and non-Jewish ones, also fell. For example, in Berlin, the elimination of hundreds of Jewish lawyers reduced the overall number of lawyers from 3,433 to 2,880.[26] For the remaining lawyers, less competition was doubtless good for business, at least for the moment,[27] but it was an ominous sign, and a step toward cheapening the status of the legal profession.

Discrimination and Degradation: Jewish Lawyers Coping with Nazism

Although Hitler became Germany's chancellor on 30 January 1933, the Nazis did not take control of Bavaria, Germany's most independent province, until 9 March. Early the next morning police arrested the Jewish lawyer Max Hirschberg. Throughout the Weimar Republic, he had been Munich's leading Social Democratic, anti-Nazi lawyer. Before being led away, he sneaked a call to Philipp Loewenfeld, his partner of fourteen years, and a politically active labor lawyer. Later that day, Loewenfeld slipped out of Germany into Switzerland. Hirschberg remained in prison for almost half a year, then picked up a moribund legal practice for eight months, and finally quit the country in April 1934. Five years later, in May 1939, Loewenfeld wrote a letter to a former colleague that included a striking remark: his friendship with Hirschberg had "suffered a rupture when, after his release from custody, he felt bound to make himself an organ of Nazi justice."[28]

The thought of the rupture between these two men—who for years had practiced law together, engaged in political struggles together, and defied dangers together—is painful. But Loewenfeld's accusation against Hirschberg was ill-founded. In 1933, Jewish lawyers in Nazi Germany, including leftists like Hirschberg, tried to maintain their legal credentials, not relinquish them as a matter of principle. To implement the Law on the Admission to the Bar, provincial governments, as in Prussia and Bavaria, suspended all Jewish lawyers and conditioned readmission on a new application in person. Jewish lawyers lined up. Bruno Blau described the scene in Berlin: "We had to wait for hours in front of the [bar association] building in the rain and under the watch of SA rogues, until we were let in one by one." Of 1,835 Jewish lawyers in Berlin, 1,761—all but 74—reapplied.[29]

By April 1933, the first exodus of Jewish lawyers from Nazi Germany had already occurred. In the wake of the Reichstag fire, Fritz Ball wrote: "Whoever was politically active against the Nazis and is still able, flees." Leftists, such as Hans Litten and Max Hirschberg, were arrested; others, such as Phillip Loewenfeld, fled. The elegant Rudolf Olden, who had represented the journalist Carl von Ossietzky, made a court appearance, headed south, and skied over the border into Czechoslovakia.[30] Some prominent, but less political lawyers, such as Max Alsberg, realized that the risk of arrest grew by the day and they made for the exit. But most lawyers stayed in the hope of preserving their livelihoods and weathering the storm.

How did the vast majority of Jewish lawyers, those who remained, respond? There were at least three types of responses, representing varying strategies, whether as a matter of principle or exigency. Each one ultimately proved futile.

How did Jewish lawyers respond to discrimination?

When Max Alsberg shot himself to death, he did not rely on skill in packing a pistol acquired as a front-line soldier. Alsberg had not fought in the war. As a criminal defense lawyer, scholar, and methodical German, he studied how to shoot himself from a text on guns.[31] Unlike Alsberg, however, in 1933 most Jewish lawyers at the height of their careers were veterans. They had the best argument against disbarment: their sacrifice in serving their country in war-time. The argument appealed to German patriotism and honor.

The argument for Jewish war veterans came from the gut. Max Hirschberg was arrested by police in Munich in early March, and while, after waiting, he finally answered routine questions, he mentioned that he had served on the front and earned the Iron Cross, First Class. Tired, frustrated and indignant, he then leaned forward and asked the policeman to add the sentence that adorned the standard military notices to next-of-kin that their loved one had died in the war: "Rest assured that the fatherland is grateful."[32]

The argument for Jewish war veterans made strategic sense. It resonated with Germans, even anti-Semites. One veteran who had fought under Hirschberg's command opposed his disbarment and imprisonment, writing: "Am personally a big follower of the national movement, but we have enough 'Christian Jews' who may be imprisoned; a good soldier who did more than his duty should be free, even if he's a Jew."[33] The comment was no exception. The files of Jewish German lawyers in Berlin are replete with letters from former comrades who praised their patriotism and courage, and from former clients who could not fathom why Jews who had risked their lives for Germany should lose their jobs.[34]

The argument for Jewish war veterans made political sense. The obvious audience was Paul von Hindenburg, the eighty-five year-old president who had appointed Hitler chancellor and was one non-Nazi who still wielded some real power. Jewish veterans wrote him. Hindenburg did not disappoint. On 4 April, he wrote Hitler about the plight of disabled veterans, front-line fighters, and families of the fallen: "If they were good enough to fight and shed their blood for Germany, they should be good enough to continue serving the Fatherland in their profession." Hitler assured Hindenburg that the upcoming law would include the appropriate exceptions. Hitler added, of course, that the German people needed to defend themselves against Jewish domination of intellectual professions, such as law, where in Berlin and other cities Jews occupied up to 80 percent of all positions—an obvious exaggeration.[35]

Coming from the gut, resonating with the populace, and appealing to a national leader, the argument for Jewish war veterans had much in its favor. It met with success. The most important exception to the exclusion of Jews from the judiciary and the bar was the one for front-line veterans. The success of the argument made a difference, sparing most Jewish judges from forced retirement, at least in 1933, and most Jewish lawyers from disbarment.

Still, the argument for Jewish war veterans suffered inherent flaws. One flaw is apparent from a liberal perspective. In relying on honor, the argument abandoned notions of both Jewish emancipation and legal equality. This illiberal tack had consequences; it separated Jewish lawyers from each other. By privileging front-line veterans, it discriminated against the rest. Was a tactical victory worth the sacrifice of principle? One Jewish lawyer, Kurt Jacob Ball-Kaduri, later reported that the exception for Jewish war veterans aroused "mixed feelings" within Jewish circles. Some thought that pushing through this exception represented a great success. Others disagreed. "While not begrudging an individual the maintenance of his existence, splitting Jews into groups of losers and winners seemed inappropriate." The exception created a generational divide, wiping out young Jewish lawyers. Some of them wrote the Prussian Ministry of State in mid-June 1933, complaining that the Law on the Admission to the Bar, which authorized but did not require the exclusion of Jewish lawyers, had become "a general and undifferentiated threat to many upright citizens." The complaint hardly seems to have resonated, either with Nazis or other Jewish lawyers. The exception for Jewish war veterans also created a gender divide, eliminating women Jewish lawyers. The first German women were admitted to the bar only in 1922. Just over a decade later, in 1933, Berlin counted twenty Jewish women lawyers. Soon the number dwindled to one.[36]

Another flaw in the argument for Jewish war veterans is apparent from a conservative perspective. Based on nationalism, the argument easily degenerated. At its most unexceptional, the point was simply that Jewish Germans were as German as anyone else, immersed in their country's culture and committed to fighting in its defense. At its worst, the point was that Jewish Germans could be loyal to the state. That was the view of the right-wing lawyer, Max Naumann, who in 1921 had founded the League of National-German Jews (*Verband nationaldeutscher Juden*). In 1933, he wanted to convince the Nazis that some Jews could assimilate into the German national community and serve the Nazi state.[37] While representing a tiny minority of Jews, his views pressed the limits of devotion to the state; they exposed the flaw in the impulse toward loyalty. Reconciliation between being Jewish and supporting Nazism was impossible. Jewish lawyers, even the veterans, could never be loyal to the Nazi state, to its leadership principle, and to Adolf Hitler—they could only be dependent. In early April 1933, Berlin's chief appellate court judge and his colleagues on the provincial courts decreed that all Jewish lawyers had to reapply for admission to the bar and at the same time acknowledge the government and its regulations; Jewish lawyers complied.[38] Jewish war veteran lawyers clung to their sense of honor until bowing to the humiliation of Nazi subjugation.

The exception allowing Jewish war veterans to continue as lawyers garnered support from Jews and Nazis. Both groups accommodated to the exigencies of the moment, but they took positions that united in anticipation of goals that diverged. From the Jewish lawyers' perspective, the immediate strategy served to blunt Nazi blows, but the accommodation sacrificed liberal equality in favor of questionable loyalty. From the perspective of governing Nazis, their concession was a matter of political expediency, appeasing Hindenburg. It was also a matter of economic necessity. The regime could not uproot Jewish lawyers in one fell swoop without troublesome economic disruption.

Although it was an accommodation for both sides, the exception allowing Jewish war veterans as lawyers was bound to be temporary because it was inherently unstable. The Nazis had the upper hand, not only because of their consolidation of power, but also because of the underlying logic in both the Law on the Admission to the Bar and this exception. That logic was to break liberal principles and replace them with hierarchical ones. Thus, the law presented the Nazis with no dilemma in principle. The very characteristics that should have disturbed Jews heartened Nazis: the law replaced liberal equality with Nazi hierarchy—Aryans before Jews, Jewish war veterans before other Jews. If society was hierarchical, if Aryans were superior to Jews, then the Nazi government could discriminate against Jewish lawyers and also among them. Furthermore, the logic of the law put a premium on loyalty. While giving a nod to a soldier's sacrifice, the Nazis were shifting the notion of loyalty from any person's devotion to Germany to a so-called Aryan's devotion to the Nazi state. Max Naumann aside, both Nazis and Jews knew that the Nazi state could not be the object of Jewish fervor.

The underlying logic of the exception for Jewish war veterans turned on loyalty, which ultimately hurt not just Jewish lawyers but German lawyers in general. What Jews could not achieve from the outside, German jurists had to display from the inside: loyalty to the Aryan community, the Nazi state, and its leader Adolf Hitler. Compared with judges, the nature of a lawyer's role struck closer to the heart of liberalism, because lawyers represent individuals or entities and advance their separate interests, whether against each other or against the state. How could lawyers reconcile their loyalty to the Aryan community with their obligation to individual clients? What was the role of the lawyer, caught between loyalty to the Nazi state and client representation? The original dilemma of the loyalty of Jewish jurists previewed the dilemma of loyalty of all German jurists.

How did Jewish lawyers respond to degradation?

Max Hachenburg was a doyen of the legal profession. An expert in commercial and corporate law, a legal commentator admired by lawyers, and an active member of bar associations, he wrote his autobiography in 1927 when he was sixty-seven years old. There he cautioned fellow Jewish lawyers to avoid anti-Semitism by conducting themselves with professional restraint. In May 1933, as a long-time columnist for the leading publication for German lawyers, *Deutsche Juristen-Zeitung*, he felt that the Law on the Admission to the Bar presented him with a dilemma. Some might construe his silence on the law as cowardice, while others might reject his views as self-interested. But comment he did. On the one hand, he was not surprised at the reaction against the heavy reliance on Jews in public positions that had appeared since 1919. On the other hand, he could not say that Jewish jurists influenced the German legal system "only in an unfavorable or un-German way." In the end, he cautioned that measures "should not go overboard" in "restraining the excessive influence of Jewish jurists." He hoped that authorities would exercise their discretion under the law "to spare men who conducted themselves with utmost honor, rooted only in Germanness, from being driven to despair." He commented that the recent suicide of a young aspiring law student "should give pause." He also noted that the possibility of denying non-Aryans admission to the bar "ripped the first hole in the freedom of the legal profession."[39]

In his article, Hachenburg struck the restrained tone that he had counseled. He spoke with a patriarchal voice, like a contemplative grandfather who listened to both sides of the story and only hesitantly, only reluctantly, and ever so gently tapped his finger on one side of the scale. But his apparent attempt at moderation was less a liberal call for tempered debate than an illiberal suggestion for milder forms of discrimination. His liberal concern for the freedom of the legal profession paled before his illiberal uneasiness with Jewish emancipation. He retreated to defending the Jewish lawyers who were at least honorable. And beyond giving his rendition of the debate about discrimination against Jewish lawyers, he mentioned violence against them only once: one Jew's self-inflicted suicide. Perhaps by 1933, Hachenburg was simply out of touch. If his thinking included an element of liberalism, it was a liberalism that was exhausted, pathetic, and cut loose from a passion for equality.

Most Jewish lawyers did not assert any kind of liberalism, exhausted or otherwise. When a mugger springs out from the dark, victims confront the moment rather than first principles. In describing the Nazi seizure of court houses, one Jewish lawyer, Bruno Blau, later wrote: "In almost all cases, people yielded to the violence."[40] As violence in public waned, Jews and non-Jews alike still yielded, now to Nazi intimidation and economic manipulation. Jewish lawyers were preoccupied with lost clients and shrinking legal practices.

For most Jewish lawyers under the new Nazi rule, the meaning of liberalism shifted from its political possibilities to its sociological circumstances, from individual freedom to social isolation. With little room for public debate, most Jewish lawyers struggled as solitary individuals trying to protect their own economic self-interest. Jewish lawyers were atomized, separated from other German lawyers, and from each other. This atomization resulted, at least in part, because Jewish lawyers had little organized response to the Nazis' accumulation of governmental power. During the Weimar Republic, Jewish lawyers had gained influence in German bar associations. Nazis in power put an end to that. Through intimidation and fiat, they expelled the Jews, took over the associations, and thwarted possible alternatives—all accomplished between March and May 1933, with the finishing touches in place by year's end. Once they were expelled, Jewish lawyers had nowhere to go. They lacked an independent bar association of their own, and attempts to fill the organizational void were at best sputtering.[41]

The struggle of Jewish lawyers to protect their individual economic self-interest proved a losing battle due to Nazi law and lawlessness. The Law on the Admission to the Bar and follow-up ordinances dried up business. Jewish lawyers lost income because the Nazis barred most from entering courthouses, pressured courts to stop assigning them to represent the poor, and leaned on companies to stop retaining them as outside counsel.[42] Christian lawyers abandoned their Jewish partners, whether eagerly, like Alsberg's partner, or reluctantly. In regard to their lawlessness, the Nazis leveraged their early acts of violence into persistent intimidation. They warned that good Germans would never seek a Jew's legal advice. Thus, as a result of Nazi law and lawlessness, clients deserted their Jewish lawyers.

Choked economically and isolated socially, Jewish lawyers felt humiliated. In describing Jewish lawyers waiting for hours in the rain to reapply for admission to the bar, Bruno Blau wrote: "This process was the height of degradation, as it was intended to be."[43] Upon learning that his non-Jewish partner insisted on dissolving their partnership, Max Alsberg fell into despair.[44] How could Philipp Loewenfeld have written about Max Hirschberg, his compatriot and friend, with such contempt? Throughout the Weimar Republic, they had struggled together, but in 1933 they were separated, suffered the deprivation of their professional lives in isolation, and lost their meeting of the minds. Perhaps in losing some self-respect, the two men lost some mutual respect.

The one countervailing tendency, a source of economic, as well as emotional, support, was other Jews. In separating Jews from other Germans, the Nazis aimed to discourage not only Jewish lawyers from representing Germans, but also German lawyers from representing Jews. Jews needed to turn to Jewish lawyers. In light of anti-Semitic discrimination, such as the Nuremberg Laws of 15 September 1935, Jews needed legal help more than ever—in defending themselves in disputes involving property, housing and employment, and in resolving their affairs before emigrating.[45]

The Nazis discriminated against and degraded Jewish lawyers first with a sudden ferocity and then with unrelenting pressure. As the discrimination and degradation dug deeper roots and took firmer hold, sporadic examples of defiance appeared among Jewish lawyers. To understand that defiance, we must first look at Nazi policy against Jewish lawyers in the mid-1930s.

Defiance: Nazi Lawyers against Jewish Lawyers, and Two Jewish Lawyers against Nazism

The logic already inherent in the two laws on Jewish judges and lawyers in April 1933 advanced on a schedule that accommodated politics and economics, first striking Jewish judges and later Jewish lawyers. When the Nuremberg Laws of 15 September 1935, in the words of the historian Henry Friedlander "stigmatized Jews as citizens of lesser worth,"[46] the notion of a Jewish judge became impossible. The Ministries of Justice and the Interior acted immediately to retire all Jewish judges by year's end. But conditions were not yet ripe for disbarring the remaining Jewish lawyers; their disbarment would have risked triggering economic disruption and foreign policy troubles in light of the upcoming 1936 Olympics planned for Berlin.[47] In 1936, there were still 2,552 Jewish lawyers out of 18,854 lawyers in Germany, just over 13 percent of the total. In Berlin, more than one thousand lawyers were Jewish, just over one third.[48]

With new forms of legal discrimination against Jewish lawyers lagging behind economic discrimination and anti-Semitic rhetoric, Nazi academics inflamed the matter with a new forum for propaganda. In May 1936 Carl Schmitt, the influential reactionary political theorist and passionate convert to the Nazi cause, announced a conference for early October in Berlin entitled "Jewry in Jurisprudence." The conference drew over one hundred jurists, teachers and guests, and generated eight pamphlets of the conference's papers, published between November 1936 and late 1937.[49]

While not there in person, Nazi Germany's leading jurist, Hans Frank—head of the National Socialists Lawyers' Association, president of the Academy for German Law, and cabinet minister without portfolio—sent an opening statement for public reading. He denounced Jewish emancipation because it subverted German legal scholarship with the peculiarly Jewish tendency to disintegrate and uproot the legal order with liberal individualism. He called for an end to German-Jewish jurisprudence since "creative, interpretive, or instructive work or commentary by Jews on German law ... is impossible." He announced four goals: (1) Jews may not appear in the name of German law; (2) German scholarship must be the reserve of German men; (3) new editions of German legal works by Jewish authors must cease; and (4) libraries must segregate the works of Jewish authors since they "do not have the slightest thing to do with" German jurisprudence.[50]

After Frank's opening, Carl Schmitt tried to rouse the crowd for the victory that National Socialism had made possible: the liberation of the German spirit from Jewish lies. "Do not forget," Schmitt declared, "what it means that year after year, semester after semester, for almost one hundred years thousands of young Germans, future judges and lawyers, have been schooled by Jewish legal teachers, that standard texts and commentaries in the most important legal disciplines are by Jews, that influential legal journals were dominated by them."[51]

In one talk, Karl Siegert, a Nazi law professor in Göttingen, explained that he was about to provide the first overview ever of the Jewish impact on the criminal procedure. He mentioned Max Hachenburg and belittled Hans Litten, but the lawyer that he targeted as the epitome of what was wrong with criminal procedure was Max Alsberg. In the last years before 1933, this "Jewish being" was the "mightiest and most fateful."[52]

Siegert handled Alsberg with the morbid curiosity of an anatomy professor displaying an archetypal skull. The evil of Alsberg's efforts lay in his promoting abstract individual rights, which lawyers advanced at the expense of the Aryan community and Nazi judges. Siegert turned his attention to Alsberg's writings. In his essay on offering evidence during proceedings, Alsberg had been concerned only with the rights of the parties rather than "[t]he idea of justice, the protection of the general good." In his lecture on the philosophy of criminal defense, Alsberg had worshiped disembodied law rather than striving for justice, he had promoted individualism rather than comprehending the needs of the community, and he had subverted "the figure of the eternally truth-seeking German judge." In his recommendations for the reform of criminal procedure, Alsberg had written that the parties in the proceedings were supposed to "be able to exercise a continuous control over the measures taken by the presiding judge—the opposite of our leadership principle." For Siegert, Alsberg the lawyer was the foil for "judicial sovereignty" and "judicial power," i.e., for Nazi sovereignty and power.[53]

The focus on Alsberg marked a subtle but important shift. Alsberg may have been the most prominent lawyer in the Weimar Republic, but he had never triggered the Nazis' worst rage. The Nazis had reserved that for leftist political lawyers, the ones hunted down immediately after the Reichstag fire on 27 February 1933. But at the conference in October 1936, Siegert turned his attention from lawyers who had engaged in leftist politics to one who represented liberal lawyering. While Siegert's anti-Semitism was bad for Jewish lawyers, his anti-liberalism was bad for all lawyers.

One lawyer who did not make it to Berlin in October 1936 for the conference "Jewry in Jurisprudence" was Hugo Sinzheimer. A Jew hailing from Frankfurt, Sinzheimer was as important in German labor law as Max Alsberg in criminal law and Max Hachenburg in commercial law. He devoted his career to the peaceful advance of the collective bargaining rights of workers within a capitalist society. After the Reichstag fire in late February 1933, the Nazis arrested him. Once he was released, he fled Germany, and soon accepted an offer to teach at the Universities of Amsterdam and Leyden.[54] Learning of the 1936 Nazi conference, he did not like what he read. Unlike Jewish lawyers still in Germany, he was not intimidated by the threat of violence; unlike exiles like Max Alsberg, he was not suffocated by foreign surroundings. Instead, he put pen to paper and by August 1937 had finished his response: *Jüdische Klassiker der deutschen Rechtswissenschaft* (*Jewish Classical Writers in German Jurisprudence*). Sinzheimer had never before written about Jews. But now he challenged the Nazi jurists and defended Jewish equality with a German idea of liberalism.

Sinzheimer explored whether Hans Frank and Carl Schmitt had engaged in polemic or, as they claimed, scholarship. Sinzheimer had always assumed that scholarship turned on the content of ideas, not the ethnic origins of the thinker. In its search for truth, scholarship also turned on factual inquiry. The factual inquiry needed to test Frank's and Schmitt's theses was this: How did Jewish jurists influence German jurisprudence? Sinzheimer asked "whether one can speak of a characteristic intellectual structure of Jewish legal scholars and what its nature is," and "what the significance is of the Jewish dimension in the development of German jurisprudence, whether it was creative or not." To answer these questions, Sinzheimer devoted one chapter each to twelve Jewish jurists, most from the nineteenth century.[55]

Sinzheimer concluded that the historical facts disproved the assertion of a specifically Jewish mentality. He found that Jewish jurists were influential not in infusing Jewish ideas into German legal thinking, but in explicating German legal thinking itself. "It is German spirit that is the foundation of the 'Jewish influence,'" he wrote. With its creative contributions, "Jewish work is … an inextricable part of German scholarship." Nazi scholars may look the other way and stop citing Jewish German scholarship, but they cannot eliminate it.[56]

Furthermore, Jewish scholars included notions of both community and individual rights, each of which could not exist without the other:

> There is no moral form of the community without recognition of the intrinsic value of each person. But there is also no moral form of the individual without recognition of the intrinsic value of the community.

At its foundation, the development of a true community requires human rights—one of the great spiritual creations, developed by thinkers of many nations, and an inextricable part of German intellectual history. But great German thinkers, Jewish and non-Jewish alike, never recognized an unlimited power of the community over the individual, and certainly not in the hands of an absolute individual.[57]

By the end, Sinzheimer had made three points. First, Frank and Schmitt were factually wrong in asserting that Jewish jurists had poisoned German law with some evil doctrine of their own. Second, Jews were equal to other Germans because they were like other Germans, influential not as Jews but as Germans. Third, unlike Nazism's perverse idea of a community that excluded Jews, the notion of community in German law included a commitment to individual rights.

Jewish Classical Writers in German Jurisprudence stands out because Sinzheimer attacked the Nazi arguments head-on. At home, no politician dared debate the Nazis in public, and few lawyers dared confront them in court. But from abroad, Sinzheimer struck back, and he struck back as a scholar. Unlike Max Hachenburg, Sinzheimer did not value commentary detached and above the fray. Rather, his scholarship was engaged. He attacked Nazi politics by using real scholarship to strip bare the Nazis' pseudo-scholarship. Sinzheimer struck back as a German. Unlike front-line fighters, he did not insist upon personal honor. Rather, Sinzheimer turned to Germany's cultural heritage, emphasizing not personal love for it, but the objective study of some of its leading jurists. And Sinzheimer struck back as a liberal, as a German liberal. He did not espouse a negative idea of freedom, of the isolated individual pitted against the state, as championed in the Anglo-American world by the post-World War II political philosopher and intellectual historian Isaiah Berlin. Rather, Sinzheimer's idea of freedom included not only the individual's rights, but also the individual's bond within a community—in Germany within a German community. Sinzheimer had devoted his pre-Nazi legal career to the peaceful reconciliation of employers and organized workers. He now argued for the peaceful integration of Jews into a liberal German community.

In the early 1920s, Sinzheimer was the dissertation advisor to Ernst Fraenkel. While Sinzheimer fled Nazi Germany in 1933, Fraenkel remained. He continued to practice law. He worked in what he later called "inner emigration."[58] By this he hardly meant compliance encasing hidden doubts. Rather, he took on political cases, one of the only Jewish lawyers to have done so.[59] He wrote anti-Nazi articles for underground distribution and ultimately his *pièce de résistance, The Dual State*. Smuggled out of Germany in 1938 and published in the United States in English translation in early 1941, the book, as the editor of his collected writings has noted, was the only contemporaneous, comprehensive, critical analysis of the Nazi regime written from within Nazi Germany.[60] While eluding arrest in part by random luck, Fraenkel tested the boundaries of anti-Nazi defiance.

In 1935, Fraenkel wrote an article, "The Point of Illegal Work," which countered the despair of Max Alsberg, the timid liberalism of Max Hachenburg, and the demoralized isolation of struggling Jewish lawyers. Smuggled from Berlin to Switzerland to Paris (there published under a pseudonym in the exile journal *Sozialistische Warte*) to Holland (there printed as a pamphlet) and back into Germany for distribution,[61] the article set forth a theory of resistance to Nazi rule. It asked: in light of propaganda that the Nazis have converted most of the bourgeoisie and proletariat and cowed the rest, and in light of censorship, arrests and sacrifices, does illegal work by socialists serve any purpose? Fraenkel's answer was that illegal work was justifiable, indeed crucial.

Fraenkel believed that Nazism needed popular support to survive. The critical conflict was between the regime shoring up popular support and the resistance creating instability by unsettling such support. The propaganda machine of Joseph Goebbels endangered the resistance with its "whispering campaign," which was luring both the bourgeoisie and the proletariat into complacency by misleading them into believing that even workers were backing the regime. Socialists, Fraenkel argued, must counter-attack. They must show the lack of popular support that Goebbels claimed, and they must thwart the consolidation of such support in order to destabilize the regime.[62] Fraenkel made four points about the most effective form for illegal work.

Fraenkel first argued that illegal work only made sense if it was visible: "Invisible illegal work is ineffective illegal work." To have political significance, the work must be visible to both the Gestapo and the populace. Socialists must keep the petty bourgeoisie from feeling "comfortable [*gemütlich*] in the German fatherland," and the worker from "finding a place where … he can feel at home [*heimisch*]." Illegal work must stir anxiety in the ruling classes and a consciousness of being "spiritually homeless" among workers. Then popular unease would infect the Gestapo with "a feeling of insecurity." Knowing that the populace was seething, the Gestapo would fear conspiracies among a wider array of groups and repress them with a hardened state of siege. In short, visible illegal work would drive more groups, and people, into opposition.[63]

Second, Fraenkel argued that "illegal socialist work must also be visible to the individual socialists." After socialism's shameful collapse in Germany in 1933, visible illegal work could rebuild its moral authority and political power. Anyone knew that "who has pressed a flyer into the hand of a comrade, who saw the flash in his eyes as he, who until then had felt forsaken, said with hardly contained excitement, 'Yes, there is still such a thing!'" By renewing the psychological strength of individual Social Democrats, visible illegal work can restore the moral authority needed for "a rebirth, or better put, a new birth," of German socialism's political power.[64]

Third, illegal socialist work must strike at the opponent's vulnerabilities. "At the moment," Fraenkel wrote, "the power apparatus of the state in Germany is unassailable." But the major weakness in Nazi rule was the leadership's self-deception about popular sentiments. Nazi leaders hindered their own grasp of those sentiments by suppressing free expression, and they could not fill in the blanks with Gestapo spying. Illegal work should target "the line of communication between populace and government." By doing so, illegal work would help destroy the last vestiges of free expression and also disorient the ruling powers and keep them from "feeling the pulse of the populace."[65] Thus, Fraenkel wanted to make a virtue out of necessity. He wanted to accomplish what was possible in the short run, namely, to increase rather than decrease repression; and watch increased repression deceive the Nazis into believing that the regime had popular support, on the one hand, and take them off guard when popular dissatisfaction shook the regime's foundations, on the other. Ultimately, "the proud edifice of the Third Reich is built on a volcano."[66]

Finally, while illegal work should be visible, resisters themselves would remain invisible. The point was neither action for action's sake nor unnecessary risk-taking. With that precaution, resisters needed to engage in their illegal work then, in late 1935. They had to put their freedom and their lives on the line, to be sure, and they had to be ready "to fall into the hands of the bloodhounds of the Third Reich." But the immediate need for visible illegal work was too great to allow a select few to save themselves for some future time when they might actually build a socialist society. He wrote: "Whoever is too good to endanger himself in the time of white terror is not good enough to join us in the moment of socialist rebuilding."[67] On this point, Fraenkel was emphatic. If imprisoned or murdered, the illegal worker inspires other resisters. Fraenkel concluded:

> Yes, we have become "criminals." ... If we were not empowered by our illegal activity, I fear that we too would sink into the smog that oppresses Germany. Because we work illegally, we keep ourselves fresh. ...
>
> That is the point of illegal socialist work in the Third Reich: to infuse the workers with strength, the waverers with trust, the sufferers with hope and the rulers with fear. Does illegal work have a point? What would Germany be without illegal work?[68]

In "The Point of Illegal Work," Fraenkel set forth a theory of political action. He argued how a socialist commitment to the rule of law could attack Nazi power. For one thing, socialist resisters should implement liberal values as best they can. They should smuggle their socialist views into the open and flaunt them in public. For another thing, resisters should push the Nazi state to follow its own repression to its logical conclusion. They should force the Nazi state to reject liberal values in full, such as freedom of expression, and then watch it suffer the consequences of misreading popular opinion. In exposing the Nazi state's anxiety about popular opinion, socialist resisters could drive a wedge between Hitler and the populace, assaulting the leadership principle at the heart of the Nazi theory of the state. Increased repression would trigger increased resistance. Finally, Fraenkel rejected a politics of martyrdom. Resisters should dodge exposure but, when exposed, turn any resulting arrests and executions to good use.[69]

In setting forth his socialist commitment to the rule of law, Fraenkel differed from many Jewish lawyers. He refused to cast away principle in the teeth of Nazi terror. Unlike Jewish front-line soldiers, he did not ask the Nazi state to spare some jobs because of prior military service. Unlike Max Hachenburg, he did not suggest cutting a slightly better deal. If stuck on the behemoth—as his colleague Franz Neumann later called the Nazi state—Fraenkel still urged fighting for principle, even if furtively striking blows from somewhere behind the eyes.

Fraenkel set forth not just a theory but also a practical philosophy for opposing tyranny. Others recoiled before two barriers that Fraenkel defied, namely mortality and professionalism. First, Fraenkel insisted that resistance requires a willingness to die for the cause. Mortal fear could not excuse biding one's time interminably. Socialists must act now, not wait. This insistence broke the paralysis that beleaguered so many Jewish lawyers. On the one hand, it implicitly rejected the stance of those who hoped to wait out the Nazi regime, to muddle through until the scourge passed. On the other hand, it offered solidarity, the affinity among the like-minded arising from political action that might ease the economic and social isolation afflicting so many Jewish lawyers. After World War II, Fraenkel rarely referred back to his life under Nazi rule. But on one occasion, when he did, he stressed the life-line that fellow resisters had provided in small gatherings, long walks and intense talks—contacts that "spared us suffocating spiritually and emotionally from the loneliness of the inner emigration."[70] For Fraenkel in the mid-1930s, death, if the result of resistance, would not be a lonely act of despair, as in Alsberg's suicide, but an unavoidable sacrifice, an inspiration to other resisters.

The second barrier that Fraenkel defied was professionalism. He could think more freely than his professional cohort because lawyering was his craft, not his identity. Other Jewish lawyers clung to their profession desperately, as the embodiment of who they were. They were consumed by their pride in their learning, their need for their livelihood, and the injustice of their victimization. They let go only when they had to—when they lost their law licenses or finally saw no choice but to emigrate. But Fraenkel held his professional identity at a distance. He could do so because he maintained an identity as a socialist as well as a lawyer, because he was young enough that his identity as a lawyer had not yet consumed his being, and because he had no children to support. His professional identity did not curb his thinking. He was hardly unique in accusing Nazism of turning legal values upside down, but he stood out as a lawyer who argued that the forum for advancing justice had shifted from the courts to illegal work. A man clinging to his professional status as a lawyer would not have labeled himself, as he did, a criminal, and would not have advocated, as he did, the commission of crimes, even political crimes as defined by a tyranny.

In short, Hugo Sinzheimer and Ernst Fraenkel were two Jewish lawyers who stuck to their belief in the rule of law and defied Nazi discrimination, degradation, and oppression.

Destruction: The Elimination of Jewish Lawyers in 1938

At approximately midnight of 4–5 February 1938, in a latrine in the Jewish barracks at the Dachau concentration camp, Hans Litten hanged himself. He had earlier decided that he could not endure more than five years in the camps. After the SS had murdered a fellow inmate and seemed poised once again to brutally interrogate Litten, he could not go on. His funeral at a crematorium in Munich was a small affair, attended only by his mother and one of her friends. His mother insisted that the organist play a passage from Bach's *St. Matthew's Passion* that she had recently discussed with her son, a passage that she doubtless thought resonated with his isolation and death, the passage after Jesus was taken prisoner before his crucifixion and the Evangelist declared, "Then all his disciples forsook him and fled."[71]

His mother had not forsaken Litten in the five years that she had fought to save his life. When he died, she cast his death in the mold of Christian martyrdom—not of Homeric heroism, not of the unfulfilled hopes of a promising bourgeois professional, and not of a Jewish scapegoat. By February 1938, Litten saw little future for himself anyway, certainly not in law or politics. As early as 1934, he had told a fellow inmate, Kurt Hiller, that he was politically spent and that "even if he should one day recover his liberty he would no longer be a very useful combatant." That same year Ernst Fraenkel had written his article, "The Point of Illegal Work," and declared that the underground must craft the fate of Nazi prisoners into myths and legends. As news of Litten's death leaked out, émigrés wrote obituaries recounting events, painting the character, and formulating the lessons. Litten's mother, after fleeing Nazi Germany, wrote a memoir telling the tale of trying to save her son. When published in 1940, it stirred the Allied war effort more than the anti-Nazi underground.[72]

Litten did not last five years in concentration camps, and Jewish lawyers could not last much longer in Nazi Germany. In 1938, the Nazi regime finally resolved its problem with Jewish lawyers. The number of Jewish lawyers had remained substantial, with only a modest drop in the two years between 1936 and 1938. In early 1936, Germany had 2,552 Jewish lawyers out of a total of 18,854, just over 13 percent. In early 1938, Germany had 1,753 Jewish lawyers out of 17,360, approximately 10 percent. In Berlin, the proportion of Jewish lawyers had declined from 34 percent in early 1936 to 28 percent in early 1938.[73]

The fragile solution from 1933, the Law on the Admission to the Bar, shattered on the Nazi annexation of Austria in March 1938. Vienna, the symbol of Jewish cosmopolitanism and racial mixing, had a higher proportion of Jewish lawyers than Berlin had ever had: almost 80 percent and, even after disbarring Jews pursuant to the Law on the Admission to the Bar, more than 65 percent still remained. With the rush of events, Jewish lawyers in Germany had a sense of foreboding. In a letter of 30 June 1938, to the Reich Ministry of Justice, Julius Fliess, an unofficial spokesman for Jewish lawyers, pressed his best argument. It was the same argument as five years earlier, on behalf of Jewish war veteran lawyers: the legal situation created by the 1933 Law on the Admission to the Bar should continue because most remaining Jewish lawyers were veterans who had served the fatherland. The argument had lost its punch. It made less strategic sense, with Hindenburg long since dead; it had less popular appeal, in light of Germany's remilitarization without Jewish participation; and it even stirred less Jewish indignation, after five years of economic burdens and demoralization.[74]

The process of eliminating Jewish lawyers combined Nazi law and lawlessness. On 27 September 1938, Hitler signed a decree that disbarred all Jewish lawyers as of 30 November 1938.[75] In between those two dates, the Nazi regime staged its infamous pogrom of 9–10 November, the so-called *Kristallnacht* or "Night of Broken Glass," when Nazis burned synagogues, ransacked Jewish businesses and homes, murdered one hundred or so Jews, and rounded up tens of thousands of Jewish men, including lawyers.

For dealing with the legal problems of Jews—emigration, property transfers, lawsuits, criminal prosecutions—the Nazis created a new position, that of Jewish *Konsulent,* or legal advisor. As of 1 December 1938, a tiny, restricted number of Jewish legal advisors—set at 172, or 10 percent of the remaining Jewish lawyers—could represent the interests of Jews.[76] But Jewish lawyers did not rush to become legal advisors in the fall of 1938 the way they had lined up for readmission to the bar in the spring of 1933. Julius Meyer, a lawyer in Frankfurt, wrote: "Several colleagues have declined ... to apply [for permission to become a legal advisor]; they want to emigrate in any case, and they don't want to roam the courts as inferior 'protected Jews' who are pitied and scorned." The few who became legal advisors were scattered remnants: some older veterans, too tired to leave Germany; some breadwinners, still grasping for economic survival, even if they hoped to emigrate; some dyed-in-the-wool moralists, chronically afflicted with a Prussian sense of duty; some community-minded souls, committed to helping fellow Jews. Probably indulging a desperate if foolhardy opportunism, one advisor reportedly acted as a Gestapo informer.[77]

In conjuring up the position of Jewish legal advisor, the Nazis separated Jews from other German lawyers. In their rhetoric about legal advisors, the Nazis insulted Jews. In their exercise of power, the Nazis isolated Jews further. But the Nazis failed to transform their theory of lawyering into a theory that made sense. In 1936, Nazi jurists had begun referring to lawyers as guardians of the law and requiring them to swear to upholding Nazism. Erwin Noack, the Vice-President of the Reich Bar Association (*Reichsrechtsanwaltskammer*), set forth the theory of Jewish legal advisors:

> The Jewish legal advisor may not under any circumstances be addressed as guardian of the law or even as a lawyer-like actor. He is nothing but a representative of the interests of a Jewish party. Only judges and lawyers can protect justice as officers of the court.[78]

Measured by their actual function rather than Nazi theory, Jewish legal advisors were lawyers, even if they had a limited client base. To the extent that German lawyers stopped performing those functions, i.e., representing the interests of their clients, they were the ones who ceased acting like lawyers. One flagrant example was a defense attorney who, in representing a defendant accused of conspiring to assassinate Hitler on 20 July 1944, told the People's Court that his client's acts horrified him. Then he demanded the death penalty. Some Nazis understood the implications of their own theory and opined that in the Nazi state, lawyers were no longer necessary. Even Hans Frank, who was devoting his career to developing Nazi law, wrote in his statement prepared for the 1936 conference "Jewry in Jurisprudence" that the "ethical training" of the people would render "criminal procedure more and more superfluous." However much they tried, however deeply they wished, the Nazis could not develop a theory that made any sense in the real world of disputes and conflicts, a theory where lawyers did not represent the individual interests of their clients.[79]

Hitler never held the law in high esteem, and theoretical subtlety was never the Nazis' strong suit. Hitler and his henchmen cut down law with power. A decree of 1 July 1943 handed over the prosecution of Jews from the administration of justice to the police,[80] and Jewish legal advisors essentially lost their raison d'être. By then, the Nazi state had already deported the vast majority of Jews still present in Germany at the outbreak of war to the east and murdered them. Power unchecked by law showed its prowess at destruction.

By the war's end, Jewish lawyers such as Max Alsberg and Hans Litten had long since committed suicide. Hugo Sinzheimer survived in hiding in Holland, only to die from exhaustion in 1945. Max Hachenburg, the quintessential nineteenth-century German lawyer, left Germany in June 1939, lived in England during the war, and finally moved to Berkeley, California, where he died in 1951 at the ripe old age of ninety-one. Both Max Hirschberg and Ernst Fraenkel lived well into the postwar era, Hirschberg in New York, Fraenkel in Berlin. Hirschberg would still write about fairness in criminal justice and Fraenkel about pluralistic democracy, both men working to secure the rule of law in pluralistic democracies.

Notes

1. For their helpful and insightful comments on an earlier draft of this article, I thank Professor Renate Bridenthal; my wife, Professor Marion Kaplan; and the anonymous reader for the press. All translations are my own unless otherwise indicated.

2. Curt Riess, *Der Mann in der Schwarzen Robe: Das Leben des Strafverteidigers Max Alsberg* (Hamburg, 1965), 324–28, 332.
3. Anecdote related to the author by Werner Angress.
4. Gerhard Junger, "Max Alsberg (1877–1933): Verteidigung als ethische Mission," in Kritische Justiz, ed., *Streitbare Juristen* (Baden-Baden, 1988), 141–152; Tillmann Krach, "Max Alsberg (1877–1933): Der Kritizismus des Verteidigers als schöpferisches Prinzip der Wahrheitsfindung," in *Deutsche Juristen jüdischer Herkunft*, eds. Helmut Heinrichs, et. al., (Munich, 1993), 655–65; Riess, *Der Mann in der Schwarzen Robe*, 334–35.
5. Kenneth F. Ledford, "Lawyers, Liberalism, and Procedure: The German Imperial Justice Laws of 1877-79," *Central European History* 26 (1993): 165–93.
6. Angelika Königseder, *Recht und nationalsozialistische Herrschaft: Berliner Anwälte, 1933–1945. Ein Forschungsprojekt des Berliner Anwaltsvereins* (Bonn, 2001), 114–15; Konrad H. Jarausch, "Jewish Lawyers in Germany, 1848–1938: The Disintegration of a Profession," *Leo Baeck Institute Year Book* 36 (1991): 173–77 (for Berlin and Breslau); Tillmann Krach, *Jüdische Rechtsanwälte in Preussen: Über die Bedeutung der freien Advokatur und ihre Zerstörung durch den Nationalsozialismus* (München, 1991), 414–16 (for the Prussian numbers).
7. Benjamin Carter Hett, *Crossing Hitler: The Man Who Put the Nazis on the Witness Stand* (Oxford, 2008), 125.
8. *Reichsgesetzblatt* (RGBl) 1933, I, 83; Ernst Fraenkel, *Der Doppelstaat*, 2nd ed., ed. Alexander von Brünneck, (Hamburg, 2001), 55–58.
9. Irmgard Litten, *Eine Mutter kämpft gegen Hitler* (Rudolstadt, 1985), 17; Simone Ladwig-Winters, *Anwalt ohne Recht: Das Schicksale jüdischer Rechtsanwälte in Berlin nach 1933* (Berlin, 1998), 28.
10. Litten, *Eine Mutter kämpft gegen Hitler*, 153.
11. Douglas G. Morris, *Justice Imperiled: The Anti-Nazi Lawyer Max Hirschberg in Weimar Germany* (Ann Arbor, 2005), 303–04.
12. Litten, *Eine Mutter Kämpft gegen Hitler*, 19.
13. Wolfgang Benz, "Von der Entrechtung zur Verfolgung und Vernichtung: Jüdische Juristen unter dem nationalsozialistischen Regime," in Heinrichs, *Deutsche Juristen*, 813–52, here 814; Weber, Reinhard, *Das Schicksal der jüdischen Rechtsanwälte in Bayern nach 1933* (Munich, 2006), 50; "Ich werde mich nie mehr bei der Polizei beschweren—I will never again complain to the Police," www1.yadvashem.org/yv/en/exhibitions/our_collections/.../index.asp, last accessed Dec. 27, 2011.
14. Benz, "Von der Entrechtung zur Verfolgung," 815.
15. Ibid., 814-15; Krach, *Jüdische Rechtsanwälte*, 172–73.
16. Benz, "Von der Entrechtung zur Verfolgung," 817–18; Krach, *Jüdische Rechtsanwälte*, 180–83 (quotation on 183).
17. Benz, "Von der Entrechtung zur Verfolgung," 820–21; Krach, *Jüdische Rechtsanwälte*, 184–85.
18. Krach, *Jüdische Rechtsanwälte*, 241.
19. Kurt-Jacob Ball-Kaduri, *Das Leben der Juden in Deutschland im Jahre 1933: Ein Zeitbericht* (Frankfurt, 1963), 93; Benz, "Von der Entrechtung zur Verfolgung," 821.
20. RGBl 1933 I, 175 (Law on the Restoration of the Professional Civil Service); RGBl 1933 I, 188 (Law of the Admission to the Bar); see also Krach, *Jüdische Rechtsan-*

wälte, 422 for reprint of the latter; Benz, "Von der Entrechtung zur Verfolgung," 823–25; Saul Friedländer, *Nazi Germany and the Jews: Volume I: The Years of Persecution* (New York, 1997), 27–28. The Nuremberg Laws of 15 September 1935 were the "Reichsbürgergesetz," and the "Gesetz zum Schutz des deutschen Blutes und der deutschen Ehre," RGBl 1935 I, 1146.

21. Krach, *Jüdische Rechtsanwälte,* 207–08.
22. Kenneth C. H. Willig, "The Bar in the Third Reich," *The American Journal of Legal History* 20 (1976), 1–14, here 4.
23. Eberhard Haas and Eugen Ewig, "Max O. Friedlaender (1873–1956): Wegbereiter und Vordenker des Anwaltsrechts," in Kritische Justiz, ed., *Streitbare Juristen,* 555–69, 563–65; Krach, *Jüdische Rechtsanwälte,* 60–66; Kenneth F. Ledford, "German Lawyers and the State in the Weimar Republic," *Law and History Review* 13 (1995): 317–49, 342–46.
24. Friedländer, *Nazi Germany and the Jews,* 29 (for Germany); Krach, *Jüdische Rechtsanwälte,* 246, 418 (for Prussia); Ladwig-Winters, *Anwalt ohne Recht,* 8, 43 (for Berlin); Königseder, *Recht und nationalsozialistische Herrschaft,* 16, 114–15 (for percentage reduction in Berlin).
25. Krach, *Jüdische Rechtsanwälte,* 210; Ladwig-Winters, *Anwalt ohne Recht,* 41–42.
26. Königseder, *Recht und nationalsozialistische Herrschaft,* 114.
27. Ibid.; Krach, *Jüdische Rechtsanwälte,* 200–02; Ladwig-Winters, *Anwalt ohne Recht,* 42.
28. Morris, *Justice Imperiled,* 300, 303, 320 (with quotation).
29. Horst Göppinger, *Juristen jüdischer Abstammung im "Dritten Reich": Entrechtung und Verfolgung* (Munich, 1990), 87–90; Ladwig-Winters, *Anwalt ohne Recht,* 8, 10, 37–9, 43 (quotation at 38); Morris, *Justice Imperiled,* 320.
30. Ball-Kaduri, *Das Leben der Juden in Deutschland,* 60 (quotation); Krach, *Jüdische Rechtsanwälte,* 166–67; Ladwig-Winters, *Anwalt ohne Recht,* 29, 34.
31. Riess, *Der Mann in der Schwarzen Robe,* 331–32.
32. Morris, *Justice Imperiled,* 300.
33. Ibid., 311–12.
34. Ladwig-Winters, *Anwalt ohne Recht,* 42.
35. Benz, "Von der Entrechtung zur Verfolgung," 824–25; Krach, *Jüdische Rechtsanwälte,* 204 (quotation), 205; Ladwig-Winters, *Anwalt ohne Recht,* 44–45.
36. Ball-Kaduri, *Das Leben der Juden in Deutschland,* 94 (first two quotations); Krach, *Jüdische Rechtsanwälte,* 263–64 (third quotation); Ladwig-Winters, *Anwalt ohne Recht,* 45–47 (on women).
37. Avraham Barkai, *"Wehr Dich!": Der Centralverein deutscher Staatsbürger jüdischen Glaubens, 1893–1938* (Munich, 2002), 138–39, 288–90; Carl J. Rheins, "The Schwarzes Fähnlein, Jungenschaft, 1932–1934," *Leo Baeck Institute Year Book* 23 (1978): 173–97, 185–89; Carl J. Rheins, "The Verband nationaldeutscher Juden 1921-1933," *Leo Baeck Institute Year Book* 25 (1980): 243–268, especially 243–47, 246 fn. 24, 252–53, 260, 263, 266, 267 fn. 147; Robert Wistrich, *Who's Who in Nazi Germany* (New York, 1982), 216–17.
38. Ladwig-Winters, *Anwalt ohne Recht,* 38.
39. Max Hachenburg, "Juristische Rundschau," in *Deutsche Juristenzeitung* 38 (1 May 1933), 607–11, 608-610 (quotations); Jarausch, "Jewish Lawyers in Germany," 171; Krach, *Jüdische Rechtsanwälte,* 159, 284–85.

41. Benz, "Von der Entrechtung zur Verfolgung," 834–35; Krach, *Jüdische Rechtsanwälte*, 172, 177–80, 215–36, 264, 307, 307 note 2.
42. Ladwig-Winters, *Anwalt ohne Recht*, 49.
43. Ibid., 38.
44. Riess, *Der Mann in der Schwarzen Robe*, 324.
45. Ladwig-Winters, *Anwalt ohne Recht*, 51; Willig, "The Bar in the Third Reich," 8.
46. Friedlander, Henry, "German Law and German Crimes in the Nazi Era," in *The Holocaust's Ghost: Writing on Art, Politics, Law and Education*, eds F.C. Decoste and Bernard Schwartz, (Edmonton, 2000), 283–89, here 285.
47. Benz, "Von der Entrechtung zur Verfolgung," 838; Göppinger, *Juristen*, 77; Krach, *Jüdische Rechtsanwälte*, 384.
48. Königseder, *Recht und nationalsozialistische Herrschaft*, 114–15.
49. Göppinger, *Juristen*, 154; "Die deutsche Rechtswissenschaft im Kampf gegen den jüdischen Geist," in *Das Judentum in der Rechtswissenschaft — Ansprachen, Vorträge und Ergebnisse der Tagung der Reichsgruppe Hochschullehrer des NSRB am 3. und 4. Oktober 1936* (Berlin, 1936–38), Nr. 1, p. 5. While the literature on Carl Schmitt is immense, important interpretations available in English include the following: Joseph W. Bendersky, *Carl Schmitt, Theorist for the Reich* (Princeton, 1983); Raphael Gross, *Carl Schmitt and the Jews: The "Jewish Question," the Holocaust, and German Legal Theory*, transl. Joel Golb (Madison, 2007); Jan-Werner Müller, *A Dangerous Mind: Carl Schmitt in Postwar European Thought* (New Haven, 2003); George Schwab, *The Challenge of the Exception: An Introduction to the Political Ideas of Carl Schmitt between 1921 and 1936* (New York, 1989).
50. "Die deutsche Rechtswissenschaft," in *Das Judentum in der Rechtswissenschaft* (1936/1937), Nr. 1, at 7, 8 (first quotation), 10 (second quotation).
51. Ibid., 15.
52. Karl Siegert, "Das Judentum im Strafverfahrensrecht," in *Das Judentum in der Rechtswissenschaft*, Nr. 4, 32.
53. Ibid., 34 (first quotation); 35 (second quotation); 33 (third quotation); 36 (fourth quotation).
54. Rainer Erd, "Hugo Sinzheimer (1875–1945): Aufruf zur Befreiung des Menschen," in *Kritische Justiz, Streitbare Juristen*, 282–294, 292.
55. Hugo Sinzheimer, *Jüdische Klassiker der deutschen Rechtswissenschaft* (Amsterdam, 1938), 9, 13, 15 (first quotation), 16 (second quotation), 17.
56. Ibid., 293 (first quotation), 295 (second quotation); 301.
57. Ibid., 299 (quotation), 300–01.
58. Ernst Fraenkel, "Vorwort zur deutschen Ausgabe (1974)," in Fraenkel, *Der Doppelstaat*, 41.
59. Krach, *Jüdische Rechtsanwälte*, 351–53.
60. Alexander von Brünneck, "Vorwort zu diesem Band," in Ernst Fraenkel, *Gesammelte Schriften: Band 2—Nationalsozialismus und Widerstand*, eds. Alexander von Brünneck, Hubertus Buchstein, Gerhard Göhler (Baden-Baden, 1999), 22.
61. Ernst Fraenkel, "Der Sinn illegaler Arbeit" (1935), in Fraenkel, *Gesammelte Schriften: Band 2*, 491–97, 49.
63. Ibid., 493 (first quotation, emphasis in original); 493 (second quotation); 494 (third quotation); 494 (fourth quotation); 493 (fifth quotation).

64. Ibid., 495 (first quotation, emphasis in original), 495 (second quotation), 495 (second quotation).
65. Ibid., 495 (first quotation), 495–96 (second quotation), 496 (third quotation).
66. Ibid., 493.
67. Ibid., 496 (first quotation), 496–97 (second quotation).
68. Ibid., 497.
69. Ibid., 493–97.
70. Fraenkel, "Vorwort," in Fraenkel, *Der Doppelstaat,* 43 (quotation), 43–45; Ernst Fraenkel, "Erklärungen von Ernst Fraenkel über die Tätigkeit von Gegnern des Regimes 1933 bis 1938" (1948, 1953, 1956), in Fraenkel, *Gesammelte Schriften: Band 2,* 622–27.
71. Knut Bergbauer, Sabine Fröhlich and Stefanie Schüler-Springorum, *Denkmalsfigur: Biographische Annäherung an Hans Litten, 1903–1938* (Göttingen, 2008), 273, 276, 289, 292–96; Hett, *Crossing Hitler,* 220–22, 224, 237, 240–43; Litten, *Eine Mutter kämpft gegen Hitler,* 238–39.
72. Bergbauer, *Denkmalsfigur,* 296–99, 315–18; Fraenkel, "Der Sinn illegaler Arbeit," in Fraenkel, *Gesammelte Schriften: Band 2,* 495, 497; Hett, *Crossing Hitler,* 187, 244–45, 249.
73. Königseder, *Recht und nationalsozialistische Herrschaft,* 114–15, 118.
74. Ibid., 116–117; Krach, *Jüdische Rechtsanwälte,* 388, 390.
76. RGBl. 1938 I, 1403, 1439; Göppinger, *Juristen,* 94–97; Königseder, *Recht und nationalsozialistische Herrschaft,* 116–18; Krach, *Jüdische Rechtsanwälte,* 386–95; Ladwig-Winters, *Anwalt ohne Recht,* 55, 58.
77. Benz, "Von der Entrechtung zur Verfolgung," 845 (quotation); Ladwig-Winters, *Anwalt ohne Recht,* 58–60.
78. Benz, "Von der Entrechtung zur Verfolgung," 839 (quotation); Ladwig-Winters, *Anwalt ohne Recht,* 54.
79. "Die deutsche Rechtswissenschaft," in *Das Judentum in der Rechtswissenschaft,* Nr. 1, at 12 (quotation); Krach, *Jüdische Rechtsanwälte,* 398, 400; Ladwig-Winters, *Anwalt ohne Recht,* 55; Müller, 64.
80. RGBl 1943 I, 372; see also Benz, "Von der Entrechtung zur Verfolgung," 848.

Defendants at the Nuremberg "Justice Case," 1947. Front row (left to right): Franz Schlegelberger, Curt Rothenberger (standing), and Ernst Lautz. Back row (left to right): Rudolf Oeschey and Josef Altstötter
Source: U.S. Army, Office of the Chief Counsel for War Crimes

Chapter 6

EVADING RESPONSIBILITY FOR CRIMES AGAINST HUMANITY

Murderous Lawyers at Nuremberg

Harry Reicher

THE TRIBUNAL IN THE JUSTICE CASE[1] at Nuremberg summed it up very powerfully, "The dagger of the assassin was concealed beneath the robe of the jurist."[2] With these words, said in April 1949, the Tribunal delivered a somber and sobering lesson: Lawyers are capable of committing hideous crimes, extending even to mass murder, and even while ostensibly carrying out their "normal" functions as lawyers.[3]

After the principal trial at Nuremberg, which concluded on 1 October 1946, the United States, acting under international law and by agreement with the other allied victors in the Second World War, conducted a series of twelve trials in the U.S. zone of occupation. These trials brought leading figures in the Nazi political and military establishments, who were both alive and in captivity, to the bar of justice. One of these subsidiary trials—known colloquially as the Justice Case—had sixteen defendants, judges, prosecutors, and Ministry of Justice officials during the Nazi era. They were charged with having perverted Germany's legal system and converting it into an instrument of brutality and terror. In considering how a legal system can be distorted beyond recognition, the tribunal in the Justice Case taught important lessons for constitutional democracies in the post-Holocaust era. Intimately bound up with this is the destruction of legal ethics by countless legal practitioners, with consequent lessons for lawyers practicing their profession in the post-Nazi era.

In light of the Tribunals' particularly harsh characterization of the role of lawyers in Nazi Germany, one of the interesting questions which arises is, how did the lawyers on trial at Nuremberg defend themselves? What legal rationalizations, justifications, or excuses did they offer in seeking to exculpate themselves? In addressing these issues, this chapter focuses on a central line of defense proffered by the defendants: They were compelled by law, either as expressed in the form of requirements set out in laws that were promulgated, or otherwise, to do what they did. It weaves this defense into the *Führerprinzip*—the leader principle—a cornerstone of the methodology by which the Nazi legal system functioned. Its essence was the aggregation of all governmental power—legislative, executive, and judicial—in very few sets of hands, and ultimately in one set of hands, namely those of the Führer himself. It was the absolute antithesis of United States-style constitutional separation of powers, with its built-in system of checks and balances. Under the *Führerprinzip*, Hitler was, at once, the chief executive, the chief legislator, and the chief justice.

The thesis presented here is that the principal line of argument developed by the defendants was in fact implicit in the *Führerprinzip*, such that the defense was actually a natural corollary or outgrowth of it. Illuminating the defense's reasoning in this way serves to underscore lessons about individual responsibility, particularly as articulated by the Nuremberg Tribunals.

The Justice Case[4]

After the conclusion of the first trial, which ended in October 1946, the United States conducted its series of twelve trials roughly by profession,[5] and the Justice Case commenced on 17 February 1947, some four-and-a-half months after the principal trial ended. Of the sixteen defendants, four were judges, six were prosecutors, and nine were officials of the Ministry of Justice.[6]

The main charge against them, for present purposes, was crimes against humanity.[7] In the context of lawyers—particularly those ostensibly practicing their profession—the charge of crimes against humanity was deeply incongruous. As a criminal offense, it was articulated for the first time in the principal trial, which had commenced some two-and-a-half years earlier in November 1945[8] and was then the most egregious crime in the international legal lexicon.[9] Crimes against humanity are normally associated with mass atrocities, such as murder, along with slave labor, torture, and inhumane treatment. In the context of the Holocaust, they evoke, in the public mind, images of concentration camps and death camps; of gas ovens and crematoria; of the *Einsatzgruppen* (the mobile killing squads that roamed the Soviet Union, shooting Jews into mass graves which they themselves had been forced to dig); of slave labor; and of torture on a large scale. Crimes against humanity are not naturally associated with practice of the legal profession.

When we—in the Anglo-American—world think of lawyers, we think, first and foremost, of judges, wearing judicial robes, sitting in detached objectivity, listening carefully and impartially to the evidence, and deciding cases fairly and in strict accordance with the admissible evidence and a reasonable interpretation of the applicable law. In criminal cases, we think of them bending over backwards to be fair to defendants, ensuring that no one is convicted unless the case against them is proven beyond a reasonable doubt. In short, judges embody all that we associate with the term "justice." In Western systems of justice, we often view the role of prosecutors as not that of obtaining convictions at any cost, but as officers of the court whose duty is to inform the court fully and candidly, advise the defense fairly and fully what the case against it is, and furnish it with potentially exculpatory information.

Finally, we think of civil servants in the employ of ministries of justice as faithful administrators of the law, acting under a legal duty to act fairly and properly vis-à-vis the general population affected by the law and applying it impartially to every person. All of this leads directly into the central question: How can these three categories of lawyers commit crimes against humanity while pursuing their professional calling?

In fact, the net of legal culpability was cast very wide by Control Council Law No. 10,[10] which constituted the charter governing the Tribunal's jurisdiction. It brought within the purview of the Tribunal not only principals, but also anyone who was "an accessory to," who had "ordered or abetted," who "took a consenting part" in, or was "connected with plans" relating to acts which constituted crimes against humanity:[11] namely "murder, extermination, enslavement, deportation, imprisonment, torture, rape, or other inhumane acts…or persecutions on political, racial or religious grounds."[12]

The allegation was that the defendants had committed acts that resulted in atrocities, and that they had done so in their capacity as lawyers. To paraphrase the summary offered by Brigadier General Telford Taylor in his opening address for the prosecution, the essence of the charge was that the defendants perverted the legal system, emptying it of all content and meaning, and then used the remaining shell, or façade, to bring about atrocities.[13] "The charge, in brief," said the Tribunal, was "that of conscious participation in a nationwide government-organized system of cruelty and injustice, in violation of the laws of ... humanity, and perpetrated in the name of law by the authority of the Ministry of Justice, and through the instrumentality of the courts."[14] In a word: "judicial murder."[15]

The Markus Luftglass and Leo Katzenberger Cases

Two case studies serve to illustrate the sort of conduct considered by the Tribunal and which involved the defendants in the commission of crimes against humanity. Franz Schlegelberger was the senior-most bureaucrat in the Justice Ministry, and was Acting Minister of Justice in October 1941, when he played a central role in the tragic case of Markus Luftglass, an elderly Jew who was convicted on a charge of stealing a large quantity of eggs and sentenced to two-and-a-half years' imprisonment. A brief report of the case, appearing in a Berlin daily newspaper, was brought to the attention of Hitler himself, who expressed the view that the sentence was manifestly inadequate. Schlegelberger received a cold-blooded letter, telling him that "the Führer wishes Luftgas [sic][16] to be sentenced to death" and instructing him "urgently to instigate what is necessary."[17] Correspondence involving Schlegelberger, and passing among relevant departments, resulted in the final letter, signed by Schlegelberger himself, reporting that, "in accordance with the order of the Führer ... I have handed over to the Gestapo for the purpose of execution, the Jew Markus Luftglass."[18]

The correspondence was chilling in several respects: most importantly for present purposes, Hitler's deep, personal reach into the daily workings of the legal system. The Führer Principle as applied to a legal proceeding is the antithesis of U.S.-style separation of powers.

The case of Markus Luftglass was by no means an exception, and Schlegelberger was involved many times. Indeed, the Tribunal stressed the fact that he "supported the pretension of Hitler in his assumption of power to deal with life and death in disregard of even the pretense of judicial process ... Schlegelberger contributed to the destruction of judicial independence."[19] Moreover, he "personally ordered the murder of the Jew Luftglass on the request of Hitler, and assured the Führer he would, himself, take action if the Führer would inform him of other sentences which were disapproved."[20]

If it had happened once, as in the case of Markus Luftglass, that would have been murder; if it had happened twice, that would have been two counts of murder. But having happened enough times, it became a crime against humanity. This was how Franz Schlegelberger, the senior civil servant, carried out his "duties."

Oswald Rothaug, the Chief Judge of the Special Court at Nuremburg, presided over the infamous and tragic case of Leo Katzenberger in March 1942.[21] Rothaug resorted to blatant distortions and machinations in order to guarantee that the hapless Leo Katzenberger, who was charged with "racial pollution" arising out of an alleged relationship with an Aryan woman, was sent to his death on the basis of no credible evidence.

When Rothaug walked into the courtroom to preside over the case he had two clear items on his agenda: first, the Jew had to lose; and second, the Jew had to be eliminated, i.e., sentenced to death.[22] Each of these two objects encountered an obstacle that, in other circumstances, would have been insurmountable.

The goal of finding Katzenberger guilty faced the difficulty of absolutely no credible evidence against him. Such evidence as there was consisted of rumor, hearsay, gossip, and flimsy circumstantial material. Indicative of what was put before the court was the way one neighbor of Irene Seiler's put it, in 1938, when asked about the "affair" between Leo Katzenberger and Seiler: "Even the sparrows are singing it from the rooftops."[23] The only credible witness in the case was Seiler herself, who consistently and adamantly—and, indeed, heroically, considering her ultimate fate—insisted that there had been no affair between them. What had transpired, she said, were normal expressions of affection between herself and a man whom she regarded as exceptionally kind and as a father figure.[24] Her evidence unqualifiedly exonerated Katzenberger.

Rothaug overcame this obstacle by having Seiler charged with perjury, based on what she had testified in pre-trial interrogation. He, then, conducted the perjury trial of Seiler concurrently with the trial of Katzenberger for racial pollution, and first found Seiler guilty of perjury. This, of course, meant that he could discount her evidence entirely. If, in denying that there had been an affair between them, Seiler was lying, it followed that they had in fact had an affair. That still left the object of ensuring that the death sentence was imposed. Here, too, there was a difficulty in Rothaug's path. The crime of "racial pollution" arose under the Law for the Protection of German Blood and German Honor,[25] one of the infamous Nuremburg Laws enacted on 15 September 1935. But the penalty for that crime was set at a maximum of a prison term or hard labor;[26] nowhere did the law make provision for the death penalty. In this light, a curious aspect of the judgment in the Katzenberger case suddenly takes on a different color. Although the charge against Katzenberger was "racial pollution," the judgment elided into another crime, namely that of being a "public enemy." Remarkably, this first appeared, out of the blue, some two-thirds of the way into Rothaug's judgment.[27] When Katzenberger was ultimately sentenced, it was for that crime, in addition to the crime with which he had originally been charged. The difference, and therefore the importance of superimposing the additional crime even though the case had begun on a very different footing, lay in the fact that the penalty for being a public enemy was death. In this way, Rothaug manipulated the proceedings to send the hapless Leo Katzenberger to the guillotine for a crime he did not commit. And, for her trouble, Irene Seiler was sentenced to two years' imprisonment with hard labor for perjury.

So far as Rothaug was concerned, the Tribunal in the Justice Case determined that the execution of Leo Katzenberger "was in conformity with the policy of the Nazi State of persecution, torture, and extermination." It concluded that "the defendant Rothaug was the knowing and willing instrument in that program of persecution and extermination" and that "from the evidence it is clear that [his] court, in spite of the legal sophistries which he employed, was merely an instrument in the program of the leaders of the Nazi State of persecution and extermination."[28] Ultimately, Rothaug was driven by results.

These two case studies clearly expose the sort of people with whom we are dealing: leading professionals with highly-educated legal minds, who, as the Tribunal put it about Rothaug, became "sadistic and evil."[29] At the same time, the cases vividly illustrate the kind of behavior at issue. In particular, they make clear what the Tribunal had in mind when it talked about a system in which the outward, formal trappings of a legal system were retained—courtrooms, robes, and rituals. In a case such as Katzenberger's, there was even the respectable veneer of a formal judgment.[30] Underneath it all though, the system was rotten, perverse, and constituted a debasement of the very notion of law.

The Central Defense

As illustrated by the two case studies, people were actually murdered as a direct consequence of the actions of the defendants. In other cases, if not murdered, they suffered terribly cruel and inhuman treatment. Despite all this, not a single one of the defendants pleaded guilty to the charges.

Given that the sort of outrageous and lethal conduct described in the Markus Luftglass and Leo Katzenberger cases took place and was repeated time after time by so many of the defendants, the questions are: What defenses did the defendants raise? What justifications or rationalizations could they offer? What could people such as Franz Schlegelberger and Oswald Rothaug say to exculpate themselves, when clearly innocent people had been put to death as a direct result of their actions?

In the event, a broad range of justifications and rationalizations was put before the Tribunal in support of pleas of innocence. This chapter will focus on one of those, which is central—indeed, fundamental—not only to the Justice Case itself, but also, more generally, to the context of the Nazi regime and its underlying ideology. It may be summarized as follows: I was following the law, and the law required me to do it. The implication was: I was required to do what I did; I had no choice and, therefore, I had no responsibility.[31]

In studying the legal dimension to the Holocaust, the extent to which there was actually an internal logic to the legal system implemented by the Nazi regime is striking. There was an underlying ideology at the heart, driving the regime. The more clearly that is understood, the more the legal system that emerged from it makes sense. The central defense in the Justice Case fell into that framework.

That the Nazi regime was constructed on, and driven by, its egregious underlying racial ideology is well known. What is less well known is the methodology by which the regime, and the legal system in particular, operated. That may best be summarized in one word: *Führerprinzip*. The point was proclaimed in dramatic fashion by Rudolf Hess, Hitler's deputy, at the Nazi Party rally in Nuremberg in September 1934: "The party is Hitler. Hitler, however, is Germany, just as Germany is Hitler."[32] It sounded very much like demagogic hyperbole which, at one level, it was. However, at the same time, it was also a statement of a constitutional principle. That constitutional principle was summarized by an expert witness in the Justice Case, Professor Jahrreis of Cologne University, an authority on constitutional and international law:[33] The "entire power of the State in the German Reich is combined in the hand of that one man who quite arbitrarily can use that power to decide individual cases or to set new norms. It depends only on him."[34]

The *Führerprinzip* had dimensions other than that of constitutional principle. The dimension which is relevant here consisted in the quasi-Messianic, cult-like aura which enveloped Hitler. He was regarded by many and promoted—even "sold"—to the masses as a superhuman demi-god, having emerged and come to power as the savior who would bring about the resurrection of the Fatherland after its crucifixion in the Treaty of Versailles, which was widely perceived as inflicting a massive humiliation on Germany:[35] Hitler was to bring about the Fatherland's restoration to former glories.[36]

When these two dimensions were put together, an inexorable logic emerged in light of the underlying racial ideology. In this scheme of things, the Führer was not merely elected.[37] Rather, he rose mystically from among the *Volk*, personifying the racial ideal and the perfection which it represented. As a consequence, he knew or instinctively sensed what was needed to implement the racial ideology and what was good for the people. Seen in that light, it made eminent sense to regard anything and everything he said and did as correct, indeed perfect. It was a short step from there to giving everything he said and did the force of law.

In its application to the judiciary, the *Führerprinzip* was articulated in the infamous "Rothenberger Memorandum" of 31 March 1942,[38] written by Curt Rothenberger,[39] a lower court judge who aspired to the position of State Secretary of the Ministry of Justice, the civil service position just under the minister himself. Rothenberger was acutely conscious that, in order to realize his ambition, he had to tell Hitler what Hitler wanted to hear and ensure that the message reached Hitler's ears. He therefore composed a Memorandum, ostensibly on the subject of "judicial reform."[40] The Memorandum, to which Rothenberger ultimately attributed his appointment as State Secretary,[41] contained three statements which fairly leaped out of the page, and which constituted a neat summary of the Führer Principle, as applied to the judiciary:

1.) "Law must serve the political leadership."[42]
2.) "The Führer is the supreme judge; theoretically, the authority to pass judgment is only his."
3.) "A judge who is in a direct relation of fealty to the Führer must judge like the Führer."

The message could not have been clearer: There was no such thing as judicial independence;[43] the role of judges was no more than execution of the political will, specifically, to judge as the Führer would want them to judge. Each of these statements will now be examined, in turn.

1.) "Law must serve the political leadership." This was perfectly consistent with the underlying ideology. In his major work, *The Myth of the Twentieth Century: An Evaluation of the Spiritual-Intellectual Confrontations of Our Age,* published in 1930, Alfred Rosenberg, an intellectual guru of the Nazi movement, laid out the Nazi theory of law in a section entitled, "Nordic-German Law."[44] Rosenberg scoffed at the notion of "independence of law," accusing those who advocated the concept of "overlook[ing] that this so-called freedom is without relation to a shaping center and is to be held responsible for the present condition of lawlessness."[45] Simply put, law had to be molded by, and subservient to, an outside force—a "shaping center," as he put it.

Furthermore, "law and politics represent only two different expressions of the same will which stands in the service of our highest racial value."[46] The judge's "first duty," accordingly, was not to uphold the Constitution or apply the law, let alone to mete out justice. Rather, it was "to protect the *Volk* honor through his pronouncements from every attack."[47] The underlying racial ideology, therefore, was the "shaping center."

The courts were thus anchored in politics, specifically matters of race, and existed to implement the racial ideology. The idea was graphically illustrated by scenes of judges entering courtrooms and immediately throwing the "Heil Hitler" salute before assuming their seats on the bench.[48] In this way, they signaled that this was not a system of government under law, but actually the opposite. Indeed, the judges' oath of allegiance was not directed to upholding the Constitution or any abstract notions of justice. Rather, allegiance was sworn to the Führer himself.[49]

2.) "The Führer is the supreme judge; theoretically, the authority to pass judgment is only his." The Markus Luftglass case vividly illustrated the point. Hitler, in his capacity as "the supreme judge," had no hesitation whatsoever in "pass[ing] judgment" in the case after it had been decided by a court and certainly without having bothered to consider the evidence. We can break down Hitler's actions in the case into their component elements, and apply a traditional lawyer's analysis: Hitler, in his capacity as Chief Justice, and therefore the final appellate authority, initiated an appeal *sua sponte;*[50] the appeal was to himself; he alone decided the appeal, upholding it and overturning the sentence below; he handed down judgment, substituting his own sentence, and then gave the order that his substituted sentence be carried out. That was the end of the matter. He, being the only one with "authority to pass judgment," had the last word; there was no appeal from his decision, regardless of how it was attained.)

3.) "A judge ... must judge like the Führer." This may be viewed from two perspectives, approach and substance. An excellent framework for understanding the approach was established by Ernst Fraenkel in his seminal 1941 work, *The Dual State*,[51] in which he painted a picture of judicial systems operating side by side in Nazi Germany, the "prerogative state" and the "normative state."[52] To Fraenkel, a Jew who practiced law in Germany until 1938 before escaping to the United States, the latter term implied a normal system that operated according to normal principles of law and procedure, as one would expect in any civilized society.[53] It applied when no issues of a political—especially, racial—nature were involved.[54] More to the point for present purposes, in circumstances where political or racial issues were involved, the prerogative state ruled, meaning, as Fraenkel defined it, "that governmental system which exercises unlimited arbitrariness and violence unchecked by any legal guarantees."[55]

The approach denoted by "prerogative state" was powerfully illustrated, albeit in extreme form, by the performance of Roland Freisler[56] in presiding over the trial of the plotters who attempted to assassinate Hitler on 20 July 1944. Freisler, who was described by William Shirer, in his widely read book, *The Rise and Fall of the Third Reich: A History of Nazi Germany*, as a "vile, vituperative maniac,"[57] was recorded for posterity in archival film footage, hysterically screaming abuse at defendants. It was a decidedly unjudicial and injudicious performance, but it brought to life Ernst Fraenkel's phrase, "unlimited arbitrariness and violence" in what today would be called ugly and brutal verbal abuse. More than that, it dropped all pretenses of judicial objectivity and impartiality; the court became a party to the proceedings, and in fact became the accusatory party. It was a ruthless performance, and therefore, in a political case, an instance of judging like the Führer, in terms of the approach it represented. Put another way, it converted the extreme callousness which Hitler displayed in the Markus Luftglass case into a method of judging in court. By the demeanor of judging, the courtroom was transformed into something alien.

At the level of substance, the goal of judging like the Führer was represented by Oswald Rothaug in the Katzenberger case. Consistent with the judicial function, as enunciated by Curt Rothenberger, Rothaug had determined the result before he entered the courtroom to preside over the case,[58] just as the Führer would have done. And, indeed, as the Führer did in fact do, for instance, before the commencement of the trial of the plotters who attempted to assassinate him on 20 July 1944, when he fumed:

> "The criminals will be given short shrift. No military tribunals. We'll hail them before the People's Court. No long speeches from them. The court will act with lightning speed. And two hours after the sentence it will be carried out. By hanging—without mercy."[59]

Having predetermined the result, Oswald Rothaug then simply worked backwards. He had his clear "legal" objectives when the case began, and he went about grinding relentlessly towards their attainment, systematically bulldozing his way through such obstacles as they presented themselves along the way. The Katzenberger case was an example of how Rothaug "made his court an instrumentality of terror," as the Tribunal put it.[60] At the substantive level, it was the prerogative state in full flight. Leo Katzenberger "was tried and executed only because he was a Jew."[61]

Corollaries of the Führerprinzip

In the kind of system described above, operating under the Führer Principle as translated into the judicial system by the Rothenberger Memorandum, the ultimate corollary was: There is no room for individual responsibility. All the basic decisions were made at the top, where governmental policy was formulated, and all instructions on how to act were communicated downward, either directly or indirectly. Lawyers—whether judges, prosecutors, or Ministry of Justice officials—were there simply to carry out the Führer's wishes and to ensure the implementation of his ideas. The judiciary was, in no sense, independent. There was, accordingly, no room for independent, individual decision-making, or for independent, individual thinking in an official capacity. Rothenberger made it clear that, at each point in the judicial process, the overriding consideration by which the judge had to be guided was: How would the

Führer decide this case (or a question or issue along the way to deciding the case), and how would he want me to decide it?

It followed, therefore, that there was no room for individual responsibility. If one took the Führer Principle to its logical conclusion, no one could be held personally accountable; no one was acting—or at least supposed to be acting—of his own accord. Guilt implies—indeed, requires—the requisite volitional element, which, in turn, implies free will and choice. But that was precisely what the Führer Principle nullified. In essence, that summarized the key line of defense in the Justice Case.

As one defendant judge put it, "I was a German judge. I followed the laws of my country,"[62] even, as another defendant judge added, if what he was doing was unpleasant, and he disagreed with it.[63] Under the Führer Principle, Hitler was the chief legislator. As such, his word was law.[64] Thus, it was argued, there was no room to maneuver; a judge was bound to both obey and apply the law. Oswald Rothaug himself expressed it this way: "[B]oth in the service as a judge and prosecutor, I applied the laws of my country in the manner in which they were intended, to the best of my conscience and belief."[65]

The Defense Considered

The case of Oswald Rothaug is a useful vehicle for scrutinizing the defense considered here. The question is: Against the background of Rothaug's role in the Katzenberger case, could it really be said, as he claimed, that "I applied the laws of my country in the manner in which they were intended, to the best of my conscience and belief"?

At one level, the answer is clearly "No." The law under which Leo Katzenberger was charged plainly did not require that the death penalty be meted out. A prison sentence, with or without hard labor, would have sufficed for Rothaug to have "applied the laws of [his] country." Where Katzenberger was charged with racial pollution, the law did not require that the entirely new charge of being a public enemy, with which he had not been charged, be introduced by the court itself at the end of the trial, some two-thirds of the way through the judgment, and purely to achieve a particular sentencing result. Furthermore, at the more basic level of culpability, before even getting to sentencing, application of the law under which Katzenberger was charged did not require Rothaug's evidentiary machinations to enable him to come to what was so evidently a pre-determined conclusion. On the best available evidence, Katzenberger was innocent of the crime of racial pollution, and the law did not, in its terms, require that intellectual gymnastics be engaged in to ensure that he was found guilty. At another level altogether, though, the answer is "Yes": Rothaug could justifiably be said to have "applied the laws of [Germany]," and moreover, to have done so "in the manner in which they were intended."

Law in Nazi Germany: Three Concentric Circles

The "laws of Germany" as an instrument of oppression in the Nazi era manifested themselves in several forms, which may be thought of as three concentric circles with Hitler at the epicenter, by virtue of the Führer Principle. Those three concentric circles accord neatly with the underlying Nazi racial ideology, as it permeated the regime's theories of law and the legal system. Although it is true that the decline of the German legal system was not uniform, and the degree and pace of the decline did not proceed evenly across the country, what is depicted here nevertheless captures the essence of what took place.

The first concentric circle contained promulgated written laws, obliging judges to enforce deprivation of civil rights. The 1935 "Law for the Protection of German Blood and German Honor" is a stark example: It provided a prison sentence for the "crime" of marriage and engaging in other male-female relations between Aryans and Jews.

The second concentric circle comprised laws that were promulgated, but which did not explicitly prescribe deprivation of civil rights. Instead, they accomplished this indirectly, by sanctioning a perverse novelty in statutory interpretation. Adherence to the language of substantive statutes became optional: "Whoever commits an act … which deserves punishment according to … the sound sentiment of the people shall be punished."[66] This constituted retrospective law-making.[67] The "sound sentiment of the people" was not a standard that could be safely predicted by a defendant later indicted. The same statute directed the Reich Supreme Court "to effect an interpretation of the law which takes into account the change of ideology and of legal concepts which the new state has brought about."[68] Interpretation of statutes thus became subject to the changing winds of politics.

The thrust of such legislation and its purpose were summarized by Minister for Justice Thierack, who had no hesitation in inverting the usual relationship between the written law and its interpretation. "[T]he written law," he said in early 1943, "is only to be an aid to the interpretation of National Socialist ideas." [69] And the Tribunal in the Justice Case put it bluntly. Speaking of the phrase "the sound sentiment of the people," the Tribunal commented: "In application and in fact, this expression became the 'healthy instincts' of Hitler and his coconspirators."[70]

The result of this was effectively to require judges to cast aside the written law, and judge cases in accordance with their own sense of what Nazi ideology required. That extended to achieving results which were unrelated to the requirements of the written substantive law, even if those results were in contradiction to the law.

Viewing Nazi law in this light, Oswald Rothaug could point to his decision in the Katzenberger case, and assert that "I applied the laws of my country." Leo Katzenberger would have "deserve[d] punishment according to [the] sound sentiment of the people." Moreover, he could have contended that the "interpretation of the law" which he applied took into account the "change of ideology and of legal concepts which the new state ha[d] brought about."

The vice of such statutory "interpretation" was that there was no way a defendant could know in advance what "law" was going to be applied in his or her case. It is a fundamental principle of fairness and therefore of natural justice and due process that a person know or be capable of ascertaining in advance what the legal consequences of his or her actions are. That principle was ruthlessly abrogated in Nazi Germany. Yet, a judge such as Oswald Rothaug could plausibly claim to have been following the law, including those elements of the "law" that effectively abrogated one of the premises of law itself: predictability.

The third concentric circle arose squarely out of a central element and a natural corollary of the *Führerprinzip*. Judges were not only subject to Hitler's instructions to "understand the demand of the hour," combined with his blunt threats to remove them from office; he hectored them about the need to "grasp the intentions of the legislature; to implement them in spirit as in fact, and to amplify them whenever necessary."[71] Behind statements such as these was the proposition that Hitler's word equated to "law," the heart of the *Führerprinzip:*

"The Führer unites in himself all the sovereign authority of the Reich ... We must speak not of the state's authority but of the Führer's authority if we wish to designate the character of the political authority within the Reich correctly. The state does not hold political authority as an impersonal unit but receives it from the Führer as the executor of the national will. The authority of the Führer is complete and all-embracing… The authority of the Führer is not limited by checks and controls, by special or autonomous bodies or individual rights, but is free and independent, all-inclusive and unlimited."[72]

As the Organization Book of the Nazi Party summarized it explicitly in 1936: "The will of the Führer is the party's law," and "the Führer is always right."[73] Thus, when Hitler told judges to "understand the demand of the hour," and to "grasp the intentions of the legislature; to implement them in spirit as in fact, and to amplify them whenever necessary," these instructions themselves had the force of law. Oswald Rothaug could, once again, claim to have been following the law.

The three concentric circles effectively constituted the whole of "law" in Nazi Germany. There was no case, or issue within a case, that could not be decided to the satisfaction of the Führer by resorting to one or other of their components. Surrounding and suffusing the three concentric circles was an ideological penumbra.

Oswald Rothaug, like the rest of the country, was steeped in the racial ideology that permeated the society and drove the regime. That racial ideology dominated Nazi theories of law and the legal system. Within those theories of law and the legal system, insofar as punishment was concerned, Alfred Rosenberg set out a theory that was unusual, but nevertheless wholly consonant with the underlying racial ideology. Writing in 1930, he characterized the nature of punishment in these terms: "Punishment is, and here we are discussing punishment for dishonorable behavior, simply the singling out of types and natures alien to our type."[74] Traditional notions of punishment as justice for wrongs committed by effecting retribution, serving an educational purpose, or rehabilitating offenders were abandoned.[75] Punishment was, purely and simply, a means of eradicating "undesirables" from society. In the case of Nazi Germany, that meant, first and foremost, those who were alien in racial terms. This approach to penal law was summed up by Joseph Goebbels on July 1942:

"While making his decisions the judge had to proceed less from the law than the basic idea that the offender was to be eliminated from the community… *The State must ward off its internal foes in the most efficient way and wipe them out entirely.* The idea that the judge must be convinced of the defendant's guilt must be discarded completely. The purpose of the administration of the law was not in the first place retaliation or even improvement but *maintenance of the State.* One must not proceed from law but from the resolution that the man must be wiped out."[76]

Anything omitted in these concentric circles was furnished by the penumbra of racial ideology. Oswald Rothaug could turn for support to Rosenberg's theory of punishment and reason: Leo Katzenberger is a Jew in Nazi Germany; Jews are the ultimate "alien to our type"; as a judge, my task is to single him out, and eliminate him from our society; the surest and most comprehensive way of accomplishing that object is to find him guilty and impose the death penalty.

When this analysis is applied to Franz Schlegelberger's role in the Markus Luftglass case, it yields precisely the same result. Schlegelberger acted on a direct instruction from Hitler, which, by virtue of the *Führerprinzip,* had the force of law. And, of course, Markus Luftglass was a Jew. Beyond these two key elements, not much more "justification" was needed.

Inner Logic and Ultimate Fallacy

Seen against the background of the Führer Principle, the judges' claim of innocence based on having merely applied the law cohered neatly. The inner logic of the Nazi legal system was a necessary consequence of the Führer Principle.

At the same time, this highlights the fallacy at the heart of that line of defense.[77] It was the ultimate bootstrap argument; it originated in and was founded on a premise ordained by the Nazi regime itself, which then formed the basis of actions and the consequences of those actions were then sought to be justified by recourse to the original premise. It was the paragon of circular logic:

(a) The aim of the regime was to rid Germany of certain classes of people.
(b) The leaders of the regime then created an elaborate legal system to further that object.

(c) The legal system fulfilled its task.
(d) Those who implemented that legal system, some of whom had been instrumental in its creation, then pleaded that they were only following the law.

But here, too, the circularity of the argument was rooted in Nazi ideology. Alfred Rosenberg's articulation of the relationship between the political and the legal summed it up accurately: "Law and politics represent only two different expressions of the same will, which stands in the service of our highest racial value."[78] Law could then justly be viewed as politics by other means; the two were effectively interchangeable. It was therefore easy and natural to cloak the politics and political goals in law and legal procedures—a legal fig-leaf, so to speak—and then use the law as exculpation for judicial perversion in the furtherance of political goals.

To its great credit, the Tribunal in the Justice Case came to a conclusion that was squarely to the point, and went to the heart of the matter: The charge was precisely that the defendants had perverted the legal system, in order to turn it into an instrument of brutality. It was therefore a circular, bootstrap argument to plead that very legal system in their defense. The defendants committed judicial murder. And murder is still murder, even with a judicial façade. [79]

> "The laws, the Hitlerian decrees and the Draconian, corrupt and perverted Nazi judicial system themselves constituted the substance of … crimes against humanity and participation in the enactment and enforcement of them amounts to complicity in crime. … The charge, in brief, is that of conscious participation in a nationwide government-organized system of cruelty and injustice, in violation of the laws of … humanity, and perpetrated in the name of law by the authority of the Ministry of Justice, and through the instrumentality of the courts. The dagger of the assassin was concealed beneath the robe of the jurist."[80]

Of the sixteen defendants in the case, ten were convicted and four acquitted. (One was dead by then, and the proceedings against another were declared a mistrial.) Four of those convicted were sentenced to life imprisonment, and the other six who were found guilty were sentenced to prison terms of between five and ten years. Schlegelberger and Rothaug were both among those sentenced to life imprisonment.

Frustratingly, in view of the evil they had perpetrated and their contemptible manner of judicial "administration," both were released early. Schlegelberger was freed in 1950 and Rothaug, the last freed defendant, in 1956. They both died of natural causes, Rothaug in 1967 (aged 80), and Schlegelberger in 1970 (aged 94).

Lessons for Individual Responsibility

With its pointed observations and assignment of individual responsibility to the individuals who had consciously perpetrated the acts, the Tribunal enunciated a major statement about individual legal and moral responsibility. The decision applied one of the key lessons of the Nuremberg Trials to members of the legal profession. Perhaps principal among the clear and unmistakable messages sent by the main trial at Nuremberg was that individuals live, simultaneously, in two legal systems, the national and the international. It is not enough for individuals to look to the national legal system to determine what is permissible or even required under national law. Rather, the inquiry must encompass the requirements of international law and consider holding defendants to that standard, as the defendants at the main trial at Nuremberg were. The attempt by lawyers to hide behind the *Führerprinzip* was an extreme example of myopic reliance on the "requirements" of national law.

In delivering this lesson, the Tribunal was articulating a corollary of Raul Hilberg's observation that "the machinery of destruction included representatives of every occupation and profession."[81] If every segment of society was implicated in the Holocaust, prosecuting legal professionals at Nuremberg and holding them accountable in spite of what Nazi law had demanded of them was just requital.

Notes

Warm appreciation is extended to Ms. Maria Smolka-Day, Associate Director for Foreign and International Law, Biddle Law Library, University of Pennsylvania, whose help over an extended period of time has been invaluable in the preparation of this chapter. Warm thanks are also extended to Ms. Monica Sawyer, JD, University of Pennsylvania Law School, 2009, for her excellent research assistance, and to Ms. Cathy Cembrale, of Touro Law Center, for help with the typing of the draft of the manuscript.

1. The United States of America v Josef Altstoetter, et al, Military Tribunal III, Case 3, *Trials of War Criminals Before the Nuernberg Military Tribunals Under Control Council Law No. 10,* Nuernberg, October 1946–April 1949, vol III (Washington, 1951) (hereinafter cited as *Justice Case*).
2. *Justice Case,* 985.
3. In this respect, it is important to distinguish the defendants in the case from people who, whilst qualified as lawyers, were not practicing law when they committed their atrocities; for instance, Hans Frank, the Governor-General of occupied Poland, and Ernst Kaltenbrunner, who ended up controlling the Gestapo, and under whose aegis Auschwitz concentration camp was conducted.
4. Insofar as the factual and basic historical material concerning the Justice Case are concerned, this chapter draws on Reicher, "The Jurists' Trial and Lessons for the Rule of Law," in Herbert R. Reginbogin and Christoph J.M. Safferling, eds., *The Nuremberg Trials: International Criminal Law Since 1945* (Munich, 2006).
5. For a complete list of the 12 subsidiary trials, see *Justice Case,* p IX. Examples were trials of members of the medical profession, industrialists, military leaders, and leaders of the *Einsatzgruppen.*
6. At various times, some defendants served in more than one capacity, which accounts for the seeming arithmetical discrepancy.
7. They were also charged with war crimes, membership in criminal organizations, such as the SS, and conspiracy to commit war crimes and crimes against humanity. See the Indictment in the case, *Justice Case,* 15–26.
8. There had been talk of embryonic versions of crimes against humanity after the First World War, and the term was used in discussions following the Armenian genocide, but nothing came of those efforts, and the Charter of the International Military Tribunal, the Tribunal which heard the principal case, conferred on the Tribunal the jurisdiction to try the defendants before it with "Crimes Against Humanity." See Charter of the International Military Tribunal, Art 6(c), *Justice Case,* XIII–XIV. For a history of the evolution of the term "crimes against humanity" in international law, see M. Cherif Bassiouni, *Crimes against Humanity: Historical Evolution and Contemporary Application* (Cambridge, 2011), 1–50.
9. It was subsequently joined by genocide. Although that term was known by 1945, it had not yet crystallized into a crime in international law.
10. *Justice Case,* XVIII.
11. Article II(2), *Justice Case* XIX.
12. Article II(1)(c), *Justice Case,* XIX.
13. *Justice Case,* 32–3.
14. *Justice Case,* 985.
15. Per Brigadier General Telford Taylor, *Justice Case,* 32.
16. At times, in the correspondence, the name is incorrectly spelled "Luftgas," but it is corrected in the last letter (*Justice Case,* 431), and the correct spelling is used throughout here.
17. *Justice Case,* 430.
18. *Justice Case,* 431.
19. *Justice Case,* 1083.
20. *Justice Case,* 1085.

21. The Opinion and Sentence of the Nuremberg Special Court is set out in full in *Justice Case,* 653–64. The case was immortalized in Stanley Kramer's 1961 film, *Judgment at Nuremburg,* with a riveting performance by Judy Garland, as Irene Hoffman Wallner, the character based on Irene Seiler.
22. That Rothaug regularly arrived at his decisions before cases began, and before he had heard any evidence, was abundantly clear from the testimony before the Tribunal, which declared: "[W]e are firmly convinced that in numberless cases Rothaug's opinions were formed in decisions made, and in many cases publicly or privately announced before the trial had even commenced and certainly before it was concluded." *Justice Case,* 1156.
23. Christiane Kohl, *The Maiden and the Jew: The Story of a Fatal Friendship in Nazi Germany,* trans. John S Barrett (Hanover, NH, 1997), 56.
24. *Justice Case,* 657, 660.
25. *Justice Case,* 180–1.
26. "Any man violating the prohibition of article 2 [forbidding extra-marital relations between Jews and Aryans] will be punished with imprisonment or hard labor. Article 5(2), *Justice Case,* 181.
27. After beginning on 653 of the *Justice Case* volume, the Opinion and Sentence mentions the offence of being a public enemy for the first time on 661, and the Judgment ends on 664.
28. *Justice Case,* 1155.
29. *Justice Case,* 1156.
30. For instance, Rothaug went through the motions of carefully analyzing the evidence, and establishing the first two basic elements of the offense, as required by law, namely that Katzenberger was a Jew and that Seiler was an Aryan. He examined the proof of Katzenberger's ancestry, based on birth registers, going back two generations, and then went through an analogous process in order to establish that Seiler was Aryan. *Justice Case,* 654–6. The meticulous consideration of the evidentiary material would have done justice to a judge in any civilized legal system.
31. This defense in fact represents a strong echo of the defense of "superior orders," which permeated so many trials of Holocaust-era perpetrators, beginning with the main trial at Nuremberg. This study focuses on the peculiar slant given by the lawyers to that more general defense, within the specific context of the Nazi legal system.
32. He is seen dramatically making his proclamation in Leni Riefenstahl's classic propaganda film, *Triumph of the Will,* which revolved around, and chronicled, the 1934 Nazi Party rally at Nuremberg.
33. *Justice Case,* 252. Jahrreiss' testimony must be read with a note of caution, as he was a witness for the defense. It was in the interests of the defendants to minimize their responsibility, and one of the ways of doing that was to maximize Hitler's authority. Nevertheless, the quoted passage from his testimony is an accurate summary of the Führer Principle.
34. Ibid, 266.
35. Under the Treaty, Germany lost territorial possessions, was compelled to disarm, was burdened with crippling reparations obligations and, under Article 231, was required to accept full responsibility for "all the loss and damage" suffered by the allied powers.

36. On the multifaceted role of "the Führer" in the Nazi movement and the Third Reich, see Ian Kershaw, *The "Hitler Myth": Image and Reality in the Third Reich*, 2 ed. (Oxford, 2001).
37. See, e.g., Alfred Rosenberg, *The Myth of the Twentieth Century: An Evaluation of the Spiritual-Intellectual Confrontations of Our Age*, trans. Vivian Bird (Newport Beach, 1982), 342–43. This work constituted the second major pillar of Nazi ideology, along with Hitler's own *Mein Kampf*.
38. *Justice Case*, 469–83.
39. He was President of the Hanseatic Court of Appeal. See *Justice Case*, 483–9.
40. "Reflections on a National Socialist Judicial Reform." *Justice Case*, 469.
41. *Justice Case*, 144, 497. See also, 467–68
42. See cross-examination of Rothenberger, *Justice Case*, 498, for collation of all three quotations dealt with here.
43. In cross-examination at the Justice Case, which reads like a passage out of *Alice in Wonderland*, Rothenberger insisted (presumably with a straight face) that his memorandum was in fact an argument for judicial independence. *Justice Case*, 498–502.
44. Ibid, 367.
45. Ibid, 360.
46. Ibid, 361.
47. Ibid.
48. The scene may be viewed in the video recording *Traitors to Hitler* (Bonn: Deutsche Reportagefilm, 1979), available through the German Information Center in New York.
49. "I swear I will be true and obedient to the Führer of the German Reich and people, Adolf Hitler…"
50. Spontaneously, without an appeal having been filed or an application made.
51. Ernst Fraenkel, *The Dual State* (New York, 1941). For more see the chapter by Douglas Morris in this volume.
52. Ibid, xiii.
53. Ibid.
54. "Political" was defined, quite simply, as encompassing whatever the politicians said was political. Fraenkel, *Dual State*, 42, note 57.
55. Ibid, xiii.
56. Roland Freisler (1893–1945) was State Secretary at the Reich Ministry of Justice, and subsequently President of the *Volksgerichtshof* (People's Court), a court handling political crimes. See the chapter on him by Robert D. Rachlin in this volume.
57. William L. Shirer, *The Rise and Fall of the Third Reich: A History of Nazi Germany* (New York, 1960), 1070. Shirer also describes Freisler as "perhaps the most sinister and bloodthirsty Nazi in the Third Reich after Heydrich," 1023.
58. The Tribunal found, on the facts, that Rothaug did this regularly.
59. Shirer, *Rise and Fall*, 1070, citing an officer who was present.
60. *Justice Case*, 1156.
61. *Justice Case*, 1155.
62. Defendant Guenther Nebelung, *Justice Case*, 950. Very tellingly, he went on to draw an analogy between himself and a soldier who is subject to superior orders: "Does not every soldier find himself in the same situation?" Ibid.

63. Defendant Wilhelm Von Ammon, *Justice Case*, 816.
64. There are many ways of illustrating this. For instance, the authorization sanctioning the euthanasia program consisted of a one-paragraph letter, addressed to two medical practitioners, on Hitler's personal stationery, and signed by him.
65. *Justice Case*, 947.
66. *Law of June 28, 1935, Amending the Criminal (Penal) Code*, Article 2. *Justice Case*, 177.
67. The former Article 2, which was repealed by the law of 28 June 1935, read: "[N]o punishment may be imposed unless such punishment is prescribed by statute before the act is committed. In the event of a change in the statute between the time of commission of an act and the time of rendering a decision, the most lenient statute shall apply." *Justice Case*, 177.
68. Section II. *Justice Case*, 179. In similar vein, Article 170a, of Section I, provided: "If an act deserves punishment according to the sound sentiment of the people, but is not declared punishable in the law, the prosecution will examine whether the underlying principle of a penal law can be applied to the act and whether justice can be helped to triumph by analogous application of that penal law." And Article 267a instructed the courts to take the same approach: "If the trial shows that the defendant has committed an act which deserves punishment according to the sound sentiment of the people, but is not declared punishable by law, the court will examine whether the underlying principle of a penal law applies to the act and whether justice can be helped to triumph by analogous application of that penal law." *Justice Case*, 178.
69. Statement of January 5, 1943. *Justice Case*, 1021–2.
70. *Justice Case*, 1082.
71. Ian Ward, *Law, Philosophy and National Socialism: Heidegger, Schmitt and Radbruch in Context* (1992), 21.
72. Prosecution Document 2771-PS. U.S. State Department, *National Socialism*, published by the US Government Printing Office, 1943, vol. V, 417, in Office of United States Chief of Counsel for Prosecution of Axis Criminality, *Nazi Conspiracy and Aggression*, vol. I (1946), 191.
73. Prosecution Document 1814-PS. The Organization of the NSDAP and its affiliated associations, from Organization book of the NSDAP, editions of 1936, 1938, 1940 and 1943, in Office of United States Chief of Counsel for Prosecution of Axis Criminality, *Nazi Conspiracy and Aggression*, vol. I (Washington, 1946), 191–2.
74. Rosenberg, *Myth of the Twentieth Century*, 364.
75. In fact, Rosenberg said so explicitly: "Punishment is not in the first instance a means of education as our humanitarians wish to persuade us. Punishment is also not revenge." ibid.
76. *Justice Case*, 1021–22.
77. As does, for that matter, the argument propounded by some that the defendants in Nuremburg should have been tried under German law.
78. Rosenberg, *Myth of the Twentieth Century*, 361.
79. The analogy to the defense of superior orders is very close indeed; in fact, the pleas of the defendants in the Justice Case which are examined here are really just a branch of it. Superior Orders, after all, consisted of express orders or laws which were effectively orders. The charter for the principal trial, and also Control Council

Law No. 10, contemplated the defense of superior orders, but not as an exculpatory defense; rather, as a basis for an argument in mitigation of sentence, after a verdict of guilty. See Charter of the International Military Tribunal, Article 8, *Justice Case,* XIV, and Control Council Law No 10, Article II(4) (b), *Justice Case,* XX.
80. *Justice Case,* 984–5.
81. Raul Hilberg, *Perpetrators, Victims, Bystanders: The Jewish Catastrophe 1933–1945* (New York, 1992), 65.

Der Rütli-Schwur vor dem höchsten Gerichtshof.

The first page of the Deutsche Richterzeitung of 25 October 1933, showing German jurists taking a Nazi oath in front of the Reichsgericht in Leipzig. The banner on the court building reads "German Law to the German People through National Socialism."
Source: Case Western Reserve University Libraries

Chapter 7

JUDGING GERMAN JUDGES IN THE THIRD REICH
Excusing and Confronting the Past

Kenneth F. Ledford

IN THE EARLY 1990S, A criminal judgment and sentence embroiled the insular world of the German judiciary in a great debate about Holocaust denial and the independence of the judiciary, reminding Germans and the world of earlier failures of German justice. On 22 June 1994, the Superior Court in Mannheim imposed a one-year suspended sentence upon Günter Deckert, leader of the neo-Nazi National Democratic Party, who stood accused and convicted of inciting the public, compounded by slander and defamation, disparagement of the memory of the dead, and fomenting race hatred.[1] In November 1991, Deckert had propagated Holocaust denial doctrines by hosting Fred Leuchter at a public meeting in Weinheim, and marketing videocassettes that propounded Leuchter's notorious claim that the gas chambers at Auschwitz could not have killed significant numbers of Jews, and by speaking approvingly of Leuchter's claims at the meeting. In calculating the proper punishment, the presiding judge, Rainer Orlet, considered as mitigating factors Deckert's previously clean criminal record; the fact that his hate-speech statements were spontaneous expostulations upon hearing Leuchter's claims for the first time; the fact that the meeting led to no violence or breach of the peace; the fact that Deckert earned no money personally from his activity and thus showed loyalty to principle rather than profit; and the "fact" that from Deckert's point of view, his only goal was to strengthen the power of the German people to resist the claims of the Jews. Two comments made by Judge Orlet were the most inflammatory. First, he took judicial notice of the circumstance that, nearly fifty years after the end of the Second World War, Germany remained saddled with political, moral, and financial claims because of its earlier persecution of the Jews, while the "mass crimes" of other peoples remained unatoned for; and second, that Deckert's financial sacrifices for his political convictions, including the loss of his prior career as a secondary school teacher because of his beliefs, "were judged by the panel to be the result of a decision of conscience that should be respected."[2]

Ultimately, in December 1994, the German Supreme Court (*Bundesgerichtshof, BGH*) reversed the Superior Court of Mannheim and remanded the case for resentencing. Holding that "the mass murder of Jews in the gas chambers of concentration camps during the Second World War is a manifest historical fact," it instructed the lower court to consider Deckert's dedication to his cause to be "better characterized as stiff-necked stubbornness than as strength of character and consciousness of responsibility" when it recalculated its sentence.[3] Nonetheless, the lower court's judgment had already unleashed a firestorm of criticism. The SPD fraction in the state parliament of Baden-Württemberg discussed filing a constitutional action to remove Judge Orlet from office if he were not subjected to internal judicial discipline.[4] The supervising judge of the superior court of Mannheim ultimately reassigned Orlet to another judicial panel and he later took temporary "sick leave," ultimately opting for early retirement, all of course for reasons unrelated to his opinion in the Deckert case.[5]

Contemporary commentary placed the case in the contexts of right-wing extremism in the newly-unified Germany, Holocaust denial worldwide, and the general question of judicial independence. But two judicial observers quickly located the controversy in the context of a debate that had occupied the Federal Republic since before its foundation, that of the inheritance of the judiciary of the Third Reich for the second German republic. Günter Bertram, presiding judge of the superior court in Hamburg, quickly warned, "we should expect that the 'unmastered' Nazi era of the justice system will again become a great theme … and because the old Nazis have since died or are retired, it will now be about their spirit, which naturally could have been transmitted through a hundred pores."[6] Rudolf Wassermann, a retired appellate court president and legal historian, specifically invoked the ghost of Weimar-era right-wing political justice and warned against a quick resort to incursions into the realm of judicial independence, pointing out social and political differences in the composition of the Federal Republic's judiciary from that of Weimar, which resulted in far broader social and political diversity on the bench, and called for renewed efforts to educate Germans about the Holocaust and German responsibility.[7]

But no new outpouring of historical research needed to occur to provide the materials for the educational process that Wassermann invoked. All of this critique of the German judiciary built upon a historiography of controversy that had extended from the beginning of the postwar period. This chapter aims to explore this whole phenomenon in four stages. First, it will build from my own work on the Prussian judiciary between 1848 and 1914 to sketch the emergence of an independent judiciary before and during the Second Empire, in order to highlight the critique of that judiciary's role during the Weimar Republic, and to outline the framework of purge and submission during the Third Reich. Second, it will explore the history of how interpreters of the behavior of the German judiciary during the Third Reich imposed competing master narratives to explain it. Third, it will analyze the wave of critical histories from the 1980s that provided the immediate context for the Deckert affair. And fourth, it will attempt to highlight new historical work that seeks to transcend the often simplistic polemic that shaped the debates during the first sixty years after 1945, offering us new insight by means of a return to empirical study.

German Judges 1878–1945

Germany remained, until the beginning of the twentieth century, a legally multifarious place, both in its substantive law and in its trial procedure and judicial system. A congeries of kingdoms, duchies, principalities, counties, and free cities, even after 1871 the new empire retained its federal structure, reserving many powers to the constituent states.[8] After 1819, however, a general framework for legal education, judicial appointment, and judicial careers emerged, and the Constitution of 1871 conferred on the Imperial government the power to legislate in realms of substantive and procedural law. Between 1871 and 1878, liberal parliamentarians and centralizing state officials shepherded through the Reichstag a set of enactments known as the Imperial Justice Laws, which established national standards for education, training, and examination for judges, but left their selection, appointment, and advancement to the Ministries of Justice in each of the German states.[9]

Graduates of neo-humanist classical secondary schools qualified for admission to German universities where they could choose to study in the legal faculty. After six semesters' study, candidates could sit for the first of two state bar examinations concerned with legal history and substantive and procedural law, after which they engaged in a four-year period of practical legal training at various courts, practitioners' offices, and government general administrative offices, all without regular salary. After passing the final bar examination, law graduates could select from several careers, one of which was the judiciary, which required the favor of a state Ministry of Justice for appointment.[10] By the 1890s, overcrowding in the employment market meant that before most applicants could obtain a permanent judicial post, they first had to spend years serving as temporary substitute judges whenever they could (*Assessoren*), receiving at most per diem salaries.[11] Usually only after several years of this tenuous and insecure existence could they attain appointment to permanent positions provided in the state budget.

This arduous and penurious preparation for a career as judge bore social selectivity implications obvious to contemporaries. Only aspirants possessed of substantial capital resources could afford to pursue this occupational path. Other factors affected social selectivity as well. Throughout the Second Empire, German Catholics attended university at a lower rate than Protestants, leaving Catholics under-represented in the judiciary, especially in Prussia.[12] And although Jews, who experienced their final legal emancipation from civil disabilities in 1869, flocked to university in higher numbers than their proportion of the general population, they found themselves discriminated against in appointment to judicial positions. Those Jews who studied law tended to enter private practice, which after 1879 was the unqualified right of all qualified lawyers who passed the second bar examination.[13]

Already in the 1890s, the Social Democratic Party of Germany began to articulate a critique of the social and political beliefs of German judges, especially in their rulings in criminal cases, denouncing them for practicing "class justice."[14] In the socialist periodical press and in a vibrant pamphlet literature, each harsh sentence imposed on a worker, especially one who belonged to the Social Democratic organizations and milieu, met with a stinging attack of the hypocrisy of claims to judicial independence, impartiality, and loyalty to the rule of law.[15] This kind of polemic only gained momentum after the experience of the First World War, the German Revolution of 1918–19, and the creation of the Weimar Republic.

German judges returned from their service in the war effort to a new Germany reduced in geographic size and locked in the throes of profound economic dislocation, in which Ministries of Justice sought to absorb judges from territories lost in the Versailles settlement at a time of shrinking salary budgets. Spectacular judicial decisions favoring right-wing perpetrators of political violence soon brought renewed critique of the disloyalty of a monarchist judiciary in a democratic republic in which the Social Democratic Party often was the largest single vote-getter in state and national elections.[16] By the final years of the Weimar Republic, two voices arose to articulate this criticism most clearly. In January 1927, Ernst Fraenkel, a Social Democrat, published a pamphlet, *On the Sociology of Class Justice*, harshly dismissing the German judiciary as merely an instrument of class rule. He recapitulated the prewar argument that the social selection process for recruitment of judges, including most frequently a year's service as a reserve officer, guaranteed a profoundly conservative judiciary, from which no proletarian should ever expect justice in any meaningful sense.[17] In March 1932, Robert M.W. Kempner, then an official in the Prussian Ministry of the Interior and later a prosecutor for the United States at Nuremberg, published under a pseudonym a book titled *Twilight of Justice: Prelude to the Third Reich*. This was a catalog of authoritarian miscarriages of justice stretching back to Frederick the Great and the Miller Arnold case, through the class justice of the Imperial era, through the immediate postwar coddling of right-wing assassins, up to the failure of the criminal justice system to stop Nazi violence in the streets since 1930.[18]

Although the criticisms advanced by Fraenkel and Kempner showed the very real shortcomings of parts, indeed the majority, of the Weimar judiciary, the personnel policies of the new republic permitted some expansion of the social and political diversity of German judges. Social Democrats and left-liberals headed many of the state Ministries of Justice and expanded the compass of their appointments to vacancies. As early as 1922, Social Democratic and left-liberal judges formed the League of Republican Judges with a nation-wide organization and as many as 500 judges as members—as compared with some 12,000 members of the German Judges' League, the major professional organization.[19] Room for success and prominence for Jews in legal professions also proved very real. During the Weimar Republic, Jews rose to leading positions in German legal faculties, as leaders of the German Bar Association (*Deutscher Anwaltverein*), and made modest inroads into the judiciary.[20]

While the Weimar Republic may have been targeted by its right-wing opponents as a "Jew republic," the Jewish presence in the judiciary certainly rose to no level of dominance. Although the proportion of Jews in the judiciary increased over that of the openly discriminatory years of the Second Empire, it still lagged far behind the proportion of Jews who qualified for legal careers and who entered private practice instead.

TABLE 1: Jews in Prussian Legal Professions, 1925–1933[21]

	1925	%	1927	%	1931	%	1933	%
Trainees			192	9.0	161	5.2	174	4.5
Judges			312	5.8	392	6.8	401	7.0
Lawyers	2,208	26.2					3,370	28.5
Berlin	1,179	45.4					1,879	48.3

Jewish judges attracted the hostility of anti-Semites because of their warm embrace of the republican form of government and their continued visibility. The leadership of the League of Republican Judges included prominent Jewish judges such as Fritz Bauer, district court judge in Stuttgart; Arnold Freymuth, court of appeal judge in Hamm; Wilhelm Israel Kroner, presiding superior court judge in Berlin; and Alfred Orgler and Siegfried Rosenfeld, judges of the *Kammergericht* in Berlin—although by no means were all pro-republic lawyers and judges Jewish, and both Robert Kempner and former Social Democratic Minister of Justice Gustav Radbruch also served as prominent leaders of the League.[22] Prominent Jewish practitioners also attracted hostility for their visibility in high-profile political and criminal litigation. Douglas Morris has recently provided an excellent treatment of the practice of the Jewish lawyer in Munich, Max Hirschberg, whose pro-republican political practice included a withering and embarrassing cross-examination of Adolf Hitler in a libel action that Hitler himself had brought over accusations that he had betrayed Germandom in the South Tyrol by accepting money from Mussolini.[23] Benjamin Carter Hett has likewise recently explored the oppositional legal practice of Hans Litten, whose cross-examination of Hitler in the Eden Dance Palace trial in 1931 exposed Hitler to accusations of perjury. Litten paid for his defiance by being arrested on the night of the Reichstag fire, ultimately hanging himself out of despair in Dachau in February 1938.[24]

The story of judges during the Third Reich interweaves two important narratives, first, that of those who were excluded because of their political orientation or "racial" identity, and second, that of the behavior of those judges who remained in office. The systematic exclusion of Social Democrats and other leftists, and especially of Jews, from the ranks of the judiciary after the Nazi rise to power on 30 January 1933 is a sadly familiar tale.[25] Both before and after the Reichstag Fire on 28 February 1933, Jewish judges, like all Jews, had to endure SA (*Sturmabteilung*, Storm Troopers) organized assaults, harassment, and humiliation. On the night of 31 March 1933, the SA invaded the venerable *Kammergericht* in Berlin and roughed up Jewish lawyers, judicial trainees, and judges.[26] The nation-wide boycott of Jewish businesses on 1 April specifically included Jewish private practitioners. Legislative restriction for judges began on 7 April with the enactment of the "Law for the Restoration of the Professional Civil Service."[27] The decree ordered the immediate dismissal of all "non-Aryan" civil servants except for those appointed before 1 August 1914, or, at the insistence of President Paul von Hindenburg, who had been Field Marshal and supreme commander during the war, those who had fought for Germany or its allies at the front during the First World War, or whose father or son had died at the front in the war.[28] This decree also permitted exclusion of civil servants, including judges, who were political opponents of National Socialism, a measure aimed primarily at Social Democrats and left-liberals. On 23 April 1933, the representatives' assembly of the German Judges' League demanded that the League dissolve itself and be absorbed into the National Socialist lawyers' organization, the League of National Socialist German Jurists, effective 31 December 1933.[29]

Nazi officials increasingly excluded Jews from the judiciary, prevented Jews from enrolling in the universities in the legal faculties, purged those faculties of their Jewish professors, and found ways to challenge those judges who claimed exemption under the two exceptions contained in the "Law for the Restoration of the Professional Civil Service."[30] By 30 April 1934, some 574 Jewish judges and prosecutors had lost their jobs. The Nuremberg Laws of September 1935, particularly the Reich Citizenship Law, and the subsequent decrees issued in accordance with it, increasingly restricted the freedom to practice for the remaining Jewish jurists. The Fifth Supplemental Decree of 17 September 1938, which definitively disbarred all remaining Jews, permitting practice only as representatives of Jewish clients, "*Judenkonsulenten*" ("Jew-counselors"), excluded the remaining 2,300 practitioners.[31] Reinhard Bendix describes with poignancy the humiliating exclusion that his father, Ludwig, felt as he faced first dismissal from his position as judge on the labor court in Berlin, and then a lawsuit against him by the Berlin Bar Association for "unfair competition" because of his successful practice as a *Judenkonsulent*, after which he ultimately emigrated.[32]

Nationwide studies of the fates of lawyers and judges excluded during the Third Reich are absent, but the Berlin *Kammergericht* has enjoyed particular attention by researchers.[33] After the Nuremberg Laws of 1935, virtually all of the 536 Jewish judges and prosecutors there were excluded from office. Some emigrated, some remained and survived, and many perished, as reflected in Table 2.

TABLE 2: Fate of Jewish Judges in Kammergericht District, 1933–45[34]

	Number	%
Died	169	39.21 %
—Deported	106	24.59 %
—Died in custody	6	1.39 %
—Suicide	13	3.02 %
—Died in war	5	1.16 %
—Natural causes	39	9.05 %
Survived	262	60.79 %
—Liberated	7	1.62 %
—Emigration	173	40.14 %
—Hid	7	1.62 %
—Mixed marriage	39	9.05 %
—Mixed ancestry	35	8.12 %
—Unknown circumstances	1	0.23 %
Total	431	100.00 %
Total in 1933	536	

Although some Jewish judges either remained in Germany and survived or returned after 1945 from emigration, the rich Jewish contribution to the German legal professions, like the rich symbiosis of German-Jewish culture, perished in the murderous catastrophe of the Third Reich.

The second narrative of judges during the Third Reich is that of the enthusiastic embrace of National Socialist legal ideology by those judges who remained in office. Not only did supervising judges carry out the purge of socialists and Jews that was ordered by the state Ministries of Justice (and in the case of Prussia, the Reich Ministry of Justice, as the Reich government absorbed the responsibilities formerly borne by Prussia), but in everyday jurisprudential decision-making, judges actively embraced the Nazi notion that they should issue rulings governed by the material norm of *gesundes Volksempfinden,* or "healthy popular instinct."[35]

In a book published in 1941, Edith Roper, who served as the courtroom reporter for the *Deutsche Allgemeine Zeitung* and the *Frankfurter Zeitung* from early 1937 until March 1939 under the vigilant supervision of the Ministry of Propaganda (and who subsequently emigrated to the United States), detailed to the outside world the corrupt workings of the courts of the Third Reich. She outlined a series of prosecutions of Catholic clergy for alleged sexual abuse of children, all orchestrated to maximum effect to discredit the church; the prosecution of the Protestant pastor Martin Niemöller in Berlin-Dahlem for his oppositional sermons; trials of Jews for ordinary criminal offenses, as well as for racial defilement and circumvention of foreign-exchange laws, all leading to harsh outcomes; and finally, politically motivated criminal trials such as that against the pacifist Carl von Ossietzky.[36] One contemporary reviewer summed up her account, "Roughly speaking, criminal justice in Naziland has become a political weapon which spreads terror and disgrace on the morally defenseless and legally disarmed opponents of the regime."[37]

A large part of the speed and contempt for process that Roper describes stemmed from the creation in March 1933 of "Special Courts," initially one for each court of appeal district, but later vastly expanded in number.[38] These courts did not derive from an original concept by the National Socialists, but rather built upon presidential decrees dating to the Brüning and von Papen chancellorships to create courts of special jurisdiction in regions of particular turmoil— specifically Berlin, the Ruhr, and Silesia— in order to respond to political street-violence in a swift and summary fashion.[39] Expanded nationwide by the Nazis, these courts had expedited procedures that offered fewer protections for the accused, and no rights of appeal.[40] Staffed by three judges from the courts of ordinary jurisdiction, these Special Courts specialized in political trials, especially prosecutions for criminal malicious mischief (*Heimtücke*)—a broad and indeterminate offense that inscribed depravity of character onto petty offenses such as jokes about Hitler, sarcastic commentary on National Socialist policy, or later on the course of the war, and other behavior reflecting independence of judgment and conduct. With minimal formality and maximal speed, the Special Courts used ordinary judges to impose harsh sentences against those targeted by Nazis as enemies of the state and the German people.

One of the great specialties of the Special Courts, and also of the courts of ordinary jurisdiction in criminal cases, was the death penalty. In 1941, Edith Roper quoted a Ministry of Justice official as indicating that by 1938, more than twenty executions took place per day in Germany.[41] Ingo Müller in the late 1980s estimated a total of 80,000 cases of capital punishment following at least summary legal proceedings, if one tallied all cases from courts of ordinary jurisdiction, Special Courts, the People's Court, and courts-martial throughout Germany and German-occupied Europe.[42] By the 1950s, and especially by the 1980s, this promiscuous imposition of capital punishment for the smallest of offenses, especially by 1945 when it had become obvious to all that the war was lost, loomed large in the renewed criticism of the continuity of personnel on the bench between Third Reich and Federal Republic.

Postwar Efforts to Grapple with the Past: Narratives of Blame and Exculpation

The wartime Allies who occupied Germany after 1945 had already determined to de-Nazify the country, including its judicial system.[43] Initially, the occupiers removed from office all state officials, including judges, who had been members of the Nazi Party or Nazi organizations, which included virtually all judges, and they arrested many judges.[44] Famously, the second wave of war crimes trials included the Justice Case, which ran from 4 January to 4 December 1947.[45] Known also by the name of the first-listed defendant as *United States v. Josef Altstötter, et al.*, this trial convicted Franz Schlegelberger and other state secretaries from the Reich Ministry of Justice, the chief prosecutor of the People's Court, and prosecutors and judges from the Special Courts and People's Courts, for implementing laws that were obviously inhumane.[46] One of the Special Court judges convicted there, Oswald Rothaug from Nuremberg, presided over the Katzenberger case of racial defilement, which formed the basis for the 1961 film *Judgment at Nuremberg*.[47] The Justice Case established the Allied narrative of the miscarriage of justice by the German judiciary in its ringing phrase:

> The charge, in brief, is that of conscious participation in a nation wide government-organized system of cruelty and injustice, in violation of the laws of war and of humanity, and perpetrated in the name of law by the authority of the Ministry of Justice, and through the instrumentality of the courts. The dagger of the assassin was concealed beneath the robe of the jurist.[48]

Many American occupation officials believed strongly in the need for continued de-Nazification and democratic education of German elites and masses alike, but pragmatic and ideological considerations intervened to thwart a lasting reconstitution of the German judiciary. German judicial leaders also reasserted themselves in efforts to slow or halt the process of purging the German judiciary, notably Hodo Freiherr von Hodenberg, President of the Court of Appeal in Celle in the British zone.[49] For the practical reason that the vast majority of those Germans qualified to serve as judges were tainted by their associations with the Nazi regime, and because of distractions caused by growing tensions with the Soviet Union in the emerging stages of the Cold War, de-Nazification of the judiciary, like de-Nazification generally, came to a discredited end by 1948, and Nazi-era judges returned to the bench after authority returned to the Germans.[50] Contemporary observers, such as Karl Loewenstein, and later critics bitterly denounced both the denial of justice and cynicism embedded in this action.[51]

One powerful exculpatory justification for this restoration of a brown-tinted judiciary had emerged in 1946 from an unexpected source. Gustav Radbruch, legal philosopher and Weimar-era minister of justice for the Social Democratic Party, published in the *Süddeutsche Zeitung* a short essay called "Statutory Lawlessness and Supra-Statutory Law."[52] In a passionate call for judges and lawyers to interrogate positive law in order to do justice in their jurisprudence, Radbruch began from the supposition that the postivistic legal thinking that dominated German legal education and practice had rendered the concept "statutory lawlessness" a contradiction in terms. This in turn left German judges defenseless against applying the inhumane but procedurally and correctly adopted legal norms of the Nazis as they ruled on cases before them, "Positivism, with its principle that 'a law is a law,' has in fact rendered the German legal profession defenseless against statutes that are wholly arbitrary and criminal."[53] In his short essay, Radbruch distinctly did not seek to exculpate German judges who imposed sentences such as that in the Katzenberger case, nor did he seek to undermine judges' fidelity to duly-enacted law. What he sought to do was to create space and a set of guidelines for when judges should know how to resort to "supra-statutory law," finding it in notions of purposiveness and justice that must stand alongside the valuable principles of legal certainty and judicial modesty which lie at the root of statutory positivism.[54]

But Radbruch's starting assumption that German judges lay trapped in the stranglehold of positivism fueled a second narrative, one of exculpation, which dominated the German discussion until the later 1950s.[55] Fidelity to the posited law formed the centerpiece of the defense of the judges on trial at Nuremberg, although the presiding court rejected the theory. Eberhard Schmidt, a leading theorist of criminal law who had himself served during the Second World War as a military judge sitting in court-martial, delivered a lecture in Karlsruhe in 1952 that explored the role of positivism in limiting the choices available to judges during the Third Reich. He laid the blame for unjust laws at the foot of the legislator and restricted the province of the judge to mere application of the law. Celebrating the replacement of a lawless (Nazi) legislator with a democratic one in the Bundestag of the Federal Republic, Schmidt concluded his speech: "Positivism is dead; long live positivism!"[56]

Radbruch's positivism formula (*"die Radbruchsche Formel"*) received its greatest resonance and broadest exposition in the English-reading world in the great debate on legal positivism between the English legal philosopher H.L.A. Hart and Harvard Law School professor Lon Fuller in the *Harvard Law Review* in 1958.[57] Drawing upon the tradition of Benthamite utilitarianism and Austinian positivism, Hart contended that Radbruch's formula was flawed, thereby proving that positivism was the only bulwark against judicial lawmaking and unjust activism; judges cannot permit their notions of morality to divert them from faithful application of the posited law. Fuller replied that Radbruch had really argued that Nazi "law" was so manifestly unjust as not to constitute law, so that if judges applied this "law" "faithfully," they actually committed injustice. A trigger for the debate, and a centerpiece of both scholars' argumentation, was the affirmation by the Court of Appeal of Bamberg of a 1949 conviction of a wife for denouncing her husband to the Nazis for violating Nazi laws, in which the court ruled that the Nazi statute "was contrary to the sound conscience and sense of justice of all decent human beings."[58] To Hart and other positivists, this "activism" on the part of the democratic German court in rejecting defenses based upon National Socialist enactments, this departure from fidelity to the literal law, opened the door to judicial injustice.[59]

Despite the Radbruchian decision by the Bamberg Court of Appeal, the jurisprudence of German courts, like the politics of the early Adenauer administration, reinforced efforts to excuse the actions of the judiciary during the Third Reich.[60] At the same time that German courts were acquitting German soldiers accused of war crimes and members of SS *Einsatzgruppen* accused of genocide, the German Supreme Court in 1956 acquitted Prosecutor Walter Huppenkothen and Presiding Judge Otto Thorbeck for having tried and sentenced to death leading members of the anti-Nazi resistance, including Wilhelm Canaris, Dietrich

Bonhoeffer, and Hans Oster, at a drumhead court-martial on 8 April 1945, when the war was clearly lost.[61] In the mid-1950s, then, German courts in their rulings embraced the outcomes that the positivist defense of judges' actions during the Third Reich were justified in theory, exculpating judges as having had no choice but to apply Nazi law in order to maintain their fidelity to "the law" and their calling as judges.

By 1959, the legal positivist and other exculpatory defenses had solidified in theory and in scholarship. In that year, Hubert Schorn, a district court judge who later retired as president of the superior court of Cologne, produced a massive apologetic volume on *The Judge in the Third Reich*, in which he argued passionately that the accusations of failure to resist Hitler directed at the judiciary since the war, especially the judgment in the Justice Case, were wrong.[62] The great bulk of this work is an alphabetical list of judges who were persecuted or prosecuted by the Nazi regime, together with analyses of the heroic ways in which they stood up to Nazi pressure, "Judges as Protectors of Law and Justice." Schorn's exculpatory argument had four parts: first, that judges widely resisted arbitrary Nazi laws and decrees; second, that judges were victims of their positivist legal training and education; third, that judges legitimately feared for their jobs and their lives if they did not apply the law in the ways the regime wanted; and fourth, that they honestly believed that they provided better fidelity to the law and to justice than their likely successors would if they were removed from office.[63]

Schorn's account received new power and credibility because of an attack on the brown background of the Federal Republic's judiciary from a new source, one that utterly lacked credibility at the height of the Cold War. Indeed, Schorn specifically referenced this attack as a reason for publishing the book. The German Democratic Republic had embarked in 1956, but with organized rigor beginning in May 1957, on a campaign to identify publicly those judges on the bench in the Federal Republic who had served the Third Reich, releasing in May 1957 a pamphlet entitled "Yesterday Hitler's Blood Judges—Today the Justice Elite of Bonn" which named 118 sitting West German judges who had also served the Nazis.[64] Because most of the archival documents of the Reich Ministry of Justice ended the war in Soviet, and later East German, hands, the German Democratic Republic held a treasure-trove of proof of the complicity of West German judges with Nazi practices and policies.[65] In edition after edition until 1968, the East Germans under the leadership of Albert Norden, head of the "Committee for German Unity," published ever expanding "Brown Books" listing the "war and Nazi criminals" active in the state, the economy, the army, the administration, the justice system, and higher education and research in the Federal Republic.[66] In the context of the Cold War, these denunciations from the German Democratic Republic made it easy to dismiss all criticisms of the West German judiciary, from whatever source, as communist propaganda.[67] Although the Adenauer government made concessions—such as to establish the Central Office of the State Ministries of Justice for the Investigation of National Socialist Crimes in Ludwigsburg to try previously unprosecuted Nazi war criminals, to extend the statute of limitations on Nazi-era murders in 1964 after the Eichmann trial, and to try Auschwitz guards in 1964—it never engaged in any consequential effort to weed its judiciary of judges who had enthusiastically served the Third Reich.[68] Annette Weinke has recently shown persuasively how the Adenauer government's effort to avoid extending the statute of limitations for murder prosecutions backfired. It only encouraged the East Germans, who discovered vast troves of Nazi-era documents made available to the Polish government by the Soviet Union and promptly incorporated into the "Brown Book." The Adenauer policy of foot-dragging and exculpation thus led to three unwanted outcomes: First, it vitiated the argument that all those guilty of Nazi crimes had been investigated and tried already; second, foreign and domestic outcry forced the parliamentary extension of the statute of limitations despite German government reluctance; and third, the outcry and the new materials invigorated the Central Office and led to an increase in prosecutions rather than to their cessation.[69] The onset of the student movement soon after the appearance of the expanded "Brown Book" in 1968 polarized German public opinion and distracted even the social-liberal government after 1969 from focus on the issue of ex-Nazis in the judiciary of the Federal Republic.

Critical Histories beyond the Cold War

In his recent history of the postwar Federal Republic, drawing upon the path-breaking analysis of Konrad Jarausch and others, the Berlin-based journalist Paul Hockenos argues that the student movement of the 1960s marks a profound caesura in the construction of a culture of genuine democracy in Germany, laying the foundation for the politics of the 1980s and the post-unification era.[70] Integral to those debates about the democratic rule of law in Germany was a wave of popular histories of the German judiciary that renewed the language of critique of the brown background of many West German judges—from inside West Germany rather than from East Germany—and also placed the experience of the Third Reich and Federal Republic in a longer context of German history back to the nineteenth century. Prompted by the imposition of a test of loyalty to the Basic Law as a condition of employment in state service (*Berufsverbot*), by the decision to deploy intermediate range nuclear missiles, and by renewed interest in unprosecuted Nazi criminals sparked by the trial in France of Klaus Barbie beginning in 1984, a series of books appeared, although none from academic historians.[71] Much of this literature articulated New Left skepticism of the administration of justice with regard to student dissidents and Red Army Faction terrorists on the one hand, and the violent police response to student demonstrations on the other, by drawing two unflattering comparisons.[72] First, these authors contrasted the contemporary West German judiciary with what they constructed as a braver and more daring set of judges at the vanguard of the German liberal movement in the mid-nineteenth century; second, they renewed the campaign to trace intellectual and personnel continuities between the Nazi and Federal Republic judiciaries. By either measure, the contemporary judiciary suffered by comparison or by association and remained complicit in a form of class justice.

The first of these works appeared in 1982, published by the press of *Stern* magazine, as a series of essays edited by Raimund Kusserow.[73] The essays opened with an epigraph from Heinrich Simon, the Breslau City Court judge who contended with Prussian King Friedrich Wilhelm IV over judicial independence and sat as a deputy at the German National Assembly in the Paulskirche in 1848. These essays in the Kusserow volume used the nineteenth-century past to accuse the twentieth-century German judiciary of insufficient independence and commitment to substantive notions of justice rather than to formal notions of positivism. In 1983, Jörg Friedrich published an exposé and documentation of how the compromised Nazi pasts of judges in the Federal Republic far too often had been swept under the rug and left unconfronted, titling his book *Acquittal for Nazi Justice*.[74] A central part of Friedrich's technique was to reproduce large sections of the judgments of acquittal by courts of the Federal Republic, letting the lengths to which judges would go to minimize or eliminate the criminal responsibility of Nazi-era judges speak for themselves, quoting the 1950s exculpatory narrative in order to undermine it.

Ingo Müller in 1987 delivered the broadest indictment of the behavior of the German judiciary in the Third Reich and its continuities into the Federal Republic in his book, *Dreadful Jurists: The Unmastered Past of Our System of Justice,* which later in 1991 appeared in English as *Hitler's Justice: The Courts of the Third Reich.*[75] After a truncated and whirlwind history of judges in the nineteenth century and in the Weimar Republic, Müller devotes 167 pages to debunking the myth that positivism bound judges to apply Nazified law reluctantly as it was given to them. He also demonstrates how the nationalist judges who remained in office after the initial purges of the judiciary in 1933–34 enthusiastically participated in the formation of National Socialist law by vying with each other to extend the uncodified notions of Nazi ideology into their jurisprudence and rulings. He then traces continuities beyond 1945 and 1949, justifying the claim of his book's title that Germany had not "come to grips with" this tainted past.

The climax of this critical historiography arrived in 1988–89 after the publication of Müller's book, with the appearance of three additional publications. First came a two-volume work by the popular Social Democratic author Bernt Engelmann called *The Invisible Tradition,* whose second volume, treating 1919 to the present and reveling in its depiction of the Nazi background of judges in the Federal Republic, bore the title *Legal Decay, Judicial Terror, and the Burdensome Inheritance.*[76] A polemic by Heinrich Senfft, published by a small leftist press, then appeared.[77] Working from present-day controversies about tainted contemporary judges, Senfft explored a rosier nineteenth-century past and concluded with "1945: No Zero Hour," emphasizing the continuity between 1933–45 and 1945 and beyond. Finally, Bernd Rüthers in 1989 brought out a second edition of his 1967 refutation of the positivism thesis, *Degenerate Law: Law Professors and Leading Jurists in the Third Reich,* in which he assiduously demonstrated the eager way in which German nationalist legal theorists and judges internalized and absorbed Nazi ideology and incorporated it into their scholarship and jurisprudence.[78]

Thus, the Deckert case in the early 1990s unfolded against the background of this efflorescence of renewed attention focused upon the repeated failures of the German judiciary to support the Weimar Republic, to resist the Nazis in the Third Reich, and to come to grips with its own past during the Federal Republic. In the post–Cold War atmosphere of 1994, when the generation of judges whose careers stretched back to the Third Reich was disappearing at an accelerating rate, this lively muck-raking and finger-pointing had helped the old taboos to disappear almost totally. But the Deckert affair also reflected and inspired yet another, more scholarly and less activist, renaissance in empirical study of the history and contours of the German judiciary that Markus Dirk Dubber called for in his *Columbia Law Review* discussion of the English translation of Müller's book, which he identified as the patient accumulation of empirical studies of the behavior of German judges and other jurists during the Third Reich.[79]

New Historical Work, New Historical Directions

Dubber's programmatic appeal credited solid but unspectacular scholarly work already under way. The roots of this movement in the tumult symbolized in Germany by 1968 are most apparent in the contribution of the scholarly journal *Kritische Justiz. Vierteljahrsschrift für Recht und Politik*. Founded in 1968, the journal throughout its history has published articles and monographs critical of the judiciary of the Federal Republic for its continuity of personnel with that of the Third Reich, and recuperative of a more useful past for German judges and other jurists.[80] The journal's publication series played an important role in the early phases of the new critical history of the judiciary in the Third Reich.[81] The collective research of the collaborators in *Kritische Justiz* culminated in a huge volume of essays in 1998 whose title conveyed its critical position, *The Juridical Rehabilitation of the Rule of Injustice* (*Die juristische Aufarbeitung des Unrechts-Staats*).[82] Emerging from the radical left, the persistent questioning by *Kritische Justiz* not only explored the past of the West German judiciary in its own pages, but also created space for scholars to lift the veil on the continuities of the West German judiciary that had been erected by the judges and politicians of the 1950s and 1960s.[83] Powerfully expressive of the analytical precision and moral force of this research is the work of Joachim Perels, whose 1999 monograph, *The Judicial Inheritance of the "Third Reich": Breakdowns of the Democratic Legal Order*, typifies the generational revulsion expressed in the pages of the journal for the failures of the legal establishment of the early Federal Republic to face this past honestly.[84]

Other legal historians in law faculties had also been hard at work at empirical investigations, often at the level of the geographic jurisdiction of a court of appeal. Exemplary here are the works of Rainer Schröder, law professor at the Humboldt University, on civil jurisprudence in the court of appeal region of Celle in the Prussian state of Hannover during the Third Reich; and Hinrich Rüping, law professor at Halle-

Wittenberg, on the state prosecutor's office and later the private bar in the jurisdiction of that same court.[85] Rudolf Wassermann, a retired judge, stated his case in the title of his book, *Even the Justice System Cannot Exit from History*.[86] These books methodically break down the exculpatory myths cherished by German judges by showing how the institutions of the judiciary, the prosecution, and even the private bar displayed little, if any, resistance to the seizure of power or the radicalization of ideology and policy, especially after the outbreak of the war and with the imminence of defeat; even in realms allegedly remote from the interests of National Socialist doctrine, such as civil law, judges radicalized their interpretation and application of the law to pervert justice by expropriating Jewish property, denying Jews insurance proceeds, and robbing Jews of the benefits of their bargain in contract law. Anniversary Festschriften for various courts of appeal appeared steadily throughout the 1990s and the subsequent decade, celebrating the high points of their histories, but not shying from stark depictions of low points during the Third Reich and after.[87] The empirical literature of case studies of the fate of Jewish jurists during the Third Reich also grew dramatically.[88] And throughout the last two decades, the Max Planck Institut for European Legal History, and its long-time Director, Michael Stolleis, produced a long series of useful histories of the law and the judiciary during the Third Reich.[89]

Only very recent years have seen a beginning of the systematic study by historians in history departments of the efforts in the Federal Republic to grapple with the continuity of personnel on the bench between the Third Reich and Federal Republic. Marc von Miquel's book *Punish or Grant Amnesty? West German Justice and Policy toward the Past in the 1960s* provides a perceptive overview of the restoration of the bench, its reluctance to engage in self-reflection in the 1950s, and the ways in which the campaigns in the 1960s and 1970s to extend the statute of limitations on Nazi-era crimes and the Auschwitz trial brought about the shift that permitted space for the critiques of the 1980s.[90]

But despite the dispassion and meticulousness of this research, questions remain to be answered. Those histories that examine the German judiciary before the First World War tend toward the recuperative, recalling a time in the middle of the nineteenth century when Prussian judges actively sought to realize constitutional government and liberal doctrine regarded them as the guarantors of liberty. They laud the Prussian *Landtag* with which Bismarck came into sharpest conflict, the one elected in 1862, sometimes called the "District Judges' Parliament" ("*Kreisrichter-Parlament*") for the prominent role that lower court judges played in the leadership of the liberal parties and in defense of the prerogatives of the legislature.[91] These histories note with pleasure that liberal judges in rural eastern district courts so vexed Bismarck that he referred to them contemptuously as the "constitutional house doctor" ("*konstitutionelle[r] Hausarzt*"), who presumptuously insisted upon the exclusive right to interpret and rule upon the constitutionality of acts of the administration.[92] These histories also create a counter-narrative or pre-history to the Social Democratic theme of "class justice," and they contrast this oppositional tradition with the irrefutable accumulated evidence that most German judges shared a thoroughgoing authoritarianism during the Weimar era and the Third Reich, enthusiastically embracing anti-republican and racist doctrines, and competing eagerly with one another in their desire to accommodate National Socialist ideology.

Conclusion

Very soon after the decision by the German Supreme Court in the Deckert case, that tribunal handed down another landmark decision. In a case that involved post-unification prosecution of an East German judge who had handed down death sentences valid under East German law, the Superior Court of Berlin had convicted that judge of perversion of justice (*Rechtsbeugung*) and had sentenced him to imprisonment. The German Supreme Court dismissed the appeal of the accused.[93] One reason that the Court recited to justify its decision to uphold this punishment was the previous failure of the West German judiciary to grapple with similar criminal behavior by the judges of the Third Reich:

> The jurisprudence of that era [the Third Reich] is often not unjustly characterized as "blood justice" in view of the excessive imposition of the death penalty. … The death sentences imposed by the People's Court have remained unatoned for, and none of the career judges and prosecutors active on the People's Court were convicted of perversion of justice, not to mention the judges of the Special Courts and courts-martial. The jurisprudence of the German Supreme Court last but not least must bear a considerable share of responsibility for this development. This jurisprudence has met with serious criticism, which this panel views as justified.[94]

Critics were quick to criticize this decision both as a "belated confession" ("*die späte Beichte*") and as an ironic willingness of the German Supreme

Court to find a perversion of justice in Communist death sentences where the same court had refused to find one in Nazi death sentences.[95] But the fact remains that for the first time, the German Supreme Court admitted the failure of the Federal Republic to prosecute and punish judges from the Third Reich for their complicity in a murderous regime, and further confessed the complicity of the BGH in that failure.

The Deckert and death penalty and perversion of justice decisions by the German Supreme Court signaled the beginning of the end of the judicial effort to come to grips with the role of judges in the Third Reich, as courts found themselves freed by political change from Cold War binaries and by demographic inevitability from personnel continuities. Historians thus need to continue to investigate the contours and structures of the judiciary and the rule of law in a longer context, beginning in the nineteenth century in the era of German unification and industrialization during the Second Empire. Necessarily, these histories must foreground the question of whether German judges' behavior during the Third Reich represented their failure to fulfill a prescribed role in state and society, or whether judges under any circumstances can succeed as bulwarks against radically unjust political regimes. Apart from a justifiable condemnation of German judges' culpable perversion of law and justice during the Third Reich, and apart from debate about whether the Kantian distinction between law and justice enshrined in legal positivism rendered judges defenseless against Nazi "law," the question remains whether even judges fully committed to the rule of law offer any guarantee of justice, in any society, in any era, or whether, as Rudolf Wassermann commented about the Deckert case, such a guarantee comes only from political education, fearless historical research, and the vigilance of a vibrant public sphere.

Notes

1. The judgment of the Landgericht Mannheim can be found in "Leugnung des Holocausts—Fall Deckert, Zur Strafbarkeit der Volksverhetzung," *Neue Juristische Wochenschrift* 47 (1994): 2494–99. The actual charges included "Volksverhetzung in Tateinheit mit übler Nachrede, Verunglimpfung des Andenkens Verstorbener, und Aufstachelung zum Rassenhaß." Donald P. Kommers provides a brief account of the affair in English in idem, "Autonomy versus Accountability: The German Judiciary," Peter H. Russell and David M. O'Brien, eds., *Judicial Independence in the Age of Democracy: Critical Perspectives from Around the World* (Charlottesville, VA,

2001), 131–54, 132–33. See also the *New York Times,* August 10, 1994, Sec. A, p. 8, col. 1. The Deckert case had already become a teaching example of the complexity of German criminal procedure, having risen on appeal to the *Bundesgerichtshof* once before the June 1994 imposition of sentence; see "Zur Strafbarkeit des Leugnens der systematischen Tötung von Juden unter der nationalsozialistischen Gewaltsherrschaft," *Neue Juristische Wochenschrift* 47 (1994):1421–23, also found at *Entscheidungen des Bundesgerichtshofs, Strafsachen* 40 (1995): 97–106.
2. "Leugnung des Holocausts," 2498–99. The justifying paragraph of the judgment read: Finally, we cannot fail to note the difficult fate in life of the accused, who had to give up his beloved profession after a long and successful career as a teacher and who now is reduced to a penurious existence. By noting this fact, this court does not disregard the reality that the accused must attribute this evil to his own behavior. But we also must note that the State of Baden-Württemberg hired and promoted him while he was an active member of the NPD and that for many years he continued his political activity with the full knowledge of his supervisors, until a new departure in the jurisprudence of the court of last resort brought him into conflict with his duties as a state official. The fact that he thereafter could not bring himself to sever his ties to the NPD with the necessary completeness, this court must view as the result of a decision of conscience that should be respected.
3. "Strafbarkeit wegen Leugnens des Holocausts—Fall Deckert II," *Neue Juristische Wochenschrift* 48 (1995): 340–41.
4. Rudolf Wassermann, "Richteranklage im Fall Orlet?" *Neue Juristische Wochenschrift* 48 (1995): 303–04, rejecting this measure as both outside the scope of the "Richteranklage" and violative of judicial independence. For a history of the inclusion of the Richteranklage in the Basic Law and a more favorable view toward its use, see Hans Wrobel, "Geh—schmeiß ihn von dem Tribunal herunter! Bemerkungen zum 8. Mai 1945, zur Richteranklage speziell und zur jüngeren Justizgeschichte überhaupt," *Deutsche Richterzeitung. Organ des Deutschen Richterbundes* 73 (1994): 199–206. For a thoughtful and extended discussion of the dilemma posed to judicial independence by the existence of such a disciplinary action, in the context of the Deckert case, see Rolf Lamprecht, *Vom Mythos der Unabhängigkeit. Über das Dasein und Sosein der deutschen Richter* (Baden-Baden, 1996), especially 33–46.
5. Kommers, "Autonomy versus Accountability," 133.
6. Günter Bertram, "Noch einmal: Die 'Auschwitzlüge'—Anmerkungen zum Urteil der 6. Großen Strafkammer des LG Mannheim vom 22.6.1994," *Neue Juristische Wochenschrift* 47 (1994): 2397–99, 2399.
7. Rudolf Wassermann, "Einäugige Justiz? In ihren Richtern spiegelt sich die Gesellschaft wider," *Recht und Politik* 30 (1994): 227–28.
8. Diethelm Klippel, ed., *Deutsche Rechts- und Gerichtskarte. Eine Einteilung des Deutschen Reichs nach Gebieten des Bürgerlichen Rechts und nach umfassenden Gerichtsbezirken. Mit Orientierungsheft* (Goldbach, 1996; reprint of first edition, Kassel, 1896) displays this legal complexity with stunning visual clarity.
9. For a discussion of the changes made and structures created by the Imperial Justice Laws, see Kenneth F. Ledford, *From General Estate to Special Interest: German Lawyers 1878–1933* (Cambridge, 1996), 59–74, and idem, "Lawyers, Liberalism, and Procedure: The Imperial Justice Laws of 1877–79," *Central European History* 26 (1993): 165–93.

10. For a detailed account of the precise placements and seniority dates of all trainees, career judges, and prosecutors in Prussia, see, as an example, Bureau des Preußischen Justizministeriums, *Dienstlaufbahn der Preußischen Richter und Staatsanwälte* (Berlin, 1902).
11. Thomas Kolbeck, *Juristenschwemmen. Untersuchungen über den juristischen Arbeitsmarkt im 19. und 20. Jahrhundert* (Frankfurt, 1978).
12. The Prussian Ministry of Justice paid close attention to the confessional composition of its judiciary, and to its distribution among the predominantly Protestant and predominantly Catholic portions of the kingdom; see Geheimes Staatsarchiv, Preußischer Kulturbesitz, I. H.A., Rep. 84a, Nr. 11944: Konfessionsverhältnisse der höheren Justizbeamten, Bd. II, 1880–1926.
13. Barbara Strenge, *Juden im preußischen Justizdienst 1812–1918. Der Zugang zu den juristischen Berufen als Indikator der gesellschaftlichen Emanzipation* (Munich, 1996), and Peter Pulzer, "Religion and Judicial Appointments in Germany, 1869–1918," *Leo Baeck Institute Year Book* 28 (1983): 185–204.
14. One typical example is Dr. jur. A. Berthold, *Volksjustiz oder Klassenjustiz? Proletarischen Betrachtungen über Recht und Rechtspflege* (Hamburg, 1895). As a kind of summary of this massive literature, see Erich Kuttner, *Klassenjustiz!* (Berlin, 1913); see also Hubert Rottleuthner, "Die gebrochene Bürgerlichkeit einer Scheinprofession. Zur Situation der deutschen Richterschaft zu Beginn des 20. Jahrhunderts," in Hannes Siegrist, ed., *Bürgerliche Berufe. Zur Sozialgeschichte der freien und akademischen Berufe im internationalen Vergleich* (Göttingen, 1988), 154–73. Finally see the legal dissertation by Gerd Linnemann, "Klassenjustiz und Weltfremdheit. Deutsche Justizkritik 1890–1914" (Dr. jur. diss., Christian-Albrechts-Universität zu Kiel, 1989).
15. Alex Hall, *Scandal, Sensation, and Social Democracy: The SPD Press and Wilhelmine Germany, 1890–1914* (Cambridge, 1977). The most comprehensive recent examination of the issue is Uwe Wilhelm, *Das Deutsche Kaiserreich und seine Justiz. Justizkritik—politische Strafrechtsprechung—Justizpolitik* (Berlin, 2010); Wilhelm goes so far as to describe the 1890s as the "crisis of confidence" of the German justice system (*"Vertrauenskrise der Justiz"*), 323–478.
16. See the volume on the *Feme* murders by right-wing death squads written by the leftist mathematician, Emil Julius Gumbel, *Vier Jahre politischer Mord* (Berlin, 1922).
17. Ernst Fraenkel, *Zur Soziologie der Klassenjustiz und Aufsätze zur Verfassungskrise 1931–1932* (Darmstadt, 1968), "Zur Soziologie der Klassenjustiz," 1–41 (originally published January 1927).
18. Eike von Repkow, pseud. for Robert M. W. Kempner, *Justizdämmerung. Auftakt zum Dritten Reich* (Berlin, 1932); Eike von Repkow is the name of the presumed author of the medieval German law code, the *Sachsenspiegel*. For a postwar account, see also Heinrich Hannover and Elisabeth Hannover-Drück, *Politische Justiz 1918-1933* (Frankfurt, 1966).
19. Birger Schulz, *Die Republikanische Richterbund (1921–1922)* (Frankfurt and Bern, 1982), with the membership figures, and the problems in deriving them, discussed at 40–42.
20. Peter Landau, "Juristen jüdischer Herkunft in Kaiserreich und in der Weimarer Republik. Dem Andenken Ernst Landsbergs," in Helmut Heinrichs, Harald Franzki,

Klaus Schmalz, and Michael Stolleis, eds., *Deutsche Juristen jüdischer Herkunft* (Munich, 1993), 133–213.
21. Tillman Krach, *Jüdische Rechtsanwälte in Preußen. Über die Bedeutung der freien Advokatur und ihre Zerstörung durch den Nationalsozialismus* (Munich, 1991), Tabel 3, 416–17.
22. Theo Rasehorn, *Justizkritik in der Weimarer Republik. Das Beispiel "Die Justiz"* (Frankfurt, 1985); see also Schulz, *Der Republikanische Richterbund,* 206–11.
23. Douglas G. Morris, *Justice Imperiled: The Anti-Nazi Lawyer Max Hirschberg in Weimar Germany* (Ann Arbor, MI, 2005).
24. Benjamin Carter Hett, *Crossing Hitler: The Man Who Put the Nazis on the Witness Stand* (Oxford, 2008).
25. The most accessible English-language account remains Ingo Müller, *Hitler's Justice: The Courts of the Third Reich,* trans. Deborah Lucas Schneider (Cambridge, 1991), 27–119. The definitive account is Krach, *Jüdische Rechtsanwälte,* 165–402.
26. Rudolf Wassermann, *"Kammergericht soll bleiben." Ein Gang durch die Geschichte des berühmtesten deutschen Gerichts (1468–1945)* (Berlin, 2004), 109–11.
27. *Gesetz zur Wiederherstellung des Berufsbeamtentums, Reichsgesetzblatt* 1933 I, 175.
28. Wolfgang Benz, "Von der Entrechtung zur Verfolgung und Vernichtung. Jüdische Juristen unter dem nationalsozialistischen Regime," in *Deutsche Juristen,* ed. Heinrichs, Franzki, Schmalz, and Stolleis, 813–52, 823–26. See also Horst Göppinger, *Juristen jüdischer Abstammung im "Dritten Reich". Entrechtung und Verfolgung,* 2d ed. (Munich, 1990), 45–84. For Hindenburg's well-known position, see Wolfram Pyta, *Hindenburg. Herrschaft zwischen Hohenzollern und Hitler* (Munich, 2007), 832.
29. Angermund, *Deutsche Richterschaft 1919–1945,* 45–61; see also Frank Altpeter, "Der Deutsche Richterbund seit 1933. Über die Bewältigung der nationalsozialistischen Vergangenheit—von politischer Selbstaufgabe zu neuem politischen Bewußtsein im DRB," *Deutsche Richterzeitung* 73 (1995): 207–12.
30. Göppinger, *Juristen jüdischer Abstammung,* 87–97.
31. Benz, "Von der Entrechtung," 839.
32. Reinhard Bendix, *From Berlin to Berkeley: German-Jewish Identities* (New Brunswick, NJ, 1986), 99–130; this work is a translation of the earlier German version, idem, *Von Berlin nach Berkeley. Deutsch-jüdische Identitäten* (Frankfurt, 1985).
33. Most recently, see Hans Bergemann and Simone Ladwig-Winters, *Jüdische Richter am Kammergericht nach 1933. Eine Dokumentation* (Cologne, 2004), and idem, *Richter und Staatsanwälte jüdischer Herkunft in Preußen im Nationalsozialismus. Eine Dokumentation* (Cologne, 2004).
34. Bergemann and Ladwig-Winters, *Richter und Staatsanwälte jüdischer Herkunft in Preußen,* 114.
35. For an account of the absorption of the Prussian Ministry of Justice into the Reich Ministry, see Lothar Gruchmann, "Die Überleitung der Justizverwaltung auf das Reich 1933–1935," in Bundesministerium der Justiz, ed., *Vom Reichsjustizamt zum Bundesministerium der Justiz. Festschrift zum 100jährigen Gründungstag des Reichsjustizamtes am 1. Januar 1877* (Cologne, 1977), 119–59.
36. Edith Roper, *Skeleton of Justice,* trans. Clara Leiser (New York, 1941; reprint ed. New York, 1975).

37. Hans von Hentig, review of *Skeleton of Justice*, *American Journal of Sociology* 47 (1941): 497–99.
38. For a description of the enactment of the laws creating the Special Courts, see Angermund, *Deutsche Richterschaft 1919–1945*, 133–57.
39. The origin of these courts under Brüning and Papen is described in Anthony McElligott, "Dangerous Communities and Conservative Authority: The Judiciary, Nazis, and Rough People, 1932-1933," in Tim Kirk and Anthony McElligott, eds., *Opposing Fascism: Community, Authority, and Resistance in Europe* (Cambridge, 1999), 33–47, esp. at 39.
40. Karl Loewenstein, "Law in the Third Reich," *Yale Law Journal* 45 (1936): 779–815, 789–92 and 808–10 treats the many exceptional courts created by the National Socialists. Lowenstein, a political scientist from Munich, who fled in 1933 because of persecution based upon his Jewish ancestry, later served in the U.S. military government in western Germany and taught at Yale and at Amherst, before returning to the University of Munich in 1956 to assume a university chair only to immediately retire. He spent the remainder of his life in Germany, holding numerous guest professorships before his death in 1973. For a recent excellent treatment of Lowenstein's frustrated efforts to purge the German judiciary of Nazis as a member Legal Division of the American Military Government in Berlin from August 1945 through June 1946, see Rande Kostal, "The Alchemy of Occupation: Karl Loewenstein and the Legal Reconstruction of Nazi Germany, 1945–1946," *Law and History Review* 29 (2011): 1–52.
41. Roper, *Skeleton of Justice*, 286–320, the number twenty quoted on 288; Roper notes at 286–87 that of 90 persons convicted of murder in Germany in 1928, and 69 in 1929, not one suffered execution. But by 1938, when statistics ceased to be compiled, newspaper reports revealed 2 executions per day nationwide. After the beginning of the war, and accelerating in 1944, the number of death penalties levied and carried out rose even higher.
42. Müller, *Hitler's Justice*, 196.
43. For a broad account of Allied de-Nazification plans, see Peter Reichel, *Vergangenheitsbewältigung in Deutschland. Die Auseinandersetzung mit der NS-Diktatur von 1945 bis heute* (Munich, 2001), 30–41; for the changes that occurred once the Federal Republic came into being, see Norbert Frei, *Adenauer's Germany and the Nazi Past: The Politics of Amnesty and Integration*, trans. Joel Golb (New York, 2002), 1–39.
44. For an extended account of this process in the Soviet and British zones, as well as the reassertion of German agency in the process, see Martin Broszat, "Siegerjustiz oder strafrechtliche 'Selbstreinigung'. Aspekte der Vergangenheitsbewältigung der deutschen Justiz während der Besatzungszeit 1945–1949," *Vierteljahrshefte für Zeitgeschichte* 29 (1981): 477–544.
45. See the case against legal officials in *Trials of War Criminals Before the Nuernberg Military Tribunals Under Control Council Law No. 10*, Nuremberg, October 1946–April 1949, 15 vols. (Washington, 1949–53), vol. III, Case 3, *U.S. v. Alstoetter* ("The Justice Case") (Washington, 1951) (hereafter cited as "*Justice Case*").
46. For biographies of Franz Schlegelberger, see Eli Nathans, *Franz Schlegelberger* (Baden-Baden, 1990) and Michael Förster, *Jurist im Dienst des Unrechts. Leben und Werk des ehemaligen Staatssekretärs in Reichsjustizministerium, 1876–1970* (Baden-

Baden, 1995). In English see Eli Nathans, "Legal Order as Motive and Mask: Franz Schlegelberger and the Nazi Administration of Justice," *Law and History Review* 18 (2000): 281–304.

47. *Justice Case*, 1143–56; on Rothaug's role in the *Katzenberger* case, 1150–56. For the judgment of the Special Court in the Katzenberger case, sentencing Katzenberger to death, see Ilse Staff, ed., *Justiz im Dritten Reich. Eine Dokumentation* (Frankfurt, 1964), 178–91. A careful analysis of the legal issues involved is Günter Spendel, "Justizmord durch Rechtsbeugung. Ein Todesurteil wegen 'Rassenschande'," in idem, *Rechtsbeugung durch Rechtsprechung. Sechs strafrechtliche Studien* (Berlin and New York, 1984), 37–54, originally published in *Neue Juristische Wochenschrift* in 1971.
48. *Justice Case*, 985.
49. Broszat, "Siegerjustiz oder strafrechtliche 'Selbstreinigung'," 520–22; see also Devin O. Pendas, "Retroactive Law and Proactive Justice: Debating Crimes against Humanity in Germany, 1945–1950," *Central European History* 43 (September 2010): 18–19, which also discusses von Hodenberg's prominent role in the "Heidelberg Circle" of judges and lawyers who strategized how to deploy legal positivism in defense of accused German war criminals.
50. Wolfgang Benz, "Die Entnazifizierung der Richter," in Diestelkamp and Stolleis, eds., *Justizalltag*, 112–30, and Klaus-Detlev Godau-Schüttke, "Entnazifizierung und Wiederaufbau der Justiz am Beispiel des Bundesgerichtshofs," in Eva Schumann, ed., *Kontinuitäten und Zäsuren. Rechtswissenschaft und Justiz im 'Dritten Reich' und in der Nachkriegszeit* (Göttingen, 2008), 189–212.
51. For a powerful contemporary complaint, see Karl Loewenstein, "Justice," in Edward H. Litchfield, ed., *Governing Postwar Germany* (Ithaca, 1953), 236–62, especially 245–55, "Problems of Judicial Personnel," in which he attributed to this continuity of judicial personnel "the chain of recent court decisions which represent gross miscarriage of justice," 254. For a detailed study of Lowenstein's frustrations at the abandonment of de-Nazification by his superiors in OMGUS, see Rande W. Kostal, "'The Alchemy of Occupation': Karl Lowenstein and the Legal Reconstruction of Nazi Germany, 1945–1946," forthcoming in *Law and History Review.*
52. Gustav Radbruch, "Gesetzliches Unrecht und übergesetzliches Recht," Anhang Nr. 4 in idem, *Rechtsphilosophie,* 8 ed., ed by Erik Wolf and Hans-Peter Schneider (Stuttgart, 1973), 339–50. An excellent English translation is available in idem, "Statutory Lawlesness and Supra-Statutory Law," in David Dyzenhaus, Sophia Reibetanz Moreau, and Arthur Ripstein, eds., *Law and Morality: Readings in Legal Philosophy*, 3rd ed. (Toronto, 2007), 127–40.
53. Radbruch, "Statutory Lawlessness," 131.
54. The clearest explanation of Radbruch's purpose is in Markus Dirk Dubber, "Judicial Positivism and Hitler's Injustice," *Columbia Law Review* 93 (1993): 1807–32, in a review of Müller, *Hitler's Justice*. See also, Walter Ott and Franziska Buob, "Did Legal Positivism Render German Jurists Defenceless during the Third Reich?" *Social & Legal Studies* 2 (1993): 91–104, which answers the question resoundingly: "No!", and Manfred Walther, "Hat der juristische Positivismus die deutschen Juristen wehrlos Gemacht?", in Kritische Justiz, ed., *Die juristische Aufarbeitung des Unrechts-Staats* (Baden-Baden, 1998), 299–322, who also refutes the claim that positivism was the cause for German judges' actions during the Third Reich.

55. Helmut Kramer, "Juristisches Denken als Legitimationsfassade zur Errichtung und Stablisierung autoritärer Systeme," in Schumann, *Kontinuitäten und Zäsuren*, 153–63, devotes a section to "Legal Positivism as Scapegoat" ("Der Rechtspositivismus als Sündenbock").
56. Eberhard Schmidt, *Gesetz und Richter. Wert und Unwert des Positivismus. Vortrag gehalten bei der Eröffnung der Juristischen Studiengesellschaft in Karlsruhe am 23. Februar 1952* (Karlsruhe, 1952). Schmidt is the subject of a recent biography, Simone Gräfin von Hardenberg, *Eberhard Schmidt (1891-1977). Ein Beitrag unseres Rechtsstaates* (Berlin, 2009). Helmut Kramer traces Schmidt's use of positivism to defend the whole German judiciary to a speech to a jurist's convention in Bad Godesberg in 1947, "Juristisches Denken als Legitimationsfassade," 143–44.
57. H.L.A. Hart, "Positivism and the Separation of Law and Morals," *Harvard Law Review* 71 (1958): 593–629, and Lon L. Fuller, "Positivism and Fidelity to Law: A Reply to Professor Hart," *Harvard Law Review* 71(1958): 630–72.
58. Hart, "Positivism and the Separation of Law and Morals," 619.
59. Dubber, "Judicial Positivism and Hitler's Injustice," 1826, emphasizes how both Hart and Fuller typify the debate around positivism by asserting categorical truths rather than acknowledging the obvious, that legal positivism played a limited but not determining role in German judges' imbrication with the National Socialist regime.
60. For the political and legislative side of this story, see Frei, *Adenauer's Germany and the Nazi Past*, 1–91.
61. Joachim Perels, "Perceptions and Suppression of Nazi Crimes by the Postwar German Judiciary," in Nathan Stoltzfus and Henry Friedlander, eds., *Nazi Crimes and the Law* (Cambridge, 2008), 87–99, especially 92–93. For a more thorough account, see idem, *Das juristische Erbe des "Dritten Reiches". Beschädigung der demokratischen Rechtsordnung* (Frankfurt, 1999), 181–202 Kerstin Freudiger, *Die juristische Aufarbeitung von NS-Verbrechen* (Tübingen, 2002), 294–317 and 381-403, provides examples of two other cases in which postwar courts absolved judges from the Third Reich of criminal culpability for promiscuous imposition of death sentences.
62. Hubert Schorn, *Der Richter im Dritten Reich. Geschichte und Dokumente* (Frankfurt, 1959).
63. See here the summary of Schorn's book in an undated review of *Hitler's Justice*, Yitzchok A. Breitowitz, *Jewish Law Commentary: Examining Halacha, Jewish Issues, and Secular Law*, on line at http://www.jlaw.com/Commentary/book.html, accessed on April 11, 2009.
64. Ausschuß für Deutsche Einheit, *Gestern Hitlers Blutrichter—Heute Bonner Justiz-Elite* (Berlin, 1957). The definitive account of this campaign is the excellent recent monograph, Marc von Miquel, *Ahnden oder Amnestieren? Westdeutsche Justiz und Vergangenheitspolitik in den sechziger Jahren* (Göttingen, 2004), especially 27–81. For a brief overview in English of the argument in von Miquel's book, see idem, "Explanation, Dissociation, Apologia: The Debate over the Criminal Prosecution of Nazi Crimes in the 1960s," in Philipp Gassert and Alan E. Steinweis, eds., *Coping with the Nazi Past: West German Debates on Nazism and Generational Conflict, 1955-1975* (New York and Oxford, 2006), 50–63.
65. See Jeffrey Herf, *Divided Memory: The Nazi Past in the Two Germanys* (Cambridge, 1997), 181–85.

66. Nationalrat der Nationalen Front des Demokratischen Deutschland Dokumentationszentrum der Staatlichen Archivverwaltung der DDR, ed., *Braunbuch. Kriegs- und Naziverbrecher in der Bundesrepublik* (Berlin: Staatsverlag der Deutschen Demokratischen Republik, 1965); the DDR also published translations to reach non-German-reading audiences, such as idem, ed., *Brown Book: War and Nazi Criminals in West Germany* (Berlin, 1965). On these early campaigns, see Klaus Bästlein, "'Nazi-Blutrichter als Stützen des Adenauer-Regimes'. Die DDR-Kampagne gegen NS-Richter und -Staatsanwälte, die Reaktionen der bundesdeutschen Justiz und ihre gescheiterte 'Selbstreinigung' 1957–68," in Helge Grabitz, Klaus Bästlein, and Johannes Tuchel, eds., *Die Normalität des Verbrechens. Bilanz und Perspektiven der Forschung zu den nationalsozialistischen Gewaltverbrechen, Festschrift für Wolfgang Scheffler zum 65. Geburtstag* (Berlin, 1994), 408–43.
67. A critical account of the efforts of the Adenauer government to grapple with this tainted past is Annette Weinke, "Die Selbstamnestierung der bundesdeutschen Justiz 1957-1965: Der Fall West-Berlin," *Zeitschrift für Geschichtswissenschaft* 46 (1998): 622–38.
68. Two excellent recent studies recount the debates surrounding these issues in the late 1950s and early 1960s: Rebecca Wittmann, *Beyond Justice: The Auschwitz Trial* (Cambridge, 2005) and Devin O. Pendas, *The Frankfurt Auschwitz Trial, 1963–1965: Genocide, History, and the Limits of the Law* (Cambridge, 2006)
69. Annette Weinke, "The German-German Rivalry and the Prosecution of Nazi War Criminals During the Cold War, 1958–1965," in Stoltzfus and Friedlander, eds., *Nazi Crimes and the Law,* 151–72, especially 163–71. In addition, the necessity to deal with the Communist government of Poland led to a relaxation of the "Hallstein Doctrine" and thus presaged the success of *Ostpolitik* under the Brandt government.
70. Paul Hockenos, *Joschka Fischer and the Making of the Berlin Republic: An Alternative History of Postwar Germany* (Oxford, 2008).
71. Throughout the 1980s, however, Lothar Gruchmann headed a massive project at the Institut für Zeitgeschichte in Munich to investigate the administration of justice during the Third Reich, whose greatest product was the massive Lothar Gruchmann, *Justiz im Dritten Reich 1933–1940. Anpassung und Unterwerfung in der Ära Gürtner,* 2d ed. (Munich, 1990; 1st ed., 1988).
72. Ironically, it was the *Berufsverbot* that led to Günter Deckert losing his position as a school-teacher because of his neo-Nazi convictions.
73. Raimund Kusserow, ed., *Richter in Deutschland. Der längst fällige Report über die Halbgötter in Schwarz* (Hamburg, 1982).
74. Jörg Friedrich, *Freispruch für die Nazi-Justiz. Die Urteile gegen NS-Richter seit 1948. Eine Dokumentation,* überarbeitete und ergänzte Ausgabe (Berlin, 1998; 1st ed. Reinbek, 1983).
75. Ingo Müller, *Furchtbare Juristen. Die unbewältigte Vergangenheit unserer Justiz* (Munich, 1987), in English as idem, *Hitler's Justice: The Courts of the Third Reich,* trans. by Deborah Lucas Schneider (Cambridge, 1991). The translated English title fails to convey the passion and breadth of the original; a more precise translation would be *Dreadful Jurists: The Unmastered Past of Our System of Justice.*
76. Bernt Engelmann, *Die unsichtbare Tradition,* 2 vols. (Cologne, 1988–89), vol. 1: *Richter zwischen Recht und Macht 1779–1918;* vol. 2: *Rechtsverfall, Justizterror und*

das schwere Erbe. Ein Beitrag zur Geschichte der deutschen Strafjustiz von 1919 bis heute.
77. Heinrich Senfft, *Richter und andere Bürger. 150 Jahre politische Justiz und neudeutsche Herrschaftspublizistik* (Nördlingen, 1988)
78. Bernd Rüthers, *Entartetes Recht. Rechtslehren und Kronjuristen im Dritten Reich,* 2d ed. (Munich, 1989; 1st ed. Tübingen, 1967).
79. Dubber, "Hitler's Injustice," 1809.
80. For a history of the journal on the fortieth anniversary of its foundation, see Sonja Buckel, Andreas Fischer-Lescano, and Felix Haschmann, "Die Geburt der *Kritischen Justiz* aus der Praxis des Widerständigen," *Kritische Justiz* 41 (2008): 235–43. In typical fashion for the pages of the journal, the essay's authors take it to task for its belated opening to feminist legal scholarship.
81. Two volumes of critical essays are particularly important: Redaktion Kritische Justiz, ed., *Der Unrechts-Staat I. Recht und Justiz im Nationalsozialismus* (Frankfurt, 1979; 2d ed. Baden-Baden, 1983), and idem, ed., *Der Unrechts-Staat II. Recht und Justiz im Nationalsozialismus* (Baden-Baden, 1984). The Nathans biography of Schlegelberger is volume III in this series. A volume of essays celebrating famous liberal or leftist jurists is Kritische Justiz, ed., *Streitbare Juristen. Eine andere Tradition* (Baden-Baden, 1988).
82. Kritische Justiz, ed., *Die juristische Aufarbeitung des Unrechts-Staats,* presents thirty-three essays on the history of law and jurists in the Third Reich before it then presents four essays on the German Democratic Republic in a section called "Prospect: On the Juridical Treatment of the SED Dictatorship." This volume also presents a chronological listing of essays on law in the Third Reich published between 1968 and 1997, 769–78.
83. An article covering the conference in honor of the fortieth anniversary of the founding of *Kritische Justiz* in October 2008 appeared in the left-wing *Tageszeitung* ironically notes that the journal has become a "brand name" (Markenzeichen), Rudolf Walther, "Kritische Justiz zwischen Aufruhr und Mainstream," *Tageszeitung,* October 11, 2009.
84. Perels, *Das juristische Erbe des "Dritten Reichs,"* especially 11–38.
85. Rainer Schröder, *"... aber im Zivilrecht sind die Richter standhaft geblieben!" Die Urteile des OLG Celle aus dem Dritten Reich* (Baden-Baden, 1988); Hinrich Rüping, *Staatsanwaltschaft und Provinzialjustizverwaltung im Dritten Reich. Aus den Akten der Staatsanwaltschaft bei dem Oberlandesgericht Celle als höhere Reichsjustizbehörde* (Baden-Baden, 1990); and idem, *Rechtsanwälte im Bezirk Celle während des Nationalsozialismus* (Berlin, 2007).
86. Rudolf Wassermann, *Auch die Justiz kann aus der Geschichte nicht aussteigen* (Baden-Baden, 1990).
87. See, for example, Christoph Schiller, *Das Oberlandesgericht Karlsruhe im Dritten Reich* (Berlin, 1997); Martin Dreyer, *Die zivilrechtliche Rechtsprechung des Oberlandesgerichts Düsseldorf in der nationalsozialistischen Zeit* (Göttingen, 2004); and Can Bozyakali, *Das Sondergericht am Hanseatischen Oberlandesgericht: Eine Untersuchung der NS-Sondergerichte unter besonderer Berücksichtigung der Anwendung der Verordnung gegen Volksschädlinge* (Frankfurt, 2005).
88. Klaus Luig, *... weil er nicht arischer Abstammung ist. Jüdische Juristen in Köln während der NS-Zeit* (Cologne, 2004).

89. A useful compendium of essays is available in English, Michael Stolleis, *The Law Under the Swastika: Studies on Legal History in Nazi Germany,* trans. by Thomas Dunlap (Chicago, 1998).
90. von Miquel, *Ahnden oder amnestieren?*.
91. Adalbert Hess, *Das Parlament das Bismarck widerstrebte. Zur Politik und sozialen Zusammensetzung des preußischen Abgeordnetenhauses der Konfliktszeit (1862–1866)* (Cologne and Opladen, 1964), esp. 61–63. For the "doctrinaire" liberalism of lower court judges, see Eugene N. Anderson, *The Social and Political Conflict in Prussia 1858–1864* (Lincoln, 1954), 290.
92. Bismarck made this comment in the course of a debate on the floor of the North German Reichstag on April 22, 1868; Otto von Bismarck, *Die gesammelten Werke,* 15 vols. in 19 (Berlin, 1924–35), vol. 10, *Reden: 1847 bis 1869,* ed. by Dr. Wilhelm Schüßler (1928), 456–62, 458. The reference to the "constitutional house doctor" is quoted in a passage on judicial independence in Hans Hattenhauer, *Geschichte des deutschen Beamtentums,* 2d rev. ed. (Cologne, 1993), 307–13, 309. For a broader discussion of Bismarck's antipathy toward judges, replete with many examples of anti-judge epithets, see Bartolomäus, "Fürst Bismarck und der preußische Richterstand," *Preußische Jahrbücher* 99 (1900):177–81.
93. *Entscheidungen des Bundesgerichtshofs, Strafsachen* 41 (1996): 317, decision of November 16, 1995.
94. Reichel, *Vergangenheitsbewältigung in Deutschland,* 63, and Freudiger, *Die juristische Aufarbeitung von NS-Verbrechen,* 403, note this decision with approval and quote this passage.
95. Günter Spendel, "Rechtsbeugung und BGH—eine Kritik," *Neue Juristische Wochenschrift* 49 (1996): 809–12, and Otto Gritschneder, "Die späte Beichte des Bundesgerichtshofs," *Neue Juristische Wochenschrift* 49 (1996): 1239–41. Spendel in fact criticizes the court's decision for overly restricting the concept of perversion of justice and setting the stage to repeat history by again pursuing judicial injustice with insufficient vigor.

Appendix A

Article 48 of the Weimar Constitution

11 August 1919

ARTICLE 48

If any state does not fulfill the duties imposed upon it by the Constitution or the laws of the Reich, the Reich President may enforce such duties with the aid of the armed forces.

In the event that the public order and security are seriously disturbed or endangered, the Reich President may take the measures necessary for their restoration, intervening, if necessary, with the aid of the armed forces. For this purpose he may temporarily abrogate, wholly or in part, the fundamental principles laid down in Articles 114 [personal liberty], 115 [inviolability of dwelling], 117 [secrecy of postal, telephonic, and telegraphic communications], 118 [freedom of expression], 123 [freedom of assembly], 124 [freedom to form associations], and 153 [inviolability of property].

The Reich President must, without delay, inform the Reichstag of all measures taken under Paragraph 1 or Paragraph 2 of this Article. The Reichstag may vote to annul these measures. […]

Source: German Historical Institute, Washington, D.C., *German History in Documents and Images,* http://germanhistorydocs.ghi-dc.org.

Appendix B

Decree of the Reich President for the Protection of the People and State (Reichstag Fire Decree)

28 February 1933

On the basis of Article 48, Section 2, of the German Constitution, the following is decreed as a defensive measure against Communist acts of violence that endanger the state:

§ 1: Articles 114, 115, 117, 118, 123, 124, and 153 of the Constitution of the German Reich are suspended until further notice. Thus, restrictions on personal liberty, on the right of free expression of opinion, including freedom of the press, on the right of assembly and the right of association, and violations of the privacy of postal, telegraphic, and telephonic communications, and warrants for house searches, orders for confiscations as well as restrictions on property are permissible beyond the legal limits otherwise prescribed.

§ 2: If any state fails to take the necessary measures to restore public safety and order, the Reich government may temporarily take over the powers of the highest state authority.

§ 3: State and local authorities must obey the orders decreed by the Reich government on the basis of § 2.

§ 4: Whoever provokes, appeals for, or incites the disobedience of the orders given out by the supreme state authorities or the authorities subject to them for the execution of this decree, or the orders given by the Reich government according to § 2, can be punished – insofar as the deed is not covered by other decrees with more severe punishments – with imprisonment of not less than one month, or with a fine from 150 to 15,000 Reichsmark.

Whoever endangers human life by violating § 1 is to be punished by sentence to a penitentiary, under mitigating circumstances with imprisonment of not less than six months and, when the violation causes the death of a person, with death, under mitigating circumstances with a penitentiary sentence of not less than two years. In addition, the sentence may include the confiscation of property.

Whoever provokes or incites an act contrary to the public welfare is to be punished with a penitentiary sentence, under mitigating circumstances, with imprisonment of not less than three months.

§ 5: The crimes which under the Criminal Code are punishable with life in a penitentiary are to be punished with death: i.e., in Sections 81 (high treason), 229 (poisoning), 306 (arson), 311 (explosion), 312 (flooding), 315, paragraph 2 (damage to railways), 324 (general public endangerment through poison).

Insofar as a more severe punishment has not been previously provided for, the following are punishable with death or with life imprisonment or with imprisonment not to exceed 15 years:

1. Anyone who undertakes to kill the Reich President or a member or a commissioner of the Reich government or of a state government, or provokes such a killing, or agrees to commit it, or accepts such an offer, or conspires with another for such a murder;

2. Anyone who under Section 115, paragraph 2, of the Criminal Code (serious rioting) or of Section 125, paragraph 2, of the Criminal Code (serious disturbance of the peace) commits these acts with arms or cooperates consciously and intentionally with an armed person;

3. Anyone who commits a kidnapping under Section 239 of the Criminal Code with the intention of making use of the kidnapped person as a hostage in the political struggle.

§ 6: This decree enters into force on the day of its promulgation.

Berlin, 28 February 1933

The Reich President von Hindenburg
The Reich Chancellor Adolf Hitler
The Reich Minister of the Interior Frick
The Reich Minister of Justice Dr. Gürtner

Source of original German text: Verordnung des Reichspräsidenten zum Schutz von Volk und Staat, 28 February 1933, *Reichsgesetzblatt* 1933, I, 83. Source of English translation: Decree of the Reich President for the Protection of the People and State, 28 February 1933, German Historical Institute, Washington, D.C., *German History in Documents and Images,* http://germanhistorydocs.ghi-dc.org.

Appendix C

Law to Remove the Distress of the People and the State (The Enabling Act)

23 March 1933

The Reichstag has passed the following law, which is, with the approval of the Reichsrat, herewith promulgated, after it has been established that it meets the requirements for legislation altering the Constitution.

Article 1. National laws can be enacted by the Reich Cabinet as well as in accordance with the procedure established in the Constitution. This also applies to the laws referred to in Article 85, Paragraph 2, and in Article 87 of the Constitution.

Article 2. The national laws enacted by the Reich Cabinet may deviate from the Constitution as long as they do not affect the position of the Reichstag and the Reichsrat. The powers of the President remain undisturbed.

Article 3. The national laws enacted by the Reich Cabinet shall be prepared by the Chancellor and published in the Reichsgesetzblatt. They come into effect, unless otherwise specified, the day after their publication. Articles 68–77 of the Constitution do not apply to the laws enacted by the Reich Cabinet.

Article 4. Treaties of the Reich with foreign states which concern matters of national legislation do not require the consent of the bodies participating in legislation. The Reich Cabinet is empowered to issue the necessary provisions for the implementation of these treaties.

Article 5. This law becomes effective on the day of its publication. It becomes invalid on April 1, 1937; it also becomes invalid if the present Reich Cabinet is replaced by another.

Appendix C

Reich President von Hindenburg
Reich Chancellor Adolf Hitler
Reich Minister of the Interior Frick
Reich Minister for Foreign Affairs Baron von Neurath
Reich Minister of Finances Count Schwerin von Krosigk

Source of original German text: Gesetz zur Behebung der Not von Volk und Reich (Ermächtigungsgesetz), 23 March 1933, *Reichsgesetzblatt,* 1933, I, 141. Source of English translation: German Historical Institute, Washington, D.C., *German History in Documents and Images*, http://germanhistorydocs.ghi-dc.org.

Appendix D

Hitler's Call for a Nazi Lawyers' League

12 September 1928

APPEAL!

to jurists belonging to the National Socialist German Workers Party (lawyers, assessors, judges, prosecutors, administrative officials, etc.)

To advance the goals of the National Socialist German Workers Party, a "League of National Socialist German Jurists" has been formed, with its headquarters at the Party Directorate in Munich. The League is intended to adopt positions with respect to all legal questions touching the Party and its members and to develop German legal affairs, both ideally and practically, from a National Socialist point of view.

I direct the attention of all jurists belonging to the National Socialist German Workers Party in Germany and German Austria to this urgent call to join the League. The danger to German law is a compelling current concern and in the forefront of the Party's present struggle.

I have assigned to Dr. Hans Frank, 57 Barerstrasse, Munich, responsibility for furnishing legal counsel with respect to the organizational preliminaries. Applications for membership are therefore to be sent directly to him.

The League will function as a free union of National Socialist jurists, will impose no dues, and determine its own by-laws.

This appeal is to be promulgated in the facilities of the Party press.

Source: *Völkischer Beobachter*, 13 September 1928. Translated by Robert D. Rachlin.

Appendix E

Circular No. 8/1938 from Dr. Karl Leitmeyer, League of National Socialist Guardians of the Law

4 March 1938

RE: Representation of Jews by League Members

Munich, March 4, 1938

The propaganda of international Jewry against the Reich has reached such a level in recent times that, in keeping with the Führer's speech in the Reichstag on February 2, 1938, certain measures are necessary. One possible response is energetic proceedings against the Jews in Germany, who all represent the Jewish International, and henceforth must be treated accordingly, as the Führer made clear in his speech of February 24, 1938 commemorating the founding of the Party. The NSRB [League of National Socialist Guardians of the Law] must do its part.

I have therefore decided to put an end to this incomprehensible situation whereby, up to now, members of the NSRB could, without any opposition, represent Jews. Whoever thinks it consistent with his honor and League duties to consent to represent Jews, while there are still Jewish lawyers, accountants, etc., can expect nothing from the ranks of the NSRB, an association bound to the National Socialist Party. He can voluntarily resign from the NSRB or will be expelled. From now on, I will refer any representation of Jews by a member of the League to the Honor Court of the Party District [*Gauehrengericht*] for severe judgment. The deputy President of the Honor Court of the Party District has, at his own initiative, complained to me about this and has told me that the Honor Court's views correspond completely with my own.

Heil Hitler!
(signed) Dr. [Karl] Leitmeyer

Source: Bundesarchiv, NS 16 (NS-Rechtswahrerbund), file Nr. 112. Translated by Robert D. Rachlin

Appendix F

Law Amending Criminal Law and Criminal Procedure (Excerpts)

24 April 1934

[Editors' Note: The People's Court (*Volksgerichtshof*) was established by this statute.]

Article I

The first section (§§ 80 to 93) of the Second Part of the Penal Code is replaced by the following provisions:

1. High treason (*Hochverrat*)

§ 80

[1] Whoever undertakes, with force or the threat of force, to bring about the incorporation of the territory of the Reich or any part thereof into a foreign state or the severance from the Reich of any territory belonging thereto, shall be punished with death.

[2] Whoever undertakes with force of the threat of force to alter the Constitution of the Reich shall also be punished with death.

§ 81

Whoever undertakes with force or the threat of force to deprive the President of the Reich or Chancellor of the Reich or another member of the Reich Government of his constitutional power, or who by a crime or offence endangers or interferes with the general or particular exercise of his constitutional authority shall be imprisoned for not less than five years.

§ 82

[1] Whoever plans a high treasonable enterprise with another shall be punished with death, with life imprisonment, or with imprisonment for not less than five years.

[2] Whoever, in preparation of a high treasonable enterprise, enters into a relationship with a foreign government, abuses public power entrusted to him, enlists troops, or engages in weapons training, shall be similarly punished. Written approach to a foreign government suffices to constitute the act, if the writing was dispatched.

...

§ 87 "Undertaking" within the meaning of the Penal Code comprises both the completion and the attempt.

1a. Treason (*Landesverrat*)

§ 88

[1] State secrets within the meaning of [§§ 88-93a.) are writings, notes, other subjects facts or information about them, whose secrecy from a foreign government is necessary for the welfare of the Reich, in particular the interest of national defense.

[2] Whoever, with the intention of endangering the Reich, allows a state secret to be conveyed to another, in particular to a foreign government or to anyone who is active on its behalf or openly communicates with it, commits treason within the meaning of [§§ 88-93a.],

§ 89

[1] Whoever undertakes to betray a state secret shall be punished with death.

...

§ 90f.

A German in a foreign country who creates a serious danger to the reputation of the German people by producing false or grossly distorted reports of a factual nature is punishable by imprisonment.

...

§ 91b.

A German, within our outside Germany, who, during a war or threatened war against the Reich, undertakes to give an advantage to an enemy power or a disadvantage to the Reich or its allies shall be punished by death or life imprisonment.

...

Article III
People's Court (*Volksgerichtshof*)

§ 1.

[1] The People's Court is established for the severe punishment of high treason and treason.

[2] Trials in the People's Court shall be adjudicated by a panel of five members, or by a panel of three members, including the President. The President and one other member must be professionally qualified as judges. There can be multiple Senates.

[3] Authority to bring complaints is in the High Reich Prosecutor.

§2. Members of the People's Court and their deputies shall be appointed by the Chancellor for a term of five years upon the recommendation of the Minister of Justice.

§ 3. The People's Court is competent to investigate and decide cases, in the first and last instance, cases of high treason ..., treason ..., attacks against the Reich President ..., and the crime specified ... by provision 5, section 2, number 1 of the [Reichstag Fire Decree of February 28, 1933]. ...

...

§ 5.

...

[2] There is no appeal from the decisions of the People's Court.

Article IV

...

§ 3. The choice of defense counsel is subject to the approval of the court President. Approval of defense counsel can be withdrawn ...

Source: Gesetz zur Änderung des Strafrechts und des Strafverfahrens, *Reichsgesetzblatt* 1934, I, 341–48. Translated by Robert D. Rachlin.

Appendix G

White Rose - Leaflet 5

February 1943

A Call to All Germans!

The war is approaching its destined end. As in the year 1918, the German government is trying to focus attention exclusively on the growing threat of submarine warfare, while in the East the armies are constantly in retreat and invasion is imminent in the West. Mobilization in the United States has not yet reached its climax, but already it exceeds anything that the world has ever seen. It has become a mathematical certainty that Hitler is leading the German people into the abyss. Hitler cannot win the war; he can only prolong it. The guilt of Hitler and his minions goes beyond all measure. Retribution comes closer and closer.

But what are the German people doing? They will not see and will not listen. Blindly they follow their seducers into ruin. Victory at any price! is inscribed on their banner. "I will fight to the last man," says Hitler-but in the meantime the war has already been lost.

Germans! Do you and your children want to suffer the same fate that befell the Jews? Do you want to be judged by the same standards as your traducers? Are we to be forever a nation which is hated and rejected by all mankind? No. Dissociate yourselves from National Socialist gangsterism. Prove by your deeds that you think otherwise. A new war of liberation is about to begin. The better part of the nation will fight on our side. Cast off the cloak of indifference you have wrapped around you. Make the decision before it is too late. Do not believe the National Socialist propaganda which has driven the fear of Bolshevism into your bones. Do not believe that Germany's welfare is linked to the victory of National Socialism for good or ill. A criminal regime cannot achieve a

German victory. Separate yourselves in time from everything connected with National Socialism. In the aftermath a terrible but just judgment will be meted out to those who stayed in hiding, who were cowardly and hesitant.

What can we learn from the outcome of this war-this war that never was a national war?

The imperialist ideology of force, from whatever side it comes, must be shattered for all time. A one sided Prussian militarism must never again be allowed to assume power. Only in large-scale cooperation among the nations of Europe can the ground be prepared for reconstruction. Centralized hegemony, such as the Prussian state has tried to exercise in Germany and in Europe, must be cut down at its inception. The Germany of the future must be a federal state. At this juncture only a sound federal system can imbue a weakened Europe with a new life. The workers must be liberated from their condition of down trodden slavery under National Socialism. The illusory structure of autonomous national industry must disappear. Every nation and each man have a right to the goods of the whole world!

Freedom of speech, freedom of religion, the protection of individual citizens from the arbitrary will of criminal regimes of violence - these will be the bases of the New Europe.

Support the resistance. Distribute the leaflets!

Source: German Historical Institute, Washington, D.C., *German History in Documents and Images,* http://germanhistorydocs.ghi-dc.org.

Appendix H

The Sentencing of Hans and Sophie Scholl and Christoph Probst

22 February 1943

In the Name of the German People

In the action against

1. Hans Fritz Scholl, Munich, born at Ingersheim, 22 September 1918,
2. Sophia Magdalena Scholl, Munich, born at Forchtenberg, 9 May 1921, and
3. Christoph Hermann Probst, of Aldrans bei Innsbruck, born at Murnau, 6 November, 1919,

now in investigative custody regarding treasonous assistance to the enemy, preparing to commit high treason, and weakening of the nation's armed security, the People's Court, first Senate, pursuant to the trial held on 22 February 1943, in which the officers were:

President of the People's Court Dr. Freisler, Presiding,
Director of the Regional (Bavarian) Judiciary Stier,
SS Group Leader Breithaupt,
SA Group Leader Bunge,
State Secretary and SA Group Leader Koglmaier, and,
representing the Attorney General to the Supreme
Court of the Reich, Reich Attorney Weyersberg,

find:

That the accused have in time of war by means of leaflets called for the sabotage of the war effort and armaments and for the overthrow of the National Socialist way of life of our people, have propagated defeatist

Appendix H

ideas, and have most vulgarly defamed the Führer, thereby giving aid to the enemy of the Reich and weakening the armed security of the nation.

On this account they are to be punished by Death.

Their honor and rights as citizens are forfeited for all time.

Grounds

The accused Hans Scholl has been a student of medicine since the spring of 1939 and, thanks to the solicitude of the National Socialist government, has begun his eighth semester in those studies. He has served meanwhile on temporary duty in a field hospital in the campaign in France and again from July to November 1942 on the eastern front as a medical aide.

As a student he is bound by duty to give exemplary service to the common cause. In his capacity as soldier – on assignment to medical study – he has a special duty of loyalty to the Führer. This and the assistance which he was expressly granted by the Reich did not deter him in the first half of the summer of 1942 from writing, duplicating, and distributing leaflets of the "White Rose." These defeatist leaflets predict the defeat of Germany and call for passive resistance in the form of sabotage in war industries and for sabotage in general, to the end that the German people would be deprived of the National Socialist way of life and thus also of their government.

All this because he imagined that only in this way could the German people survive the end of the war!

Returning from Russia in November 1942, Scholl requested his friend, the accused Probst, to provide him with a manuscript which would open the eyes of the German people! In actuality Probst furnished Scholl with a draft of a leaflet as requested, at the end of January 1943.

In conversations with his sister, Sophia, the two decided to carry on leaflet propaganda in the form of a campaign against the war and in favor of collaboration with the plutocratic enemies of National Socialism. Brother and sister, who had quarters in the same rooming house, collaborated in the writing of a leaflet, "To All Germans." In it they predicted Germany's defeat in the war, they urged a war of liberation against

"National Socialist gangsterism," and demanded the establishment of a liberal democracy. In addition, they drafted a leaflet, "German Students!" (in later versions, "Fellow Fighters!"), wherein they called for a struggle against the Party. They wrote that the day of reckoning was at hand, and they were bold enough to compare their call to battle against the Führer and the National Socialist way of life with the War of Liberation against Napoleon (1813). In reference to their project, they used the military song, "Up, up, my people, let smoke and flame be our sign!"

The accused Scholls, in part with the help of the accused Schmorell, duplicated the leaflets and by common agreement distributed them as follows:

> 1. Schmorell traveled to Salzburg, Linz, and Vienna and put 200, 200, and 1,200 leaflets addressed to places in those cities in the mails; and in Vienna an additional 400 were directed to Frankfurt am Main.
> 2. Sophia Scholl posted 200 in Augsburg and on another occasion 600 in Stuttgart.
> 3. Hans Scholl, with the aid of Schmorell, scattered thousands of leaflets in the streets of Munich at night.
> 4. On February 18 the Scholls deposited 1500–1800 copies in bundles in the University of Munich, and Sophia Scholl let drop a large number from the third floor down the light well of the building.

Hans Scholl and Schmorell also, on the nights of August 8, 1942, and February 14, 1943, defaced walls in many places in Munich, and particularly the university, with the words "Down with Hitler," "Hitler the Mass Murderer," and "Freedom." After the first incident Sophia Scholl learned of this action, was in agreement with it, and requested – though without success – to be allowed to help in the future!

Expenses were covered by the accused themselves – in all, about 1,000 marks. Probst likewise began his medical studies in the spring of 1939 and is now in his eighth semester, a soldier on student duty. He is married and has three children aged two and a half, one and one fourth years, and four weeks. He is a "nonpolitical man" – hence no man at all! Neither the solicitude of the National Socialist Reich for his professional training nor the fact that it was only the National Socialist demographic policy which made it possible for him to have a family prevented him from writing at the behest of Scholl – in cowardly defeatism – a "manuscript" which takes the heroic struggle in Stalingrad as the occasion for defaming the Führer as a military swindler and which then progressing to a hortatory tone, calls for opposition to National Socialism and for action which would lead, as he pretends, to an honorable capitulation. He supports the promises in this leaflet by citing – Roosevelt! And his knowledge about these matters he derived from listening to British broadcasts!

All the accused have admitted the facts stated above. Probst offers as excuse his "psychotic depression" at the time he drafted the leaflet, a depression which he claims arises from Stalingrad and the childbed illness of his wife. But such explanations do not excuse a reaction *of this scope*.

Whoever has, like the three accused, committed the acts of high treason, weakening the home front and thereby in time of war the security of the nation, and by the same token has aided the enemy (Par. 5 of Special War Decree and Par. 91 b of the Criminal Code), raises the dagger for a stab in the back of the Front! That applies also to Probst, though he claims that his manuscript was not intended for use as a leaflet – since the tone and style of the manuscript proves the opposite. Whoever acts in this way – and particularly at this time, when we must close our ranks – is attempting to cause the first rift in the unity of the battle front. And German students, whose traditional honor has always called for self-sacrifice for *Volk* and fatherland, were the ones who acted thus!

If a deed of this sort were to be punished otherwise than by death, we would be forging the first links of a chain whose end – in an earlier time – was 1918. Therefore, for the protection of the *Volk* and the Reich at war, the People's Court has found but one just punishment: death. The People's Court knows that it is at one with our soldiers in this decision.

Through their treason to our *Volk*, the accused have forever forfeited their citizenship.

As criminals who have been found guilty, the accused will pay the court costs.

Dr. Freisler (signed)

Source: Inge Scholl, *The White Rose: Munich, 1942–1943* (Middletown, Conn., 1983), 114–18.

Appendix I

The Fate of Markus Luftglass: Excerpt from the Record of the Nuremberg Justice Case

October 1941

[Editors' Note: The incorrect spellings of Luftglass as "Luftgas" are present in the original documents.]

The Reich Minister and Chief of the Reich Chancellery Rk/ 15506 B

Führer Headquarters 25 October 1941
[Handwritten] 393A

1. To: Under Secretary, Professor Dr. Dr. h.c. Schlegelberger, charged with the management of the affairs of the Reich Minister of Justice
Berlin W 8 Wilhelmstrasse 65
[Handwritten] Refer to newspaper

Dear Mr. Schlegelberger :

The enclosed newspaper clipping about the sentencing of the Jew Markus Luftgas to imprisonment for 2 ½ years by the Special Court of Bielitz has been submitted to the Führer. The Führer wishes Luftgas to be sentenced to death. May I ask you urgently to instigate what is necessary and to notify me about the measures taken so that I can inform the Führer.

Heil Hitler !
Yours very truly,
(Signature of the Reich Minister)

[Handwritten] Justice 11

Appendix I

2. To: SS-GruppenFührer Julius Schaub

           Führer Headquarters

Subject : Markus Luftgas

Dear Mr. Schaub:

After receiving your letter dated 22 October 1941 I got into touch with the Reich Minister of Justice and asked him to instigate the necessary measures.

           Heil Hitler !
           Yours very truly,
           (Signature of the Reich Minister)

3. Copy of the newspaper clipping to be filed.
4. After dispatch-For the attention of Ministerial Director Kritzinger for information.
5. After 1month.

           (Signature of the Reich Minister)
           [Initial] L [Lammers]

COPY [Enclosure] to Rk. 15 506 B

           "Berlin Illustrated Night Edition"
           No: 246, Monday 20 October 1941

Jew hoarded 65,000 eggs and allowed 15,000 of them to spoil

           By wire from our reporter

Breslau, 20 October-The 74-year-old Jew Markus Luftgas from Kalwarja removed a huge number of eggs from the controlled economy and had to answer for it at the Special Court in Bielitz. The Jew had hidden 65,000 eggs in containers and in a lime-pit, 15,000 of which had already spoiled. The defendant was sentenced to 2 ½ years' imprisonment as a just punishment for a crime against the war economy regulations.

Appendix I

Berlin, 29 October 1941

The Acting Reich Minister of Justice
111g-14 3454J41

To the Reich Minister and
Chief of the Reich Chancellery
in Berlin W 8, Vossst. 6

[Initial] L [Lammers]
[Handwritten] 3/11

1. Submitted to the Minister for his information
2. To be filed. [Initial]

[Initial] KR [Kritzinger]

Subject: Case against the Jew Luftglass (not Luftgas) Sg 12
Js 340/.41 of the Chief Public Prosecutor in Katowice
-Rk. 15506 B dated 25 October 1941.

Dear Reich Minister Dr. Lammers:

In accordance with the order of the Führer and Reich Chancellor dated 24 October 1941, transmitted to me by the Minister of State and Chief of the Presidential Chancellery of the Führer, I have handed over to the Gestapo for the purpose of execution, the Jew Markus Luftglass who was sentenced to 2 ½ years' imprisonment by the Special Court in Katowice.

Heil Hitler!

Very truly yours,
[Signed] SCHLEGELBERGER

Source: NG-287, Prosecution Exhibit 88, in *Trials of War Criminals before the Nuernberg Military Tribunals under Control Council Law No. 10,* Nuremberg, October 1946–April 1949, 15 vols. (Washington, 1949–53), vol. III, Case 3, *U.S. v. Altstoetter* ("The Justice Case") (Washington, 1951), 429–31. The editors have made minor spelling changes to conform to spelling employed elsewhere in this volume.

Appendix J

Opinion and Sentence of the Nuremberg Special Court in the Case of Leo Katzenberger

13 March 1942

Sg No. 351/41

Verdict

In the name of the German People

The Special Court for the district of the Court of Appeal in Nuremberg with the District Court Nuremberg-Fürth in the proceedings against Katzenberger, Lehmann Israel, commonly called Leo, merchant and head of the Jewish religious community in Nuremberg, and Seiler, Irene, owner of a photographic shop in Nuremberg, both at present in arrest pending trial the charges being racial pollution and perjury-in public session of 13 March 1942, in the presence of-

The President– Dr. Rothaug, Senior Judge of the District Court;
Associate Judges– Dr. Ferber and Dr. Hoffmann, Judges of the District Court;
Public Prosecutor for the Special Court– Markl;
and Official Registrar: Raisin, clerk, pronounced the following verdict:

Katzenberger, Lehmann Israel, commonly called Leo, Jewish by race and religion, born 25 November 1873 at Massbach, married, merchant of Nuremberg; Seiler, Irene, née Scheffler, born 26 April 1910 at Guben, married, owner of a photographic shop in Nuremberg, both at present in arrest pending trial have been sentenced as follows :

Katzenberger-for an offense under section 2, legally identical with an offense under section 4 of the decree against public enemies in connection with the offense of racial pollution to death and to loss of his civil rights for life according to sections 32-34 of the criminal (penal) code.

Seiler-for the offense of committing perjury while a witness to 2 years of hard labor and to loss of her civil rights for the duration of 2 years.

The 3 months the defendant Seiler spent in arrest pending trial will be taken into consideration in her sentence.

Costs will be charged to the defendants.

Findings

I

1. The defendant Katzenberger is fully Jewish and a German national; he is a member of the Jewish religious community.

As far as his descent is concerned, extracts from the birth registers of the Jewish community at Massbach show that the defendant was born on 25 November 1873 as the son of Louis David Katzenberger, merchant, and his wife Helene née Adelberg. The defendant's father, born on 30 June 1838 at Massbach, was, according to an extract from the Jewish registers at Thundorf, the legitimate son of David Katzenberger, weaver, and his wife Karoline Lippig. The defendant's mother Lena Adelberg, born on 14 June 1847 at Aschbach, was, according to extracts from the birth register of the Jewish religious community of Aschbach, the legitimate daughter of Lehmann Adelberg, merchant and his wife, Lea. According to the Thundorf register, the defendant's parents were married on 3 December 1867 by the district rabbi in Schweinfurt. The defendant's grandparents on his father's side were married, according to extracts from the Thundorf register, on 3 April 1832; those on his mother's side were married, according to an extract from the register of marriages of the Jewish religious community of Aschbach, on 14 August 1836.

The extracts from the register of marriages of the Jewish religious community at Aschbach show, concerning the marriage of the maternal grandparents, that Bela-Lea Seemann, born at Aschbach in 1809, was a member of the Jewish religious community. Otherwise the documents mentioned give no further information so far as confessional affiliations are concerned that parents or grandparents were of Jewish faith.

The defendant himself has stated that he is certain that all four grandparents were members of the Jewish faith. His grandmothers he knew when they were alive; both grandfathers were buried in Jewish cemeteries. Both his parents belonged to the Jewish religious community, as he does himself.

The court sees no reason to doubt the correctness of these statements, which are fully corroborated by the available extracts from exclusively Jewish registers. Should it be true that all four grandparents belonged to the Jewish faith, the grandparents would be regarded as fully Jewish according to the regulation to facilitate the producing of evidence in section 5, paragraph 1 together with section 2, paragraph 2, page 2 of the ordinance to the Reich Civil Code of 14 November 1935 Reichsgesetzblatt, page 1333. The defendant therefore is fully Jewish in the sense of the Law for the Protection of German Blood." His own admissions show that he himself shared that view.

The defendant Katzenberger came to Nuremberg in 1912. Together with his brothers, David and Max, he ran a shoe shop until November 1938. The defendant married in 1906, and there are two children, ages 30 and 34.

Up to 1938 the defendant and his brothers, David and Max, owned the property of 19 Spittlertorgraben in Nuremberg. There were offices and storerooms in the rear building, whereas the main building facing the street was an apartment house with several apartments.

The co-defendant Irene Seiler arrived in 1932 to take a flat in 19 Spittlertorgraben, and the defendant Katzenberger has been acquainted with her since that date.

2. Irene Seiler, née Scheffler, is a German citizen of German blood.

Her descent is proved by documents relating to all four grandparents. She herself, her parents, and all her grandparents belong to the Protestant Lutheran faith. This finding of the religious background is based on available birth and marriage certificates of the Scheffler family which were made part of the trial. As far as descent is concerned therefore, there can be no doubt about Irene Seiler, née Scheffler, being of German blood.

The defendant Katzenberger was fully cognizant of the fact that Irene Seiler was of German blood and of German nationality.

On 29 July 1939, Irene Scheffler married Johann Seiler, a commercial agent. There have been no children so far.

In her native city, Guben, the defendant attended secondary school and high school up to Unterprima [eighth grade of high school], and after that, for 1 year, she attended the Leipzig State Academy of Art and Book Craft.

She went to Nuremberg in 1932 where she worked in the photographic laboratory of her sister Hertha, which the latter had managed since 1928 as a tenant of 19 Spittlertorgraben. On 1 January 1938, she took over her sister's business at her own expense. On 24 February 1938, she passed her professional examination.

3. The defendant Katzenberger is charged with having had continual extra-marital sexual intercourse with Irene Seiler, née Scheffler, a German national of German blood. He is said to have visited Seiler frequently in her apartment in Spittlertorgraben up to March 1940, while Seiler visited him frequently, up to autumn 1938, in the offices of the rear building. Seiler, who is alleged to have got herself in a dependent position by accepting gifts of money from the defendant Katzenberger and by being allowed delay in paying her rent, was sexually amenable to Katzenberger. Thus, their acquaintance is said to have become of a sexual nature, and, in particular, sexual intercourse occurred. They are both said to have exchanged kisses sometimes in Seiler's flat and sometimes in Katzenberger's offices. Seiler is alleged to have often sat on Katzenberger's lap. On these occasions Katzenberger, in order to achieve sexual satisfaction, is said to have caressed and patted Seiler on her thighs through her clothes, clinging closely to Seiler, and resting his head on her bosom.

The defendant Katzenberger is charged with having committed this act of racial pollution by taking advantage of wartime conditions. Lack of supervision was in his favor, especially as he is said to have visited Seiler during the blackout. Moreover, Seiler's husband had been called up, and consequently surprise appearances of the husband were not to be feared.

The defendant Irene Seiler is charged with having, on the occasion of her interrogation by the investigating judge of the local Nuremberg Court on 9 July 1941, made deliberately untrue statements and affirmed under oath that this contact was without sexual motives and that she believed that to apply to Katzenberger as well.

Seiler, it is alleged, has thereby become guilty of being a perjuring witness.

The defendants have said this in their defense–

The defendant Seiler– When in 1932 she arrived in the photographic laboratory of her sister in Nuremberg, she was thrown completely on her own resources. Her sister returned to Guben, where she opened a studio as a photographer. Her father had recommended her to the landlord, the defendant Katzenberger, asking him to look after her and to assist her in word and deed. This was how she became closely acquainted with the Jew Katzenberger.

As time went on, Katzenberger did indeed become her adviser, helping her, in particular, in her financial difficulties. Delighted with the friendship and kindness shown her by Katzenberger she came to regard him gradually as nothing but a fatherly friend, and it never occurred to her to look upon him as a Jew. It was true that she called regularly in the storerooms of the rear house. She did so after office hours, because it was easier then to pick out shoes. It also happened that during these visits, and during those paid by Katzenberger to her flat, she kissed Katzenberger now and then and allowed him to kiss her. On these occasions she frequently would sit on Katzenberger's lap which was quite natural with her and had no ulterior motive. In no way should sexual motives be regarded as the cause of her actions. She always thought that Katzenberger's feelings for her were purely those of a concerned father.

Basing herself on this view she made the statement to the investigating judge on 9 July 1941 and affirmed under oath, that when exchanging those caresses neither she herself nor Katzenberger did so because of any erotic emotions.

The defendant Katzenberger– He denies having committed an offense. It is his defense that his relations with Frau Seiler were of a purely friendly nature. The Scheffler family in Guben had likewise looked upon his relations with Frau Seiler only from this point of view. That he continued his relations with Frau Seiler after 1933, 1935, and 1938, might be regarded as a wrong [Unrecht] by the NSDAP. The fact of his doing so, however, showed that his conscience was clear.

Moreover, their meetings became less frequent after the action against the Jews in 1938. After Frau Seiler got married in 1939, the husband often came in unexpectedly when he, Katzenberger, was with Frau Seiler in the flat. Never, however, did the husband surprise them in an ambiguous situation. In January or February 1940, at the request of the husband, he went to the Seiler's apartment twice to help them fill in their tax declarations. The last talk he ever had in the Seiler apartment took place in March 1940. On that occasion Frau Seiler suggested to him to discontinue his visits because of the representations made to her by the NSDAP, and she gave him a farewell kiss in the presence of her husband.

He never pursued any plans when being together with Frau Seiler, and he therefore could not have taken advantage of wartime conditions and the blackout.

II

The court has drawn the following conclusions from the excuses made by the defendant Katzenberger and the restrictions with which the defendant Seiler attempted to render her admissions less harmful:

When, in 1932, the defendant Seiler came to settle in Nuremberg at the age of 22, she was a fully grown and sexually mature young woman. According to her own admissions, credible in this case, she was not above sexual surrender in her relations with her friends.

In Nuremberg, when she had taken over her sister's laboratory in 19 Spittlertorgraben, she entered the immediate sphere of the defendant Katzenberger. During their acquaintance she gradually became willing, in a period of almost 10 years, to exchange caresses and, according to the confessions of both defendants, situations arose which can by no means be regarded merely as the outcome of fatherly friendliness. When she met Katzenberger in his offices in the rear building or in her flat, she sat often on his lap and, without a doubt, kissed his lips and cheeks. On these occasions Katzenberger, as he admitted himself, responded these caresses by returning the kisses, putting his head on her bosom and patting her thighs through her clothes.

To assume that the exchange of these caresses, admitted by both of them, were on Katzenberger's part the expression of his fatherly feelings, on Seiler's part merely the actions caused by daughterly feelings with a strong emotional accent, as a natural result of the situation, is contrary to all experience of daily life. The subterfuge used by the defendant in this respect is in the view of the court simply a crude attempt to disguise as sentiment, free of all sexual lust, these actions with their strong sexual bias. In view of the character of the two defendants and basing itself on the evidence submitted, the court is firmly convinced that sexual motives were the primary cause for the caresses exchanged by the two defendants.

Seiler was usually in financial difficulties. Katzenberger availed himself of this fact to make her frequent gifts of money, and repeatedly gave her sums from 1 to 10 Reichsmark. In his capacity as administrator of the property on which Seiler lived and which was owned by the firm he was a partner of, Katzenberger often allowed her long delays in paying her rental debts. He often gave Seiler cigarettes, flowers, and shoes.

The defendant Seiler admits that she was anxious to remain in Katzenberger's favor. They addressed each other in the second person singular.

According to the facts established in the trial, the two defendants offered to their immediate surroundings, and in particular to the community of the house of 19 Spittlertorgraben, the impression of having an intimate love affair.

The witnesses Kleylein, Paul and Babette; Maesel, Johann; Heilmann, Johann; and Leibner, Georg observed frequently that Katzenberger and Seiler waved to each other when Seiler, through one of the rear windows of her flat, saw Katzenberger in his offices. The witnesses' attention was drawn particularly to the frequent visits paid by Seiler to Katzenberger's offices after business hours and on Sundays, as well as to the length of these visits. Everyone in the house came to know eventually that Seiler kept asking Katzenberger for money, and they all became convinced that Katzenberger, as the Jewish creditor, exploited sexually the poor financial situation of the German-blooded woman Seiler. The witness Heilmann, in a conversation with the witness Paul Kleylein, expressed his opinion of the matter to the effect that the Jew was getting a good return for the money he gave Seiler.

Nor did the two defendants themselves regard these mutual calls and exchange of caresses as being merely casual happenings of daily life, beyond reproach. According to statements made by the witnesses Babette and Paul Kleylein, they observed Katzenberger to show definite signs of fright when he saw that they had discovered his visits to Seiler's flat as late as 1940. The witnesses also observed that during the later period Katzenberger sneaked into Seiler's flat rather than walking in openly.

In August 1940, while being in the air-raid shelter, the defendant Seiler had to put up with the following reply given to her by Oestreicher, an inhabitant of the same house, in the presence of all other inhabitants: "I'll pay you back, you Jewish hussy." Seiler did not do anything to defend herself against this reproach later on, and all she did was to tell Katzenberger of this incident shortly after it had happened. Seiler has been unable to give an even remotely credible explanation why she showed this remarkable restraint in the face of so strong an expression of suspicion. Simply pointing out that her father, who is over seventy, had advised her not to take any steps against Oestreicher does not make more plausible her restraint shown in the face of the grave accusation made in public.

The statements made by Hans Zeuschel, assistant inspector of the criminal police, show that the two defendants did not admit from the very beginning the existing sexual situation as being beyond reproach. The fact that Seiler admitted the caresses bestowed on Katzenberger only after having been earnestly admonished, and the additional fact that Katzenberger, when interrogated by the police, confessed only when Seiler's statements were being shown to him, forces the conclusion that they both deemed it advisable to keep secret the actions for which they have been put on trial. This being so, the court is convinced that the two defendants made these statements only for reason of opportuneness intending to minimize and render harmless a situation which has been established by witnesses' testimony.

Seiler has also admitted that she did not tell her husband about the caresses exchanged with Katzenberger prior to her marriage—all she told him was that in the past Katzenberger had helped her a good deal. After getting married in July 1939 she gave Katzenberger a "friendly kiss" on the cheek in the presence of her husband on only one occasion, otherwise they avoided kissing each other when the husband was present.

In view of the behavior of the defendants toward each other, as repeatedly described, the court has become convinced that the relations between Seiler and Katzenberger which extended over a period of 10 years were of a purely sexual nature. This is the only possible explanation of the intimacy of their acquaintance. As there were a large number of circumstances favoring seduction no doubt it is possible that the defendant Katzenberger maintained continuous sexual intercourse with Seiler. The court considers as untrue Katzenberger's statement to the contrary that Seiler did not interest him sexually, and the statements made by the defendant Seiler in support of Katzenberger's defense the court considers as incompatible with all practical experience. They were obviously made with the purpose of saving Katzenberger from his punishment.

The court is therefore convinced that Katzenberger, after the Nuremberg laws had come into effect, had repeated sexual intercourse with Seiler, up to March 1940. It is not possible to say on what days and how often this took place.

The Law for the Protection of German Blood defines extra-marital sexual intercourse as any form of sexual activity apart from the actual cohabitation with a member of the opposite sex which, by the method applied in place of actual intercourse, serves to satisfy the sexual instincts of at least one of the partners. The conduct to which the defendants admitted and which in the case of Katzenberger consisted in drawing Seiler close to him, kissing her, patting and caressing her thighs over her clothes, makes it clear that in a crude manner Katzenberger did to Seiler what is popularly called "Abschmieren" [petting]. It is obvious that such actions are motivated only by sexual impulses. Even if the Jew had only done these so-called "Ersatzhandlungen" [sexual acts in lieu of actual intercourse] to Seiler, it would have been sufficient to charge him with racial pollution in the full sense of the law.

The court, however, is convinced over and above this that Katzenberger, who admits that he is still capable of having sexual intercourse, had intercourse with Seiler throughout the duration of their affair. According to general experiences it is impossible to assume that in the 10 years of his tête-a-tête with Seiler, which often lasted up to an hour, Katzenberger would have been satisfied with the "Ersatzhandlungen" which in themselves warranted the application of the law.

III

Thus, the defendant Katzenberger has been convicted of having had, as a Jew, extra-marital sexual intercourse with a German citizen of German blood after the Law for the Protection of German Blood came into force, which according to section 7 of the law means after 17 September 1935. His actions were guided by a consistent plan which was aimed at repetition from the very beginning. He is therefore guilty of a continuous crime of racial pollution according to sections 2 and 5, paragraph 1 of the Law for the Protection of German Blood and German Honor of 15 September 1935.

A legal analysis of the established facts shows that in his polluting activities, the defendant Katzenberger, moreover, generally exploited the exceptional conditions arising out of wartime circumstances. Men have largely vanished from towns and villages because they have been called up or are doing other work for the armed forces which prevents them from remaining at home and maintaining order. It was these general conditions and wartime changes which the defendant exploited. As he continued his visits to Seiler's apartment up to spring 1940, the defendant took into account the fact that in the absence of more stringent measures of control his practices could not, at least not very easily, be seen through. The fact that her husband had been drafted into the armed forces also helped him in his activities.

Looked at from this point of view, Katzenberger's conduct is particularly contemptible. Together with his offense of racial pollution he is also guilty of an offense under section 4 of the decree against public enemies. It should be noted here that the national community is in need of increased legal protection from all crimes attempting to destroy or undermine its inner solidarity.

On several occasions since the outbreak of war the defendant Katzenberger sneaked into Seiler's flat after dark. In these cases the defendant acted by exploiting the measures taken for the protection in air raids and by making use of the blackout. His chances were further improved by the absence of the bright street lighting which exists in the street along Spittlertorgraben in peacetime. In each case he exploited this fact being fully aware of its significance, thus during his excursions he instinctively escaped observation by people in the street.

The visits paid by Katzenberger to Seiler under the cover of the blackout served at least the purpose of keeping relations going. It does not matter whether during these visits extra-marital sexual intercourse took place or whether they only conversed because the husband was present, as Katzenberger claims. The motion to have the husband called as a witness was therefore overruled. The court holds the view that the defendant's actions were deliberately performed as part of a consistent plan and amount to a crime against the body according to section 2 of the decree against public enemies. The law of 15 September 1935 was promulgated to protect German blood and German honor. The Jew's racial pollution amounts to a grave attack on the purity of German blood, the object of the attack being the body of a German woman. The general need for protection therefore makes appear as unimportant the behavior of the other partner in racial pollution who, however, is not liable to prosecution. The fact that racial pollution occurred at least up to 1939-1940 becomes clear from statements made by the witness Zeuschel to whom the defendant repeatedly and consistently admitted that up to the end of 1939 and the beginning of 1940 she was used to sitting on the Jew's lap and exchanging caresses as described above.

Thus, the defendant committed an offense also under section 2 of the decree against public enemies.

The personal character of the defendant likewise stamps him as a public enemy. The racial pollution practiced by him through many years grew, by exploiting wartime condition, into an attitude inimical to the nation, into an attack on the security of the national community during an emergency.

This was why the defendant Katzenberger had to be sentenced, both on a crime of racial pollution and of an offense under sections 2 and 4 of the decree against public enemies, the two charges being taken in conjunction according to section 73 of the penal code.

In view of the court the defendant Seiler realized that the contact which Katzenberger continuously had with her was of a sexual nature. The court has no doubt that Seiler actually had sexual intercourse with Katzenberger. Accordingly the oath given by her as a witness was to her knowledge and intention a false one, and she became guilty of perjury under sections 154 and 153 of the penal code.

IV

In passing sentence the court was guided by the following considerations:

The political form of life of the German people under National Socialism is based on the community. One fundamental factor of the life of the national community is the racial problem. If a Jew commits racial pollution with a German woman, this amounts to polluting the German race and, by polluting a German woman, to a grave attack on the purity of German blood. The need for protection is particularly strong.

Katzenberger practiced pollution for years. He was well acquainted with the point of view taken by patriotic German men and women as regards racial problems and he knew that by his conduct the patriotic feelings of the German people were slapped in the face. Neither the National Socialist Revolution of 1933, nor the passing of the Law for the Protection of German Blood in 1935, neither the action against the Jews in 1938, nor the out-break of war in 1939 made him abandon this activity of his.

As the only feasible answer to the frivolous conduct of the defendant, the court therefore deems it necessary to pronounce the death sentence as the heaviest punishment provided by section 4 of the decree against public enemies. His case must be judged with special severity, as he had to be sentenced in connection with the offense of committing racial pollution, under section 2 of the decree against public enemies, the more so, if taking into consideration the defendant's personality and the accumulative nature of his deeds. This is why the defendant is liable to the death penalty which the law provides for such cases as the only punishment. Dr. Baur, the medical expert, describes the defendant as fully responsible.

Accordingly, the court has pronounced the death sentence. It was also considered necessary to deprive him of his civil rights for life, as specified in sections 32-34 of the penal code. When imposing punishment on the defendant Seiler, her personal character was the first matter to be considered. For many years, Seiler indulged in this contemptible love affair with the Jew Katzenberger. The national regeneration of the German people in 1933 was altogether immaterial to her in her practices, nor was she in the least influenced when the Law for the Protection of German Blood and Honor was promulgated in September 1935. It was, therefore, nothing but an act of frivolous provocation on her part to apply for membership in the NSDAP in 1937 which she obtained.

When by initiating legal proceedings against Katzenberger the German people were to be given satisfaction for the Jew's polluting activities, the defendant Seiler did not pay the slightest heed to the concerns of State authority or to those of the people and decided to protect the Jew.

Taking this over-all situation into consideration the court considered a sentence of 4 years of hard labor as having been deserved by the defendant.

An extenuating circumstance was that the defendant, finding herself in an embarrassing situation, affirmed her--as she knew-- false statement with an oath. Had she spoken the truth she could have been prosecuted for adultery, aiding, and soliciting. The court therefore reduced the sentence by half despite her guilt, and imposed as the appropriate sentence 2 years of hard labor. (Sec. 157, par. I, No. 1, of the Penal Code.)

On account of the lack of honor of which she was convicted, she had to be deprived of her civil rights too. This has been decided for a duration of 2 years.

Taking into consideration the time spent in arrest pending trial : Section 60, Penal Code. Costs: Section 465, Code of Criminal Procedure.

Appendix J

[Signed] Rothaug
Dr. Ferber
Dr. Hoffmann

Certified:

Nuremberg, 23 March 1942

Source: NG-154, Prosecution Exhibit 152, in *Trials of War Criminals before the Nuernberg Military Tribunals under Control Council Law No. 10,* Nuremberg, October 1946–April 1949, 15 vols. (Washington, 1949–53), vol. III, Case 3, *U.S. v. Altstoetter* ("The Justice Case") (Washington, 1951), 653–64. The editors have made minor spelling changes to conform to spelling employed elsewhere in this volume.

Appendix K

Testimony of Curt Rothenberger at the Nuremberg Justice Case (Excerpts)

1947

CURT ROTHENBERGER—State Secretary (Staatssekretär) of the Reich Ministry of Justice; deputy president of the Academy of German Law (Akademie für deutsches Recht); Gauführer of the National Socialist Lawyers League.

CROSS-EXAMINATION

MR. KING: Dr. Rothenberger, I would like to come back to Prosecution Exhibit 27, which is Document NG075. This is your memorandum to Hitler, or rather your memorandum which eventually reached Hitler, and to which you attribute your appointment to the position of State Secretary. The purpose of examining certain phrases from this memorandum is to enable me better to understand what your new program for the independence of the judiciary was. I am sure you know that memorandum much better than I do. I want to read to you several paragraphs from it. You say in one place: "Law must serve the political leadership." Then you say in another place on page 8 of the document, "He who is striving toward a new world order cannot move in the limitation of an orderly Ministry of Justice. To accomplish such a far-reaching revolution in domestic and foreign policy it is only possible if on one hand all outmoded institutions, concepts, and habits have been done away with, if need be in a brutal manner." Then you say still further on, "The Führer is the supreme judge, theoretically the authority to pass judgment is only his." Then you say still further on: "A judge who is in a direct relation of fealty to the Führer must judge like the Führer." All of these phrases which I read appear in that memorandum and based on them, I want to ask you this and perhaps several other questions. You have repeatedly said that the purpose of your program was to establish an independence of the judiciary. However, the essence of your program, as it seems clear to me from reading your memorandum, is that the Führer is the supreme judge. As you say here, theoretically the authority to pass judgment is only his. A judge in a position of direct relation of fealty to the Führer must judge like the Führer. Now my question to you, Dr. Rothenberger, is simply this: When you speak of the independence of the German judiciary, how do you reconcile that with these statements that the Führer is the supreme judge, and that only he can actually judge, and that all judges must reflect his thinking?

Defendant Rothenberger: During my direct examination I have already tried to explain the thoughts which made me write this memorandum. It is extraordinarily difficult to do so briefly, especially to state one's attitude only in regard to two or three sentences which are taken out of their context. Therefore, I am of the opinion that the memorandum as such should speak for itself, and that I leave it up to the Tribunal to form its judgment about the actual thoughts contained in the memorandum. And if in spite of that I may answer that question only very briefly in a concrete manner, I have to say the following: In 1942 the authoritarian state as such was a fact in Germany. That is to say, Hitler was also the highest judicial authority, and if any chance or possibility still existed to remove all the damage which had occurred during the course of years and all the burdens with which the administration of justice was loaded by the Party and by the SS—or, as we used to say at the time, on the part of the thousand little Hitlers who every day jeopardized the independence of the individual judge—under those conditions the only possibility to bring about any amelioration at all was Hitler himself. That it was impossible to convince Hitler I, and later on, everybody realized. But at the time I believed that it was possible to convince him, and I had to seize that possibility as a last chance. And if it would have been possible to convince him, then in effect the independence of the courts would have been reestablished again. For in that case this direct relationship between Hitler and the judiciary which I asked for would have been established and all other influences which burdened every judge every day would have been eliminated.

Q. Dr. Rothenberger, may I interrupt you at this point? I think that you are entirely too modest about the success of your program. If you

Appendix K

meant what you said in your memorandum, and I assume that you did mean what you said, then isn't it true that your program was a complete success, since the final result was that the Führer became the supreme judge? Isn't that true?

A. The fact that after only 15 months I again left my office is probably the best proof of the fact that my program was a complete failure.

Q. Dr. Rothenberger, do you distinguish between the success of your program and your own failure to get along with people in the ministry? Isn't it possible that those two factors are separable?

A. No. A second reason also speaks for the assumption that it was a complete failure—and that is the intervention of outside offices with the activity of the judges which I wanted to prevent; this did not stop at all after this memorandum was submitted, but rather became worse. The independence of the court and the lifting of the judiciary from the civil service, which I was striving for, did not become effective at all. I request the Tribunal to tell me whether I should go into more detail in regard to this problem, which of course is a fundamental problem, or whether I should not say any more about it now.

PRESIDING JUDGE BRAND: We will not interfere at this time.

MR. KING: Dr. Rothenberger, I am frankly puzzled by seemingly contradictory statements in your memorandum. Let's go over it once more. You say, on the one hand, that you want an independent judiciary. You say, on the other, that the Führer is the supreme judge, and all judges must act like the Führer. Now, unless you meant that all judges must act in accordance with the wishes of the Führer, your memorandum means absolutely nothing and is pure double-talk. If that isn't what you meant—if you didn't mean that the Führer's decisions should be the final decisions—just what do you mean by all that talk of the Führer being the supreme judge?

DEFENDANT ROTHENBERGER: I said in my memorandum that theoretically the Führer is the highest judge in Germany; I also expressed that the individual judge in his decision must be independent even in his relationship to the Führer. What I attempted to achieve first was to

Appendix K

eliminate all other influences on the judge and therefore to establish this direct connection between the Führer and the judge. Therefore, my suggestion in order to say it clearly to put in place of the influence of Bormann or Himmler, the so-called "Judge of the Führer," who would influence the Führer in the capacity of a judge, and would therefore not only try to direct the development in Germany into quite different channels in a legal respect but in every respect.

Q. Let me put this question to you. If, under your program, as you envisaged it in 1942, a judge came to a decision, and that decision was known not to be in accordance with the Führer's views, in your view whose opinion should have prevailed, as you intended it to work out?

A. The decision of the judge.

Q. Then what do you mean when you say the judge must judge like the Führer?

A. The Führer does not have the right to touch a decision made by a judge.

Q. Dr. Rothenberger, we know that that wasn't so in practice, don't we? We have seen instances where it didn't work out that way, haven't we?

A. Unfortunately, after I wrote this memorandum, especially here in this trial, and also when I was in Berlin already, I found out that the Führer acted in a different way. The purpose of this memorandum, however, was merely the following: to convince the Führer that the men who had influenced him so far and in that direction were wrong. My knowledge from Hamburg was not sufficient in order to know already at that time that the Führer himself could not be convinced. But that is not only my own tragedy, but the tragedy of the entire German people.

Q. Did you ever consider the possibility that the Führer in reading your memorandum read it literally and decided that when you said "The Führer should be the supreme judge," that you meant what you said? Did you ever consider that possibility?

A. Yes, I considered that possibility.

Q. Do you have any feeling that in practice it didn't work out that way? In fact, the evidence adduced here at this trial tends to prove, don't you believe, that by the end of the war the Führer really became the supreme judge and interfered with all judicial decisions?

A. I saw that later, and if I had known that before, I would not have undertaken this daring attempt, because there was no hope for it from the very beginning. But at the time, I thought that as a jurist I was under an obligation to make this final attempt, because I just could not accept the conditions which existed.

Q. You knew what the Party platform was, did you not? You knew what Hitler had said in *Mein Kampf,* did you not?

A. About that problem, he did not say anything in a negative way in his Party platform and not in *Mein Kampf* either.

Q. Well, as a reasonable man, Dr. Rothenberger, you knew what his attitudes were on all of these questions, and if your program embodied having him become the supreme judge, you knew fairly well how he would judge on all these questions from your prior knowledge, did you not?

A. No. I can only emphasize again and again that as long as I saw the possibility of influencing him, I considered it my duty to make this attempt; otherwise I would have been a fool.

Q. No one denies that you did influence him, Dr. Rothenberger; the implication is that you did, and that you were completely successful.

A. I did not have any success. That is just it. Hitler could not be convinced.

Q. He became the supreme judge, did he not?

A. In effect, he interfered with the administration of justice, as we know now.

Q. All of the judges in Germany were in a position of fealty to the Führer, were they not?

A. No fealty, no.

Q. What do you understand by "fealty"?

A. Dependence upon him.

Q. And you don't think judges in Germany at the end of the war were dependent on Hitler?

A. I just wanted to prevent this fealty.

Q. You wanted to prevent it?

A. Yes.

Q. That is not what you said in your memorandum. You said in your memorandum, "A judge who is in direct relation of fealty to the Führer must judge like the Führer." That doesn't sound like you were trying to prevent it. That sounds like you were trying to induce it.

A. You do not distinguish between the dependence and fealty on the one hand, and an obvious natural relationship of trust and confidence which every German and therefore every judge too should have in the Führer.

Source: *Trials of War Criminals before the Nuernberg Military Tribunals under Control Council Law No. 10,* Nuremberg, October 1946–April 1949, 15 vols. (Washington, 1949-53), vol. II, *U.S. v. Altstoetter* ("The Justice Case") (Washington, 1951), 498–502. The editors have made minor spelling changes to conform to spelling employed elsewhere in this volume.

Appendix L

Gustav Radbruch, "Statutory Lawlessness and Supra-Statutory Law" (excerpt)
1946

Positivism, with its principle that "a law is a law," has in fact rendered the German legal profession defenseless against statutes that are arbitrary and criminal. Positivism is, moreover, in and of itself wholly incapable of establishing the validity of statutes. It claims to have proved the validity of a statute simply by showing that the statute had sufficient power behind it to prevail. But while power may indeed serve as a basis for the "must" of compulsion, it never serves as a basis for the "ought" of obligation or for legal validity. Obligation and legal validity must be based, rather, on a value inherent in the statute. To be sure, *one* value comes with every positive-law statute without reference to its content: Any statute is always better than no statute at all, since it at least creates legal certainty. But legal certainty is not the only value that law must effectuate, nor is it the decisive value. Alongside legal certainty, there are two other values: purposiveness and justice. In ranking these values, we assign to last place the purposiveness of the law in serving the public benefit. By no means is law anything and everything that "benefits the people." Rather, what benefits the people is, in the long run, only that which law is, namely, that which creates legal certainty and strives toward justice. Legal certainty (which is characteristic of every positive-law statute simply in virtue of the statute's having been enacted) takes a curious middle place between the other two values, purposiveness and justice, because it is required not only for the public benefit but also for justice. That the law be certain and sure, that it not be interpreted and applied one way here and now, another way elsewhere and tomorrow, is also a requirement of justice. Where there arises a conflict between legal

Appendix L

certainty and justice, between an objectionable but duly enacted statute and a just law that has not been cast in statutory form, there is in truth a conflict of justice with itself, a conflict between apparent and real justice. This conflict is perfectly expressed in the Gospel, in the command to "obey them that have the rule over you, and submit yourselves," and in the dictate, on the other hand, to "obey God rather than men."

The conflict between justice and legal certainty may well be resolved in this way: The positive law, secured by legislation and power, takes precedence even when its content is unjust and fails to benefit the people, unless the conflict between statute and justice reaches such an intolerable degree that the statute, as "flawed law," must yield to justice. It is impossible to draw a sharper line between cases of statutory lawlessness and statutes that are valid despite their flaws. One line of distinction, however, can be drawn with utmost clarity: Where there is not even an attempt at justice, where equality, the core of justice, is deliberately betrayed in the issuance of positive law, then the statute is not merely "flawed law," it lacks completely the very nature of law. For law, including positive law, cannot be otherwise defined than as a system and an institution whose very meaning is to serve justice. Measured by this standard, whole portions of National Socialist law never attained the dignity of valid law.

The most conspicuous characteristic of Hitler's personality, which became through his influence the pervading spirit of the whole of National Socialist "law" as well, was a complete lack of any sense of truth or any sense of right and wrong. Because he had no sense of truth, he could shamelessly, unscrupulously lend the ring of truth to whatever was rhetorically effective at the moment. And because he had no sense of right and wrong, he could without hesitation elevate to a statute the crudest expression of despotic caprice. There is, at the beginning of his regime, his telegram offering sympathy to the Potempa murderers, at the end, the hideous degradation of the martyrs of 20 July 1944. The supporting theory had been provided by the Nazi ideologue, Alfred Rosenberg, writing in response to the Potempa death sentences: People are not alike, and murders are not alike; the murder of the pacifist Jaurès was properly judged in France in a different light than the attempt to murder the nationalist Clemenceau; for it is impossible to subject the patriotically motivated perpetrator to the same punishment as one whose motives are (in the view of the National Socialists) inimical to the people. The explicit intention from the very beginning, then, was that National Socialist "law" would extricate itself from the essential requirement of justice, namely, the equal treatment of equals. It thereby lacks completely the very nature of law; it is not merely flawed law, but rather no law at all. This applies especially to those enactments by means of which the National Socialist Party claimed for itself the whole of the state, flouting the principle that every political party represents only a part of the state. Legal character is also lacking in all the statutes that treated human beings as subhuman and denied them human rights, and it is lacking, too, in all the caveats that, governed solely by the momentary necessities of intimidation, disregarded the varying gravity of offences and threatened the same punishment, often death, for the slightest as well as the most serious of crimes. All these are examples of statutory lawlessness.

We must not fail to recognize—especially in light of the events of those twelve years—what frightful dangers for legal certainty there can be in the notion of "statutory lawlessness," in duly enacted statutes that are denied the very nature of law. We must hope that such lawlessness will remain an isolated aberration of the German people, a never-to-be-repeated madness. We must prepare, however, for every eventuality. We must arm ourselves against the recurrence of an outlaw state like Hitler's by fundamentally overcoming positivism, which rendered impotent every possible defense against the abuses of National Socialist legislation.

Source: David Dyzenhaus, Sophia Reibetanz Moreau, and Arthur Ripstein, eds., *Law and Morality: Readings in Legal Philosophy*, 3rd ed. (Toronto 2007). The excerpt is from pp. 131–33. Notes are omitted. Reproduced with the kind permission of Oxford University Press

Contributors

Raphael Gross is Director of the Leo Baeck Institute London, the Frankfurt Jewish Museum, and the Fritz Bauer Institute at the University of Frankfurt, where he also serves as honorary professor. He is also a Reader in History at Queen Mary College, University of London. Among his many publications are *Anständig geblieben. Nationalsozialistische Moral* (Frankfurt/Main 2010); *Novemberpogrom 1938. Die Augenzeugenberichte der Wiener Library, London* (ed.) (Frankfurt/Main 2008), and *Carl Schmitt and the Jews: The "Jewish Question," the Holocaust, and German Legal Theory* (Madison, 2007).

Konrad H. Jarausch is the Lurcy Professor of European Civilization in the Department of History at the University of North Carolina at Chapel Hill. He has written or edited about forty books in modern German and European history. Starting with Hitler's seizure of power and the First World War, his research interests have moved to the social history of German students and professions, German unification in 1989–90, historiography under the Communist GDR, the nature of the East German dictatorship, as well as the debate about historians and the Third Reich. More recently, he has been concerned with the problem of interpreting twentieth-century German history in general, the learning processes after 1945, the issue of cultural democratization, and the relationship between Honecker and Brezhnev. His most recent book is *Reluctant Accomplice: A Wehrmacht Soldier's Letters from the Eastern Front* (Princeton, 2011). His book *The Unfree Professions: German Lawyers, Teachers and Engineers, 1900–1950* (New York, 1990), is a standard work on the professions in twentieth-century Germany.

Hans-Christian Jasch is the author of *Staatssekretär Wilhelm Stuckart und die Judenpolitik. Der Mythos von der sauberen Verwaltung* (Munich, 2012). A lawyer by training, he has long been a collaborator of the Memorial House of the Wannsee Conference in Berlin, where he organizes seminars for young lawyers on the legal profession and its involvement in the Holocaust. Since 2001, Jasch has worked as a civil servant in the German Federal Ministry of the Interior. From 2007 to 2011 he was seconded to the European Commission in Brussels to work on counter-terrorism policy.

Kenneth Ledford serves in the Department of History and the School of Law at Case Western Reserve University, where he teaches German history, European legal history, the history of European legal professions, historical methods, and the history of European Union law. His main research interests include the intersection of legal thought and middle-class formation in Germany in the nineteenth and twentieth centuries, which results in his focus on the study of legal professions and legal professionals. He is author of *From General Estate to Special Interest: German Lawyers 1878–1933* (Cambridge, 1996), as well as numerous articles on the history of German law and legal professions, and is currently completing a book manuscript tentatively titled *Prussian Judges and the Rule of Law in Germany, 1848–1914*. He currently serves as Editor of *Central European History*, published by the Conference Group for Central European History of the American Historical Association; as a member of the Board of Editors of the Law and History Review, published by the American Society for Legal History; and as a member of the Board of Directors of that Association.

Douglas G. Morris is a legal historian and practicing criminal defense attorney with Federal Defenders of New York, Inc., where he represents defendants charged with federal crimes, such as drug smuggling, illegal immigration, currency smuggling, gun use by convicted felons, alien smuggling, child pornography and, occasionally, bank robbery. He is author of *Justice Imperiled: The Anti-Nazi Lawyer Max Hirschberg in Weimar Germany* (Ann Arbor, 2005). He is now writing a book on Jewish lawyers in Nazi Germany. In 2001–02, he was a Fellow at the Dorothy and Lewis B. Cullmann Center for Scholars and Writers at the New York Public Library. In 1998 he was a recipient of the Thurgood Marshall Award from the Association of the Bar of the City of New York for serving "as pro bono counsel to a human being under a sentence of death."

Robert D. Rachlin is senior director and general counsel of Downs Rachlin Martin PLLC, in Burlington, Vermont. He is also Visiting Professor at the Vermont Law School, where he has taught courses in ethics, remedies, and corporations, and is adjunct faculty in the Carolyn and Leonard Miller Center for Holocaust Studies and the Department of German and Russian, University of Vermont. He has published numerous book reviews as well as essays on the Finnish response to the Holocaust, on Nazi-era law in Germany, on early Vermont history, and on American law. A concert pianist and composer, his Sonata for 'Cello and Piano and his Trio on Jewish Festival Themes for Viola, 'Cello, and Piano have been publicly performed.

Harry Reicher has represented Agudath Israel World Organization at the United Nations, in which capacity he practiced international law and diplomacy in the field of human rights, with special emphasis on freedom of religion, protection and preservation of cultural heritage and property (especially Jewish cemeteries in Eastern Europe), as well as education. He has taught at Penn Law School for 17 years, offering courses in International Human Rights, and Law and the Holocaust. In 2004, he was appointed by President George W. Bush as a member of the US Holocaust Memorial Council, on which he served until 2008. He has published in the Columbia Journal of Transnational Law, and he edited the first indigenous Australian casebook on international law. He is presently also Scholar-in-Residence at Touro Law Center.

Alan E. Steinweis is Professor of History and Miller Distinguished Professor of Holocaust Studies at the University of Vermont, where he also directs the Miller Center for Holocaust Studies. His books include *Art, Ideology, and Economics in Nazi Germany: The Reich Chambers of Music, Theater, and the Visual Arts* (Chapel Hill, 1993); *Studying the Jew: Scholarly Antisemitism in Nazi Germany* (Cambridge, 2006); and *Kristallnacht 1938* (Cambridge, 2009). In 2011 he held the visiting professorship in Interdisciplinary Holocaust Studies and German-Jewish History at the Fritz Bauer Institute at the University of Frankfurt, Germany.

Selected Bibliography

Angermund, Ralph. *Deutsche Richterschaft 1919–1945: Krisenerfahrung, Illusion, politische Rechtsprechung.* Frankfurt, 1990.

Bendersky, Joseph W. *Carl Schmitt, Theorist for the Reich.* Princeton, 1983.

Benz, Wolfgang. "Von der Entrechtung zur Verfolgung und Vernichtung. Jüdische Juristen unter dem nationalsozialistischen Regime," in *Deutsche Juristen,* ed. Heinrichs, Franzki, Schmalz, and Stolleis.

Bergemann, Hans and Simone Ladwig-Winters. *Jüdische Richter am Kammergericht nach 1933. Eine Dokumentation.* Cologne, 2004.

Bergemann, Hans and Simone Ladwig-Winters. *Richter und Staatsanwälte jüdischer Herkunft in Preußen im Nationalsozialismus. Eine Dokumentation.* Cologne, 2004.

Bozyakali, Can. *Das Sondergericht am Hanseatischen Oberlandesgericht: Eine Untersuchung der NS-Sondergerichte unter Besonderer Berücksichtigung der Anwendung der Verordnung gegen Volksschädlinge.* Frankfurt, 2005.

Broszat, Martin. "Zur Perversion der Strafjustiz im Dritten Reich," *Vierteljahrshefte für Zeitgeschichte* 6, no. 4 (1958): 390–445.

Buchheit, Gert. *Richter in roter Robe: Freisler, Präsident des Volksgerichtshofes.* Munich, 1968.

Bundesminister der Justiz, ed., *Im Namen des deutschen Volkes. Justiz und Nationalsozialismus. Katalog zur Ausstellung des Bundesministers der Justiz.* Cologne, 1989.

Caplan, Jane. *Government without Administration: State and Civil Service in Weimar and Nazi Germany.* Oxford, 1988.

"Das Reichsministerium des Innern und die Judengesetzgebung. Aufzeichnung von Doktor Bernhard Lösener," in *Vierteljahrshefte für Zeitgeschichte* 9, (1961), 262–313.

Diestelkamp, Bernhard, ed. *Justizalltag im Dritten Reich.* Frankfurt, 1988.

Dreyer, Martin. *Die zivilrechtliche Rechtsprechung des Oberlandesgerichts Düsseldorf in der nationalsozialistischen Zeit.* Göttingen, 2004.

Dubber, Markus Dirk. "Judicial Positivism and Hitler's Injustice," *Columbia Law Review* 93 (1993): 1807–32.

Echterhölter, Rudolf. *Das öffentliche Recht im nationalsozialistischen Staat.* Stuttgart, 1970.

Engelmann, Bernt. *Die unsichtbare Tradition.* Vol. 1: *Richter zwischen Recht und Macht 1779–1918;* Vol. 2: *Rechtsverfall, Justizterror und das schwere Erbe. Ein Beitrag zur Geschichte der deutschen Strafjustiz von 1919 bis heute.* Cologne, 1988–89.

"Entnazifizierung und Wiederaufbau der Justiz am Beispiel des Bundesgerichtshofs," in Eva Schumann, ed., *Kontinuitäten und Zäsuren. Rechstwissenschaft und Justiz im 'Dritten Reich' und in der Nachkriegszeit* (Göttingen, 2008), 189–212.

Essner, Cornelia. *Die "Nürnberger Gesetze"oder die Verwaltung des Rassenwahns 1933–1945*. Paderborn, 2002.

Förster, Michael. *Jurist im Dienst des Unrechts. Leben und Werk des ehemaligen Staatssekretärs im Reichsjustizministerium, Franz Schlegelberger (1876–1970)*. Baden-Baden, 1995.

Fraenkel, Ernst. *The Dual State: A Contribution to the Theory of Dictatorship*. New York, 1941.

Frei, Norbert. *Adenauer's Germany and the Nazi Past: The Politics of Amnesty and Integration*. Translated by by Joel Golb. New York, 2002.

Freisler, Roland. *Nationalsozialistisches Recht und Rechtsdenken*. Berlin, 1938.

Gassert, Philipp and Alan E. Steinweis, eds. *Coping with the Nazi Past: West German Debates on Nazism and Generational Conflict, 1955–1975*. New York, 2006.

Göppinger, Horst. *Juristen jüdischer Abstammung im "Dritten Reich". Entrechtung und Verfolgung*. 2d ed. Munich, 1990.

Gross, Raphael. *Anständig geblieben: Nationalsozialistische Moral*. Frankfurt, 2010.

Gross, Raphael. *Carl Schmitt and the Jews: The "Jewish Question," the Holocaust, and German Legal Theory*. Translated by Joel Golb. Madison, 2007.

Gruchmann, Lothar. *Justiz im Dritten Reich: 1933–1940: Anpassung und Unterwerfung in der Ära Gürtner*. Munich, 2001.

Hachenburg, Max. *Lebenserinnerungen eines Rechtsanwalts und Briefe aus der Emigration*. Stuttgart, 1978.

Haldemann, Frank. "Gutstav Radbruch vs. Hans Kelsen: A Debate on Nazi Law," in *Ratio Juris*, Vol. 18, No.2 (June 2005), 162–78.

Herf, Jeffrey. *Divided Memory: The Nazi Past in the Two Germanys*. Cambridge, 1997.

Hett, Benjamin Carter. *Crossing Hitler: The Man Who Put the Nazis on the Witness Stand*. New York, 2008.

Heydeloff, Rudolf. "Staranwalt der Rechtsextremisten: Walter Luetgebrune in der Weimarer Republik." *Vierteljahrshefte für Zeitgeschichte* 32 (July 1984), 373–421.

Hillermeier, Heinz, ed. *"In Namen des Deutschen Volkes!"—Todesurteile des Volksgerichtshofs*. Darmstadt, 1983.

Jarausch, Konrad H. *The Unfree Professions: German Lawyers, Teachers and Engineers, 1900–1950*. New York, 1990.

Jasch, Hans-Christian. *Staatssekretär Wilhelm Stuckart und die Judenpolitik. Der Mythos von der sauberen Verwaltung*. Munich, 2012.

Kempner, Robert M.W. and Carl Haensel. *Das Urteil im Wilhelmstraßenprozess*. Schwäbisch Gmünd, 1950.

Kempner, Robert M.W. *Ankläger einer Epoche. Lebenserinnerungen*. Frankfurt, 1986.

Selected Bibliography

Koch, H.W. *In the Name of the Volk: Political Justice in the Third Reich.* New York, 1989.

Königseder, Angelika. *Recht und nationalsozialistische Herrschaft. Berliner Anwälte 1933–1945: ein Forschungsprojekt des Berliner Anwaltsvereins e.V.* Bonn, 2001.

Koonz, Claudia. *The Nazi Conscience.* Cambridge, 2003.

Kostal, Rande. "The Alchemy of Occupation: Karl Loewenstein and the Legal Reconstruction of Nazi Germany, 1945-1946," *Law and History Review* 29 (2011), 1–52.

Krach, Tillman. *Jüdische Rechtsanwälte in Preußen. Über die Bedeutung der freien Advokatur und ihre Zerstörung durch den Nationalsozialismus.* Munich, 1991.

Kulka, Otto Dov. "Die Nürnberger Rassengesetze und die deutsche Bevölkerung im Lichte geheimer NS-Lage- und Stimmungsberichte," in *Vierteljahrshefte für Zeitgeschichte* 32 (1984), 582–624.

Ladwig-Winters, Simone. *Anwalt ohne Recht: Das Schicksale jüdischer Rechtsanwälte in Berlin nach 1933.* Berlin, 1998.

Ledford, Kenneth F. *From General Estate to Special Interest: German Lawyers 1878–1933.* Cambridge, 1996.

Loewenstein, Karl. "Law in the Third Reich," *Yale Law Journal* 45 (1936), 779–815.

Luig, Klaus. *… weil er nicht arischer Abstammung ist. Jüdische Juristen in Köln während der NS-Zeit.* Cologne, 2004.

Mayer, Michael. *Staaten als Täter. Ministerialbürokratie und "Judenpolitik" in NS-Deutschland und Vichy-Frankreich.* Munich, 2010.

McClelland, Charles E. *The German Experience of Professionalization: Modern Learned Professions and their Organizations from the Early Nineteenth Century to the Hitler Era.* Cambridge, 1991.

McElligott, Anthony. "Dangerous Communities and Conservative Authority: The Judiciary, Nazis, and Rough People, 1932–1933," in Tim Kirk and Anthony McElligott, eds., *Opposing Fascism: Community, Authority, and Resistance in Europe.* Cambridge, 1999. 33–47.

Miquel, Marc von. *Ahnden oder Amnestieren? Westdeutsche Justiz und Vergangenheitspolitik in den sechziger Jahren.* Göttingen, 2004.

Mommsen, Hans. "The Civil Service and the Implementation of the Holocaust. From Passive to Active Complicity," in *The Holocaust and History: The Known, the Unknown, the Disputed, and the Reexamined.* Eds. Michael Berenbaum and Abraham J. Peck. Bloomington, 1998.

Mommsen, Hans. *Beamtentum im Dritten Reich.* Stuttgart, 1966.

Morris, Douglas G. *Justice Imperiled: The Anti-Nazi Lawyer Max Hirschberg in Weimar Germany.* Ann Arbor, 2005.

Müller, Ingo. *Hitler's Justice: The Courts of the Third Reich*, translated by Deborah Lucas Schneider. Cambridge, 1991.

Nathans, Eli. *Franz Schlegelberger.* Baden-Baden, 1990.

Neliba, Günter. *Wilhelm Frick, Der Legalist des Unrechtsstaats.* Paderborn, 1992.

Niethammer, Lutz. *Die Mitläuferfabrik. Die Entnazifizierung am Beispiel Bayerns.* Berlin, 1989.

Noam, Ernst and Wolf Arno Kropat. *Juden vor Gericht 1933–1945. Dokumente aus hessischen Justizakten mit einem Vorwort von Johannes Strelitz.* Wiesbaden, 1975.
Ortner, Helmut. *Der Hinrichter: Roland Freisler, Mörder im Dienste Hitlers.* Vienna, 1993.
Pendas, Devin O. "Retroactive Law and Proactive Justice: Debating Crimes against Humanity in Germany, 1945-1950," *Central European History* 43, No. 3 (September 2010).
Perels, Joachim. "Perceptions and Suppression of Nazi Crimes by the Postwar German Judiciary," in Nathan Stoltzfus and Henry Friedlander, eds., *Nazi Crimes and the Law.* Cambridge, 2008. 87–99
Perels, Joachim. *Das juristische Erbe des "Dritten Reiches". Beschädigung der demokratischen Rechtsordnung.* Frankfurt, 1999.
Poliakov, Léon and Joseph Wulf. *Das Dritte Reich und seine Diener. Dokumente,* 1st ed. Berlin, 1956.
Przyrembel, Alexandra. *"Rassenschande." Reinheitsmythos und Vernichtungslegitimation im Nationalsozialismus.* Göttingen, 2003.
Pulzer, Peter. "Religion and Judicial Appointments in Germany, 1869–1918," *Leo Baeck Institute Year Book* 28 (1983): 185–204.
Radbruch, Gustav. "Statutory Lawlessness and Supra-Statutory Law," in David Dyzenhaus, Sophia Reibetanz Moreau, and Arthur Ripstein, eds., *Law and Morality: Readings in Legal Philosophy,* 3rd ed. (Toronto, 2007), 127–40.
Rebentisch, Dieter. *Führerstaat und Verwaltung im Zweiten Weltkrieg. Verfassungsentwicklung und Verwaltungspolitik 1939–1945.* Stuttgart, 1989.
Redaktion Kritische Justiz, ed. *Der Unrechts-Staat: Recht und Justiz im Nationalsozialismus.* 2 vols. Baden-Baden, 1983–84.
Reicher, Harry. "The Jurists' Trial and Lessons for the Rule of Law," in Herbert R. Reginbogin and Christoph J.M. Safferling, eds., *The Nuremberg Trials: International Criminal Law Since 1945.* Munich, 2006.
Riess, Curt. *Der Mann in der Schwarzen Robe: Das Leben des Strafverteidigers Max Alsberg.* Hamburg, 1965.
Rottleutner, Hubert. *Karrieren und Kontinuitäten deutscher Justizjuristen vor und nach 1945.* Berlin, 2010.
Rüping, Hinrich. *Rechtsanwälte im Bezirk Celle während des Nationalsozialismus.* Berlin, 2007.
Rüthers, Bernd. *Entartetes Recht. Rechslehren und Kronjuristen im Dritten Reich,* 2d ed. Munich, 1989.
Schiller, Christoph. *Das Oberlandesgericht Karlsruhe im Dritten Reich.* Berlin, 1997.
Schmitt, Carl. *Staat, Bewegung, Volk.* Hamburg, 1935.
Schorn, Hubert. *Der Richter im Dritten Reich. Geschichte und Dokumente.* Frankfurt, 1959.
Schröder, Rainer. *"... aber im Zivilrecht sind die Richter standhaft geblieben!" Die Urteile des OLG Celle aus dem Dritten Reich.* Baden-Baden, 1988.
Staff, Ilse, ed. *Justiz im Dritten Reich, eine Dokumentation.* Frankfurt, 1978.
Stolleis, Michael. *The Law Under the Swastika: Studies on Legal History in Nazi Germany.* Translated by Thomas Dunlap. Chicago, 1998.

Strenge, Barbara. *Juden im preußischen Justizdienst 1812–1918. Der Zugang zu den juristischen Berufen als Indikator der gesellschaftlichen Emanzipation.* Munich, 1996.
Sweet, William. "The Volksgerichtshof: 1934–45," *The Journal of Modern History,* 46/2 (1964), 314–329.
Trials of War Criminals Before the Nuernberg Military Tribunals Under Control Council Law No. 10, Nuremberg, October 1946–April 1949, 15 vols. (Washington, 1949–53), vol. III, Case 3, *U.S. v. Alstoetter* ("The Justice Case"). Washington, 1951.
Wachsmann, Nikolaus. *Hitler's Prisons: Legal Terror in Nazi Germany.* New Haven, 2004.
Wagner, Walter. *Der Volksgerichtshof im nationalsozialistischen Staat.* Stuttgart, 1974.
Walk, Joseph, ed. *Das Sonderrecht für die Juden im NS-Staat. Eine Sammlung der gesetzlichen Maßnahmen und Richtlinien—Inhalt und Bedeutung.* Karlsruhe, 1981.
Ward, Ian. *Law, Philosophy and National Socialism: Heidegger, Schmitt and Radbruch in Context.* New York, 1992.
Wassermann, Rudolf, *"Kammergericht soll bleiben." Ein Gang durch die Geschichte des berühmtesten deutschen Gerichts (1468–1945).* Berlin, 2004.
Wassermann, Rudolf. *Auch die Justiz kann aus der Geschichte nicht aussteigen.* Baden-Baden, 1990.
Weber, Reinhard, *Das Schicksal der jüdischen Rechtsanwälte in Bayern nach 1933.* Munich, 2006.
Weinkauff, Hermann. *Die deutsche Justiz und der Nationalsozialismus: ein Überblick.* Stuttgart, 1968.
Weinke, Annette. *Die Verfolgung von NS-Tätern im geteilten Deutschland: Vergangenheitsbewältigung 1949-1969.* Paderborn, 2002.
Wieland, Günther. *Das war der Volksgerichtshof: Ermittlungen, Fakten, Dokumente.* Pfaffenweiler, 1989.
Willig, Kenneth C.H. "The Bar in the Third Reich," *The American Journal of Legal History* 20 (Jan., 1976), 1–14.

INDEX

Academy for German Law, 46, 50, 121, 224
Adenauer, Konrad, 28, 39, 172, 174
Agamben, Giorgo, 91
Alsberg, Max, 105–07, 109, 114, 119–122, 124, 127, 131
Angress, Werner, 105–06
anti-Semitism. *See* Jews
Arendt, Hannah, 16, 40, 44
Article 48 (Weimar Constitution), 191
Auschwitz trial, 27, 39, 174, 178

Backe, Herbert, 47
Ball, Fritz, 114
Ball-Kaduri, Kurt Jacob, 116
Barbie, Klaus, 175
bar associations, German, 110, 112, 114, 118, 119, 130, 165, 167
Basic Law (*Grundgesetz*), 28, 175
Bauer, Fritz, 11, 27, 166
Bauman, Zygmunt, 40
Becher, Johannes, 75
Bendix, Ludwig, 167–68
Bendix, Reinhard, 167–68
Berlin, Isaiah, 124
Bertram, Günter, 162
Best, Werner, 16, 24–25
Bismarck, Otto von, 20, 178–79
Blau, Bruno, 114–19
Bonhoeffer, Dietrich, 173
Bracher, Karl-Dietrich, 16
Brackmann, Albert, 15, 23
Broszat, Martin, 82
Brüning, Heinrich, 18, 169
Buchheit, Gert, 71
Bundesgerichtshof, (*BGH*). *See* courts, German

Bürgerliches Gesetzbuch (BGB), 80, 213

Canaris, Wilhelm, 172
Catel, Werner, 53
Central Office of the State Ministries of Justice for the Investigation of National Socialist Crimes in Ludwigsburg, 27, 174
Cicero, 83
Columbia Law Review, 177
Committee for German Unity, 173–74
common law, 64
Communists, 17, 26, 43, 77, 78, 108, 112, 174, 180, 192
Conti, Leonardo, 47
Control Council Law No. 10, 139
courts, German, 2, 4, 11, 45, 89, 95, 106, 114, 116, 124, 128, 130, 139–40, 161, 166, 172–73, 176–79
  Bundesgerichtshof, 162, 179–80
  Feme, 81–82
  Freisler and, 64–65, 68–70, 74, 80–81
  Nazi intimidation and violence in, 108–111, 119
  People's Court, 7–8, 30, 63–83, 131, 170
  Reichsgericht, 48, 72, 172
  Special Courts, 9, 10, 95–100, 140–52, 169–70, 208–10, 211–23
crimes against humanity, 138–41, 153
Critical Jurists, 28. *See also Kritische Justiz*

Index

Daluege Kurt, 43
death penalty, 127, 131, 169, 179, 180
   imposed on Werner Holländer, 9, 96–8
   imposed on Leo Katzenberger, 10, 140–52, 170, 171, 211–23
   imposed on Markus Luftglass, 10, 140–52, 208–10
   imposed by People's Court, 8, 64, 73, 75–79, 81
Deckert, Günter, 161–63, 176, 179–80
de-Nazification, 16, 27, 39, 97, 170–71
Deutsche Juristen-Zeitung, 118
Deutsche Justiz, 67
Deutsche Verwaltung, 46
Deutsches Recht, 50
Dönitz, Karl, 53
Dubber, Markus Dirk, 177

Eden Dance Palace trial, 108, 166
Eichmann trial, 27, 174
Einsatzgruppen, 23, 24, 39, 40, 139, 172
Enabling Act, 194–95
Engelmann, Bernt, 176
Eternal Jew (Der ewige Jude) (film), 93
euthanasia program, 7, 25, 53

Fallada, Hans, 75–76
Feme-justice, 81–82
Flessa, Friedrich, 25
Fliess, Julius, 129
Foreign Office, 40, 47
Four-Year Plan, 47
Fraenkel, Ernst
   and *The Dual State,* 2–3, 10, 40, 73, 108, 146
   life and activities in Nazi Germany, 124–29, 131, 165
   See also normative state; prerogative state

Frank, Hans, 24, 46, 71, 72, 121, 123, 131, 196
Free Corps, 18, 42
Frei, Norbert, 39
Freisler, Oswald, 68
Freisler, Roland, 7–8, 11, 30, 47, 62–83, 146, 204, 207
Freud, Sigmund, 91
Freymuth, Arnold, 166
Frick, Wilhelm, 42, 45, 193, 195
Friedlaender, Max, 112
Friedlander, Henry, 120
Friedrich, Carl, 16
Friedrich, Jörg, 175
Führerprinzip, 10, 11, 116, 117, 138, 140–41,143–46, 148–53
Fuller, Lon, 172

Ganzenmüller, Albert, 47
Gellately, Robert, 16
German Judges' League, 165, 167
German Jurist Assemblies, 46
German National People's Party (DNVP), 42
German Research Council, 23
Gestapo, 4, 24, 49, 75, 82, 92, 125–26, 130, 140, 210
Globke, Hans, 39, 50
Goebbels, Joseph, 52, 66–67, 76, 125, 151
Göring, Hermann, 43, 45, 47, 72, 76
Gürtner, Franz, 72, 193

Hachenburg, Max, 30, 118, 121, 122, 124, 127, 131
Haffner, Sebastian, 30
Halbwachs, Maurice, 28
Hallgarten, Fritz, 43
Hampel, Otto and Elise, 75–77
Hart, H.L.A., 172
Harvard Law Review, 172
Hassencamp, Fritz, 96–97, 102
Hegel, Georg Wilhelm Friedrich, 83
Heimtücke. See malicious mischief
Herbert, Ulrich, 16
Hess, Rudolf, 45, 143

Hett, Benjamin, 107, 166
Heydrich, Reinhard, 51, 53
High Tribunal for Population Questions in the Eastern Territories, 46
Hilberg, Raul, 80, 154
Hiller, Kurt, 129
Himmler, Heinrich, 38, 41–42, 44, 46, 72, 76, 91, 227
Hindenburg, Paul von, 9, 115, 117, 129, 167, 193, 195
Hirschberg, Max, 113–15, 120, 131, 166
Hitler, Adolf, 3, 15, 19, 20, 22, 23, 24, 38, 42, 43, 46, 47, 49, 50, 52, 92, 105, 113, 127, 131, 169, 173, 176
    charismatic authority of, 16
    at Eden Dance Palace trial, 108, 166
    and Freisler, 7, 8, 30, 63, 64–69, 71–76, 78–79, 82
    and *Führerprinzip,* 10, 11, 116, 117, 138, 140–41,143–46, 148–53
    assures Hindenburg regarding Jewish civil servants, 115
    disbars Jewish lawyers, 129
    and Nuremberg Laws, 95
    as a source of law, 65–71, 79–83, 143–54, 173, 224–32
    and Stuckart, 45
Hockenos, Paul, 174
Hodenberg, Hodo Freiherr von, 171
Holländer, Werner, 9, 95–100, 102
Huppenkothen, Walter, 172

Imperial Justice Laws, 163
International Academy for State and Administrative Sciences, 46

Jahrreis, Hermann, 143–44
Jarausch, Konrad, 174
Jehovah's Witnesses, 66
Jewry in Jurisprudence (1936 conference), 121–23, 131

Jews, 18, 19, 20, 22, 23, 24, 25, 26, 29, 30, 67, 69, 80, 81, 139, 146, 147, 161, 162, 169, 178, 197, 202, 208–210
    anti-Semitism and shame, 100–02
    role of civil service in persecution of, 6, 37–54
    and German legal professions before 1933, 5, 11, 17, 21, 106–07, 164–66
    Jewry in Jurisprudence (1936 conference), 121–23, 131
    and Law for the Protection of German Blood and Honor, 9, 10–11, 47, 48, 91–100, 140–42, 149, 152, 213, 211–23
    and Nazi morality, 7–8, 89–94
    purged from legal professions, 9–10, 22, 105–31, 166–68
    as parties before the courts, 9, 10–11, 91–100, 140–42, 211–23
    and Reich Citizenship Law, 47, 48, 167–68
Johnson, Eric, 16
Justice Case. *See* Nuremberg Trials

Kant, Immanuel, 101, 180
Kater, Michael, 16
Katzenberger, Leo, 10, 140–52, 170, 171, 211–23
Kauba, Hermann, 20
Kempner, Robert M.W., 26, 165–66
Kerrl, Hanns, 110
Kershaw, Ian, 16
Kessler, Edmund, 96–102
Kleinewefers, Paul, 24
Klemperer, Victor, 16, 22, 26
Klepper, Jochen, 26
Koch, Hannsjoachim, 79
Kogon, Egon, 26
Köhl, Lotte Gertrud, 43
Konsulent, 130, 167–68
Körner, Paul, 47
Kristallnacht, 130

Kritische Justiz, 177
Kritzinger, Wilhelm, 47, 209–10
Kroner, Wilhelm Israel, 166
Kusserow, Raimund, 175

Lammers, Hans-Heinrich, 45, 53, 209–10
Langbehn, Julius, 20
Largarde, Paul de, 20
Law for the Protection of German Blood and German Honor. *See* Nuremberg Laws
Law for the Restoration of the Professional Civil Service, 22, 111, 167, 171
Law on the Admission to the Bar, 111–14, 116–119, 129
law, rule of, 1, 8, 9, 12, 79–81
League of National-German Jews, 116
League of Republican Judges, 165–66
Leitmeyer, Karl, 197–98
Leo Baeck Institute, 26
Leuchter, Fred, 161
Liebmann, Max, 43
Litten, Hans, 108–09, 114, 121, 128–29, 131, 166
Loewenfeld, Philipp, 113–14, 120
Loewenstein, Karl, 171
Lösener, Bernhard, 48–55
Luetgebrune, Walter, 69, 71
Luftglass, Markus, 10, 140–52, 208–10
Luther, Martin, 47

Madjanek Trial, 39
Majer, Diemut, 52
malicious mischief (*Heimtücke*), 169
Max Planck Institute for European Legal History, 178
Mengele, Josef, 15
Meyer, Julius, 130
Miller Arnold case, 165
Ministries Case. *See* Nuremberg Trials
Miquel, Marc von, 178

Mommsen, Theodor, 20
Morris, Douglas, 166
Müller, Ingo, 12, 170, 175

National Democratic Party (NPD), 161
Naumann, Max, 116–17
Naumann, Werner, 47
Nazi Party (NSDAP), 3, 65, 75, 143, 145, 151, 170, 215, 222
  attraction to professionals, 16–18
  Freisler and, 7, 63, 68–69
  lawyers in, 14, 19, 21, 233, 167, 196
  Stuckart and, 6, 37–38, 41–43, 47–49
Neumann, Franz, 40, 127
Neurath, Konstantin von, 195
Niemoller, Martin, 169
Nietzsche, Friedrich, 101
Night and Fog decree, 74
Noack, Erwin, 130
Norden, Albert, 173–74
normative state, 2–3, 11, 40, 73, 108, 146. *See also* Fraenkel, Ernst; prerogative state
NSDAP. *See* Nazi Party
nulla poena sine lege (or *nullum crimen sine lege*), 8, 64, 70, 82
Nuremberg Laws, 7, 47, 51, 111, 120
  Law for the Protection of German Blood and German Honor, 9, 47, 48, 91–100, 140–42, 149, 152, 213, 211–23
  Reich Citizenship Law, 47, 48, 167–68
Nuremberg Trials, 26, 38, 40, 154, 165
  Justice Case, 10, 11, 53, 137–54, 170, 171–72, 173, 208–10, 224–29
  Wilhelmstrasse Trial (aka Ministries Case), 39, 40, 48–49, 53

Olden, Rudolf, 114
Organisation Consul, 81
Orgler, Alfred, 166
Orlet, Rainer, 161–62
Ortner, Helmut, 63, 69
Ossietzky, Carl von, 114, 169
Oster, Hans, 173

Papen, Franz von, 169
People's Court (*Volksgerichtshof*).
    See courts, German
Perels, Joachim, 177
Petri, Franz, 24, 25
Planck, Max, 22
Plötzensee Prison, 64
positivism, 4, 8, 10–12, 70–71, 75,
    171–176, 180, 230–32
prerogative state, 2–3, 40, 73, 108,
    146. *See also* Fraenkel, Ernst;
    normative state
Probst, Christoph, 78, 202–07
Protocols of the Elders of Zion, 99

Quangel, Otto and Anna (fictional
    characters). *See* Hampel, Otto and
    Elise

racial defilement (*Rassenschande*),
    88, 96, 99. *See also* Nuremberg
    Laws
Radbruch, Gustav, 11, 166, 171–72,
    230–32
Rathenau, Walther, 82
Rechtsstaat. See law, rule of
Reich Chancellery, 45, 47, 208–10
Reich Citizenship Law. *See*
    Nuremberg Laws
Reich Committee for the Protection
    of German Blood, 50–51
Reich Ministry of Agriculture, 47
Reich Ministry of Education, 43
Reich Ministry of Finance, 47
Reich Ministry of Justice, 2, 7, 10,
    29, 47, 67, 69, 70, 72, 74, 93, 97,
    120, 129, 137, 138, 140, 144,
    147, 150, 153, 168, 169, 170,
    173

Reich Ministry of Propaganda, 47,
    169
Reich Ministry of the Interior, 6–7,
    120, 165, 193, 195
    Stuckart's role in, 41, 43, 45,
        47, 51, 53
Reich Ministry of Transportation,
    47, 93
Reich Security Main Office (RSHA),
    16, 48–51
Reich, Volksordnung und Lebensraum,
    46–47
Reichsgericht. See courts, German
Reichstag Fire Decree, 108, 192–93
Reinhard, Fritz, 47
Ribbentrop, Joachim von, 108
Röhm Putsch, 72
Roman law, 64–65, 80
Roper, Edith, 169, 178
Rosenberg, Alfred, 145, 151–53,
    231
Rosenfeld, Siegfried, 166
Rothaug, Oswald, 10, 141–54, 170,
    211–23
Rothenberger, Curt, 47, 136, 144,
    147, 224–29
RSHA. *See* Reich Security Main
    Office
Rüping, Hinrich, 177–78
Rust, Bernhard, 45
Rüthers, Bernd, 176

SA (*Sturmabteilung*), 15, 19, 72, 167
    terrorizes Jews and courts,
        109–14
Salomon, Ernst von, 18
Sartre, Jean-Paul, 91, 93
Scheler, Max, 100–101
Schieder, Theodor, 24
Schiedermair, Rolf, 52
Schlegelberger, Franz, 10, 136,
    140–54, 170, 208–10
Schmidt, Eberhard, 172
Schmitt, Carl, 3, 15, 20, 71, 121,
    123
Scholl, Hans and Sophie, 78,
    202–07

Index

Schorn, Hubert, 173
Schröder, Rainer, 177
Schwarze Reichswehr, 81
Schwerin von Krosigk, Johann Ludwig Graf, 195
Seiler, Irene, 141–42, 211–23
Senfft, Heinrich, 176
Siegel, Michael, 104, 109
Siegert, Karl, 121–22
Simon, Heinrich, 175
Sinzheimer, Hugo, 10, 122–24, 128, 131
Smith, Adam, 89
Social Democrats, 11, 20, 113, 125, 127, 162, 164–68, 171, 176, 179
Special Courts (*Sondergerichte*). *See* Courts, German
Spranger, Eduard, 22
SS (*Schutzstaffel*), 2, 3, 6, 23, 24, 25, 28, 37–38, 41, 42, 44, 48, 50, 51, 71–72, 91, 128
statutory law, 67, 73
    subordination to "healthy sentiment of the people" (*gesundes Volksempfinden*), 70–71, 168
    subordination to Hitler, 65–71, 79–83, 143–54, 171–173, 224–32
statute of limitations, 174, 178
Stern magazine, 175
Stolleis, Michael, 178
Strafgesetzbuch (penal code), 64, 80, 199–201, 212, 221–22
Strawson, P.F., 89
Stuckart, Wilhelm, 6–7, 36–54

Taylor, Telford, 139
Terrible Jurists (exhibition), 27

Thierack, Otto, 29, 67, 70, 71, 74, 79, 97, 150
Thorbeck, Otto, 172
treason, 64–66, 70, 72, 75–78, 193, 199–201, 204, 207
Treitschke, Heinrich von, 20
Tugendhat, Ernst, 90
Turner, Henry Ashby, 16

universities (German), 21

Versailles, Treaty of, 20–21, 29, 144, 165
Vierteljahrshefte für Zeitgeschichte, 48
Völkisch-Sozialer Bund, 68

Wagner, Walter, 75, 79
Wannsee Conference, 7, 47, 51–54, 69, 93, 101
war youth generation, 5–6, 18, 29, 42
Wassermann, Rudolf, 162–63, 178, 180
Wehler, Hans-Ulrich, 16
Wehrmacht, 24, 40, 72, 91, 97
Weinke, Annette, 174
Weizsäcker, Ernst von, 40, 53
Wildt, Michael, 16
Wilhelmstrasse Trial. *See* Nuremberg Trials
Willensstrafrecht, 70
Wolf, Christa, 29
World War II, 2, 17, 29, 41
    effect on law, 7–8, 12, 66–68, 73–82, 95–100. *See also* Katzenberger, Leo; Luftglass, Markus
    radicalizing effects of, 24–26, 30–31, 49, 52

www.ingramcontent.com/pod-product-compliance
Lightning Source LLC
Chambersburg PA
CBHW072149100526
44589CB00015B/2159